REAL
ESTATE
COUNSELING

REAL
ESTATE
COUNSELING

AMERICAN SOCIETY OF REAL
ESTATE COUNSELORS

James H. Boykin

editor in chief

Prentice-Hall, Inc., Englewood Cliffs, N.J. 07632

Library of Congress Cataloging in Publication Data
Main entry under title:

REAL ESTATE COUNSELING.

    Includes bibliographical references and index.
    1. Real estate counselors—United States. 2. Real
estate business—United States. I. Boykin, James H.,
1936–   . II. American Society of Real Estate
Counselors.
HD278.R42 1984   333.33′0973   83-19068
ISBN 0-13-762444-1

American Society of Real Estate Counselors
edition published 1988
by Prentice-Hall
A Division of Simon & Schuster

Editorial/production supervision
   and interior design by *Richard C. Laveglia*
Cover design: *Edsal Enterprises*
Manufacturing buyer: *Ed O'Dougherty*

Printed in the United States of America

10 9 8 7 6 5 4 3 2

ISBN 0-13-762444-1

Prentice-Hall International, Inc., *London*
Prentice-Hall of Australia Pty. Limited, *Sydney*
Editora Prentice-Hall do Brasil, Ltda., *Rio de Janeiro*
Prentice-Hall Canada Inc., *Toronto*
Prentice-Hall of India Private Limited, *New Delhi*
Prentice-Hall of Japan, Inc., *Tokyo*
Prentice-Hall of Southeast Asia Pte. Ltd., *Singapore*
Whitehall Books Limited, *Wellington, New Zealand*

CONTENTS

Section I Decision Making

FOREWORD

Having turned the corner of its thirtieth year, the American Society of Real Estate Counselors takes great pride in presenting this book. *Real Estate Counseling* represents an important milestone in the organization's efforts to offer real estate professionals and those in related fields a comprehensive guide to the counseling specialty and at the same time to increase the public's awareness and understanding of the counseling function, counseling practitioners, and the place of counseling in the real estate industry.

Real Estate Counseling conveys the story of counseling through the specialized experiences and seasoned judgments of practicing counselors. Each of the nineteen chapters in the book was written by a different counselor, and all of these counselor authors are members of the American Society of Real Estate Counselors. The material was pulled together by the editor in chief, James H. Boykin of Richmond, Virginia. It is organized into three sections: Decision Making, Real Estate Analyses, and Counseling for Specific Types of Assignments. The specific areas covered include the counseling function, the activities of the counselor, the counselor-client relationship, the analytical processes used in the counselor's decision making, and the problems involved in counseling on various types of property.

The Society wishes to acknowledge the immediate past and present members of the Publications Committee for their ideas and recommendations, and especially Max J. Derbes, Jr., Jean C. Felts, and Maury Seldin, who spearheaded the development of the publication. James H. Boykin is to be highly commended for his expertise and skill as editor in chief and for his diligence and steadfastness in piloting the manuscript through its various stages.

Of course, the publication would not exist if it weren't for its contributing authors. The American Society of Real Estate Counselors is indebted to them and is proud to claim them among its more than 575 members. *Real Estate Counseling* reflects the work of some of the best talent, knowledge, and dedication in the real estate profession. It's a privilege to have brought it all together under one cover, and it's exciting to send it forth to benefit the reader.

F. Poche Waguespack, CRE
1983 President
American Society of Real Estate Counselors

PREFACE

Real estate counseling is a young profession. Indeed, the premier organization of counselors, the American Society of Real Estate Counselors, dates back only to 1953.

Public awareness of the availability of expert counsel is, in part, a function of the availability of literature to the would-be clients. Many persons who have need for expert counsel in real estate are unaware of what real estate counseling is or of how it can help them.

Practitioners in real estate who give counsel on occasion are similarly unaware of their opportunities for developing professional practice in counseling. Indeed, many of those who have achieved the status of being counselors in real estate thirst for a better understanding of the profession.

Literature that explains the principles and practices of real estate counseling meets the needs of all of the aforementioned groups. Indeed, such literature meets the needs of anyone who wishes to enhance his or her understanding of real estate analysis and decision making. This is especially true for persons who are undergoing academic preparation and for persons who are already employed in some facet of the real estate business or in one of the family of industries that relate to real estate.

An earlier work, *Real Estate Counseling: A Professional Approach to Problem Solving*, blazed a trail in providing case-type material. The present work, with the shorter title *Real Estate Counseling*, is organized differently. We were going to give it the subtitle "Principles and Practices," but it isn't that academic. We sometimes call it "Real Estate Counseling II"—because it is a second-generation work.

This book starts off with a section entitled "Decision Making." The four chapters of the section identify and explain the decisions requiring counseling, the counseling process, and the counselor's function and role. These chapters contain the most complete presentation on counseling of which we are aware.

The second section, "Real Estate Analyses," identifies some types of analysis that are frequently used in a variety of real estate counseling assignments. An extensive literature on real estate analysis is available elsewhere. The six chapters in this section on analysis are only intended to give a counseling perspective to the use of analysis.

The thrust of the book is to identify and explain what the real estate counselor does. Thus, the heart of the book is contained in the nine chapters of the third section, "Counseling for Specific Types of Assignments." The first six chapters in this section are organized by type of real estate. The last three chapters are based on the type of client rather than the type of property.

The permutations and combinations of types of properties, types of clients, decisions to be made, and analyses necessary are so great that it is mind-boggling to determine how many different examples could be given and how many ways the body of knowledge could be organized. The choice in this case was simplified because we wanted, not only to have practicing counselors tell what they do, but also to describe what counseling is and to provide an overview of real estate analysis.

Please note that all of the chapters were written by practicing real estate counselors. These are people who are willing to share with others, in a forthright manner, information on how they do what they do. The work was organized by the editor in chief with the help of a subcommittee, and it was shepherded through by the editor in chief. Thus, although each chapter presents the view of its author, the work as a whole provides pretty close to a state-of-the-art view. It is an authoritative work, and it is also very readable. Even the copy editor was specially selected because of his prior experience with similar works.

The reader may note that the book is published as a joint venture by the American Society of Real Estate Counselors (ASREC) and Prentice-Hall, Inc.. ASREC decided that it wanted to publish this book and to distribute it to the ASREC membership and to the family of societies, councils, and institutes comprised by the National Association of Realtors because we wished to communicate among ourselves. In addition, however, we wished to communicate with the rest of the world, especially the potential users of counseling services and academia. Thus, we selected an outstanding publisher with a track record in both of these areas. Irrespective of which distribution channel has introduced you to the book, we are confident that after you have read it, you will have learned a great deal about real estate counseling. We also believe that after having read this book, you will want to learn even more.

Maury Seldin, CRE
1983 Chairman, Publications Committee
American Society of Real Estate Counselors

CONTRIBUTING AUTHORS

Adler, Thomas W., CRE (Chapter 15)
Principal, Adler Galvin Rogers, Inc.

Barkan, Abram, CRE (Chapter 18)
President, James Felt Realty Services,
a division of Grubb & Ellis

Bowes, E. Nelson, CRE (Chapter 14)
Vice President, Bowes and Company

Boyce, Byrl N., CRE (Chapter 4)
Director, Center for Real Estate and Urban Economic Studies,
University of Connecticut

Brener, Stephen W., CRE (Chapter 12)
President, Stephen W. Brener Associates, Inc.

Church, Byron M., CRE (Chapter 19)
President, Byron Church Associates

Collins, Webster A., CRE (Chapter 9)
Executive Vice President, C. W. Whittier, Inc.

Dolman, John P., CRE (Chapter 2)
Chairman, Jackson-Cross Company

Farber, Joseph, CRE (Chapter 13)
President, Joseph Farber & Company, Inc.

Ford, Robert W., CRE (Chapter 16)
President, Robert Ford & Associates, Inc.

Gibbons, James E., CRE (Chapter 17)
President, Sackman-Gibbons Associates

Hagood, Wayne D., CRE (Chapter 3)
President, Hagood & Associates, Inc.

Justice, Albert N., CRE (Chapter 8)
President, Justice Corporation

Kell, Lawrence A., CRE (Chapter 5)
Senior Vice President, Ostendorf-Morris Company

Shelger, Kurt S., CRE (Chapter 6)
Senior Vice President, Landauer Associates, Inc.

Shlaes, Jared, CRE (Chapter 1)
President, Shlaes & Co.

Simmons, Richard D., CRE (Chapter 11)
Principal, Simmons Associates

Stanson, Richard S., CRE (Chapter 10)
President, S. D. Stanson Company

Steele, Robert A., CRE (Chapter 7)
Owner, Robert Anson Steele Associates

Wight, Stewart, CRE (Chapter 16)
Senior Vice President, Landauer Associates, Inc.

ABOUT THE EDITOR AND CONTRIBUTING AUTHORS

James H. Boykin, editor in chief

James H. Boykin, Ph.D., MAI, SRPA, is the Alfred L. Blake Professor of Real Estate in the School of Business, Virginia Commonwealth University. He is also the director of the Real Estate and Urban Land Development Program in the School of Business and the director of the Virginia Real Estate Research Center.

Dr. Boykin has been the recipient of numerous research grants, fellowships, and awards. These include a National Science Foundation Fellowship and the Robert H. Armstrong Award given by the American Institute of Real Estate Appraisers for the article judged to have been "the most significant contribution to real estate valuation literature published in *The Appraisal Journal* in . . . 1976."

Dr. Boykin's research monographs and articles have appeared in numerous journals in this country and abroad. His most recent books are *Mortgage Loan Underwriting, Financing Real Estate,* and *Basic Income Property Appraisal.* He has been featured in numerous newspaper stories, appeared on radio and television news programs, and been quoted in such national publications as *U.S. News & World Report* and *The Wall Street Journal,* and lectured for professional groups throughout the country.

In addition to his university teaching, Dr. Boykin has had extensive experience as a real estate appraiser and consultant. He has been employed by the Federal Housing Administration and the Urban Land Institute and has qualified as an expert real estate witness in twelve courts of law.

Chapter 1
DECISIONS REQUIRING COUNSELING

Jared Shlaes

Jared Shlaes, CRE, MAI, is president of Shlaes & Co., a Chicago-based real estate counseling and appraisal firm. His real estate specialties are property and community analyses, land use and development programs, general counseling, and appraising. He has served as first vice president and member of the Board of Governors of the American Society of Real Estate Counselors and served from 1977 to 1986 as the Society's editor in chief of *Real Estate Issues*. He is a past director of the Chicago Real Estate Board and of the Illinois Chapter of AIREA.

He has published articles in professional journals and portions of several books, including a chapter on real estate counseling, feasibility analysis, and investment analysis in the eighth edition of *The Appraisal of Real Estate*.

Chapter 2
THE COUNSELING FUNCTION

John P. Dolman

John P. Dolman, CRE, MAI, is chairman of the Philadelphia-based firm Jackson-Cross Company, with offices in Wilmington, Delaware, and Washington, D.C. He specializes in counseling and in the appraisal of industrial, commercial, and special purpose properties, including railroads. His professional offices include past president, American Society of Real Estate Counselors, and past vice president, American Institute of Real Estate Appraisers, which he served as editor in chief of *The Appraisal Journal*.

He has published articles in *The Appraisal Journal, Buildings Magazine,* and *Realtor Magazine* and has had articles reprinted in AIREA's *Readings in the Appraisal of Special Purpose Properties* and *Readings in Real Property Valuation Principles*. He also served on the editorial board of *The Real Estate Handbook*.

Chapter 3
THE COUNSELING PROCESS

Wayne D. Hagood

Wayne D. Hagood, CRE, MAI, is president of Hagood & Associates, Inc., with offices in Forth Worth and Arlington, Texas. He specializes in investment analysis and counseling on commercial, industrial, apartment, and special purpose properties.

Hagood has taught appraisal courses and seminars throughout the United States and in Canada and Puerto Rico. He is a past president of the North Texas and Central Texas chapters of the American Institute of Real Estate Appraisers. He is a past state director of the Texas Association of Realtors and has served on the Board of Governors and as vice president of the American Society of Real Estate Counselors. He is the author of a number of valuation papers.

Chapter 4
THE COUNSELOR'S ROLE IN DECISION MAKING

Byrl N. Boyce, Ph.D.

Byrl N. Boyce, CRE, is director of the Center for Real Estate and Urban Economic Studies and professor of finance and real estate, University of Connecticut. His specializations are income property, valuation and evaluation, investment analysis, feasibility, marketability surveys, and tax shelter analyses.

Dr. Boyce is a past president of the American Real Estate and Urban Economics Association and was formerly editor of its journal.

He has written a considerable number of technical reports, articles, and monographs. Among the books that he has authored or coauthored are *Analyzing Real Estate Opportunities: Market and Feasibility Studies, Industrial Real Estate, Real Estate Appraisal Terminology, and Appraising Real Property*.

Chapter 5
LOCATION ANALYSIS

Lawrence A. Kell

Lawrence A. Kell, CRE, is a senior vice president and member of the board of directors of Ostendorf-Morris Company, a Cleveland firm. He specializes in investment property analysis, appraisals, and counseling, and he heads the appraisal counseling department of the firm. He has served as vice president, chairman of the Member Services and Membership Liaison Committees, editor in chief of the THE COUNSELOR, the quarterly newsletter, and a member of the Board of Governors and Special Task Forces of the American Society of Real Estate Counselors. His twenty plus years of experience in the private sector of the real estate market have been varied both in property types and objectives. His articles have appeared in the Cleveland Area Board of Realtors publication, The Real Estate Appraisal and Analyst, and The Appraisal Journal.

Chapter 6
INVESTMENT ANALYSIS FOR PROPOSED PROJECTS

Kurt S. Shelger

Kurt S. Shelger, CRE, MAI is a principal in Buss-Shelger Associates in Los Angeles. He provides investment and marketing consulting services in the acquisition, sale, leasing, portfolio management, valuation, land use, and development planning of investment real estate.

Shelger is a past president of the American Institute of Real Estate Appraisers' Southern California Chapter and a regional vice president of the Southwest Region. He has also been a member of the Governing Council of the AIREA, and he has served as a governor of the American Society of Real Estate Counselors. His instruction of real estate appraisal courses has been on a regional basis. He has contributed to the *Silver Anniversary Papers* of the American Institute of Real Estate Appraisers and to the *Encyclopedia of Real Estate Appraising*.

Chapter 7
INVESTMENT ANALYSIS FOR EXISTING PROJECTS

Robert A. Steele

Robert A. Steele, CRE, MAI, is the owner of Robert Anson Steele Associates. He specializes in real estate investments. He was twice elected to the Board of Governors of the American Society of Real Estate Counselors, of which he is a past second vice president. He has also been a president of the Southern California Chapter, and he has served on the Governing Council of the American Institute of Real Estate Appraisers. His publications include six articles in *The Appraisal Journal* as well as articles in *The Appraiser* and in publications of the California Association of Realtors and the International Association of Assessing Officers.

Chapter 8
PROPERTY MANAGEMENT COUNSELING

Albert N. Justice

Albert N. Justice, CRE, CPM, is president of Justice Corporation, which is headquartered in Clearwater and has seven offices throughout Florida. His specialty for the past twenty-three years has been the development, leasing, and management of commercial office buildings. He has served as national president of the Institute of Real Estate Management and as past president of the Richmond, Virginia, Board of Realtors, and he was the chairman of the Community Revitalization Committee of the National Association of Realtors. Since 1968 Justice has conducted courses and seminars in every major city in the United States and Canada on the development, leasing, and management of office buildings.

Chapter 9
COUNSELING IN LEASE OR BUY DECISIONS

Webster A. Collins

Webster A. Collins, CRE, MAI, is executive vice president of C. W. Whittier, Inc., of Boston. His experience has included analysis of over $2 billion in real estate assets, and he has recently been involved in representing New England–based major national corporations in order to meet their real estate needs throughout the country. He is a past president of the New England Chapter of the American Institute of Real Estate Appraisers. As a member of the American Society of Real Estate Counselors, he has served on the Board of Governors, as a vice president, editor of *The Counselor* and author of the report, *Office Building Rehabilitation: Key Ingredient for Successful Projects*.

Chapter 10
DISTRESSED PROPERTY ANALYSIS

Richard S. Stanson*

Richard S. Stanson, CRE, SIR, is president of S. D. Stanson Company in Akron, Ohio. He specializes in rehabilitation and conversion of older and historic properties, distressed property evaluation analysis and work-out procedures. He is a past president of the Ohio Chapter of the Society of Industrial Realtors and has also served as a vice president of SIR and as a member of its board of directors. He is currently serving on the board of directors of the Akron Area Board of Realtors. He is the coauthor of the chapter "Rehabilitation and Conversion of Industrial Real Estate" in *Industrial Real Estate*.

*Assisted by James R. Webb, Ph.D.,
Associate Professor, Department of Finance,
University of Akron.

Chapter 11
COUNSELING THE RESIDENTIAL CLIENT

Richard D. Simmons

Richard D. Simmons, CRE, is the president in Simmons Associates LTD. which is located in Wakefield, Massachusetts. He concentrates his counseling practice on investment real estate, medical buildings, municipal land use, residential real estate purchase and sale, and land development. He is a past vice president of the American Society of Real Estate Counselors and has served on the Board of Governors. He is a past president of the Eastern Middlesex Board of Realtors and New England Regional Vice President of RNMI. He has also served as a regional vice president of the Massachusetts Association of Realtors. Simmons is a regular columnist on "Counseling" for the *New England Real Estate Journal*.

Chapter 12
MOTEL-HOTEL PROPERTIES

Stephen W. Brener*

Stephen W. Brener, CRE, CPM, CCIM, is president of Stephen W. Brener Associates, Inc., of New York City. He specializes in counseling private and public investors in hotel and motel development, market surveys, valuation studies, and resort time-share planning, feasibility analyses, and management reviews. He has written in such publications as *Lodging Hospitality, The Real Estate Appraiser,* and *American Banker,* and he is the financial editor of *Lodging Hospitality.* Annually since 1964 he has published the *New York Hotel Survey & Motor Hotel Survey and Report.*

*Assisted by Jeffrey C. Carter, President,
Keystone Hospitality Services, New York, New York.

Chapter 13
COUNSELING THE OFFICE BUILDING CLIENT

Joseph Farber

Joseph Farber, CRE, MAI is president of the Denver-based firm Joseph Farber and Company, Inc. He specializes in counseling, valuation, market, and feasibility studies related to unique and complex problems in real estate development, financing, sales, leasing, and syndication. He has been a participant in advanced educational seminars and a featured speaker at national conventions for professional organizations. His articles have appeared in such publications as *Up to Date Appraisal News, Commercial Investment Journal* and ASREC's *Office Building Monograph.*

Chapter 14
COMMERCIAL PROPERTY COUNSELING

E. Nelson Bowes

E. Nelson Bowes, CRE, MAI, is vice president of the Denver firm Bowes and Company. In addition to having professional real estate designations, he is also a professional engineer (PE). He specializes in valuation and counseling regarding feasibility, market studies, highest and best use, and management and marketing of income-producing real estate. He has served on several committees of the American Institute of Real Estate Appraisers and has taught real estate courses at the University of Colorado and engineering courses at the University of Denver.

Chapter 15
INDUSTRIAL PROPERTIES

Thomas W. Adler*

Thomas W. Adler, CRE, SIR, is a principal in the Cleveland firm Adler Galvin Rogers, Inc. His real estate specialties are counseling and brokerage services for all types of investment real estate; evaluation of the investment merits of properties and the negotiation for clients of purchases, sales, joint ventures, and financing arrangements involving income property. Adler has served on various committees of the American Society of Real Estate Counselors. He has actively participated in the Society of Industrial Realtors and has served as a member of its board of directors and as national chairman of its Education and Long Range Planning committees. He is a past president of the Ohio Chapter of SIR and a former member of the Board of Governors and executive committee of the National Association of Real Estate Investment Trusts. He was chairman of the committee that was assigned to the third edition of *Industrial Real Estate*.

*Assisted by James R. Webb, Ph.D., Associate Professor,
Department of Finance, University of Akron.

Chapter 16
RECREATIONAL AND RESORT PROPERTY COUNSELING

Robert W. Ford and Stewart Wight

Robert W. Ford, CRE, MAI, is president of Robert Ford & Associates, Inc., of Modesto, California. He specializes in counseling and valuation analysis of transitional properties with recreational or agricultural influence, including coastal, lakefront, range, and timbered properties. He has served as the national president of the American Institute of Real Estate Appraisers, been a member of the AIREA faculty, and is a past president of the Northern California Chapter of AIREA. He is also a past president of the Modesto Board of Realtors. He has published in ASREC's quarterly journal *Real Estate Issues*.

Stewart Wight, CRE, MAI, CPM, is a managing director of Landauer Associates, Inc. Operating from Atlanta, he specializes in counseling on commercial, multifamily, and special purpose properties and on general real estate problems. He is a past governor of the American Society of Real Estate Counselors, the American Institute of Real Estate Appraisers, and the Institute of Real Estate Management. He has also served as a regional vice president of the American Institute of Real Estate Appraisers, and he is a past president of both the Atlanta Board of Realtors and the Georgia Association of Realtors.

Chapter 17
COUNSELING FINANCIAL INSTITUTIONS

James E. Gibbons

James E. Gibbons, CRE, MAI, is president of Sackman-Gibbons Associates and of Majestic Towers Management Corporation. He specializes in mortgage banking and counseling on real estate investments and finance. He has served on several national committees of the American Society of Real Estate Counselors and has been a member of its Board of Governors. He is a past president of the New York Chapter and a former regional vice president of the American Institute of Real Estate Appraisers. He is the author of *Appraising in a Changing Economy—Col-*

lected Writings of James E. Gibbons, and his articles have been published in such journals as *The Appraisal Journal, The Appraiser,* and *The Counselor.* His writing has earned him several national awards. He is a trustee of the Jamaica Savings Bank and the chairman of its Mortgage Committee. He is also a director of the Manhattan Life Insurance Company. He is admitted to practice law in the courts of the state of New York.

Chapter 18
CORPORATE CONSULTATION

Abram Barkan

Abram Barkan, CRE, MAI, is president of James Felt Realty Services, a Grubb & Ellis Company that is headquartered in New York City and has offices in Los Angeles. He specializes in counseling services on residential and commercial real estate, including large-scale housing developments, office buildings, and shopping centers; investment analyses; and market and feasibility studies. He is a past president of the American Society of Real Estate Counselors and of the New York Chapter of the American Institute of Real Estate Appraisers. He has served as a director of the National Association of Realtors and was a member of the board of directors of the Real Estate Board of New York, Inc.

Chapter 19
GOVERNMENT AGENCY COUNSELING

Byron M. Church*

Byron M. Church, CRE, MAI, is president of Byron Church Associates in Colorado Springs, Colorado. He specializes in counseling, valuation and syndication. He has been a member of the Board of Governors of the American Society of Real Estate Counselors, and he is a past president of the Colorado Chapter of the American Institute of Real Estate Appraisers. His appraisal lecturing assignments have carried him to fifteen states. His articles have appeared in *The Appraisal Journal, The Real Estate Appraiser*, and *National Real Estate and Building Journal*, and he served as editor in chief of the ASREC quarterly newsletter, *The Counselor.*

*Assisted by Stephen C. Sampson,
Owner
Stephen C. Sampson Associates

ACKNOWLEDGMENTS

The editor in chief wishes to express his appreciation to the many helpful and knowledgeable professionals who assisted in the preparation of this book. The idea of the book was conceived and shepherded through the necessary approval stages by Max J. Derbes, Jr., who also prepared an initial draft of the chapter outlines and served as a member of the Book Subcommittee. Jean C. Felts proved most helpful in the embryonic stages of the book's development—first as chairman of ASREC's Publications Committee and next as chairman of the Book Subcommittee. During the final year of the writing of the book, Dr. Maury Seldin served as chairman of the Book Subcommittee. His willingness to promptly and capably respond to problems—actual and anticipated—made the editorial task quite agreeable. Lois Hofstetter, Executive Vice President, and Mary Christenson, Staff Editor, American Society of Real Estate Counselors, were invaluable sources of information and assistance. Both were provided by them ever so willingly.

Each chapter was read by counselors who had particular experience with and insights into the subject matter. These valuable critics were Thomas H. Bearden, The Thomas Bearden Company, Houston, Texas; Watson A. Bowes, A. G. Bowes & Son, Inc., Denver, Colorado; Malcolm L. S. Bryce, Bryce, Kipp & Company, Ltd., Calgary, Alberta, Canada; John M. Burroughs, Burke, Hansen & Homan, Phoenix, Arizona; Wallace H. Campbell, Wallace H. Campbell & Co., Inc., Baltimore, Maryland; Blaine B. Chase, Chase and Company, Denver, Colorado; John A. Clem III, Clem & Company, Inc., Staunton, Virginia; Douglas F. Collins, Bob

Collins Co., Tulsa, Oklahoma; the late Robert S. Curtiss, New York, New York; Max J. Derbes, Jr., Max J. Derbes, Inc., Realtors, New Orleans, Louisiana; Thomas B. Dupree, Jr., Waguespack, Dupree & Felts, Inc., Shreveport, Louisiana; Roger W. Foster, Foster Appraisal & Consulting Co., Inc., Fitchburg, Massachusetts; Leslie B. Gray, Pomeroy Appraisal Associates, Inc., Syracuse, New York; Hunter A. Hogan, Jr., Goodman-Segar-Hogan, Inc., Norfolk, Virginia; James C. Kafes, Miller & Kafes Associates, Inc., Fort Lee, New Jersey; Lawrence A. Kell, Ostendorf-Morris Company, Cleveland, Ohio; Neil J. King, Armond D. King, Inc., Skokie, Illinois; William N. Kinnard, Jr., Ph.D., Real Estate Counseling Group of Connecticut, Inc., Storrs, Connecticut; Irving Korb, Korb Co. Real Estate Consultants, Oakland, California; Tom H. Lang, Tom H. Lang & Co., Cleveland, Ohio; Reaves C. Lukens, Jr., Reaves C. Lukens Company, Philadelphia, Pennsylvania; Stephen C. Morris, Ostendorf-Morris Company, Cleveland, Ohio; Hunter Moss, Hunter Moss and Company, Boca Raton, Florida; Roland Rodrock Randall, Jackson-Cross Company, Philadelphia, Pennsylvania; James A. Roe, Landauer Associates, Inc., West Palm Beach, Florida; Thurston H. Ross, Ph.D., Los Angeles, California; Stephen Rushmore, Hospitality Valuation Services, Inc., Mineola, New York; Stephan M. Segal, Stephan M. Segal Associates, Trenton, New Jersey; John A. Stallings, Henry S. Miller Company, Dallas, Texas; Daniel L. Swango, Ph.D., Swango Real Estate Valuation & Counseling, Tucson, Arizona; J. Ed. Turner, J. Ed. Turner, Inc., Realtor, Hattiesburg, Mississippi; William T. Van Court, Van Court and Company, Denver, Colorado; and James S. Watkinson, Morton G. Thalhimer, Inc., Richmond, Virginia.

Another person who was quite helpful was G. William Greer, Foran & Greer, Inc., Raleigh, North Carolina.

James H. Boykin
Editor in Chief

REAL
ESTATE
COUNSELING

CHAPTER ONE
DECISIONS REQUIRING COUNSELING

This chapter defines real estate counseling, specifies some of the many kinds of problems that real estate counseling addresses, and illustrates by means of brief examples how real estate counselors can assist real estate decision makers in solving such problems. The chapter concludes with a discussion of the ethics of counseling. Ethics is emphasized at this early stage because of the vital part it plays in both the definition and the practice of the counseling profession.

REAL ESTATE COUNSELING DEFINED

Real estate counseling is the provision of advice, guidance, and support in real estate matters. As used in this book, the term *real estate counseling* is limited to the provision of such services on a fee basis by qualified professionals who have subscribed to a suitable code of ethics. The services provided may include

Acquisition planning

Alternative use studies for existing structures

Conflict management

Cost-benefit studies

Cost studies

Development planning

Disposition planning

Evaluation of proposed transactions

Feasibility analysis

1

Financial planning	Neighborhood and community analysis
Forecasting	Opinion testimony
Highest and best use studies	Portfolio design
Impact analysis	Portfolio review
Investment analysis	Property management review
Location analysis	Risk analysis
Market analysis	Site selection studies
Marketing assistance	Transaction structuring
Needs assessment	Zoning assistance
Negotiations	

Services such as these are often provided by real estate brokers, real estate managers, and mortgage bankers in the ordinary course of their work. However, they are considered counseling services only when they are rendered on a professional basis, for a fee, and not when they are rendered for commissions or as a function of a dealer in real estate.

The American Society of Real Estate Counselors has defined real estate counseling as follows:

> Providing competent, disinterested and unbiased advice, professional guidance, and sound judgment on diversified problems in the broad field of real estate involving any or all aspects of the business such as merchandising, leasing, management, planning, financing, appraising, court testimony and other similar services. Counseling may involve the utilization of any or all of these functions.
>
> Real estate counseling, then, is the offering of advice on a broad basis in all aspects of real estate as delimited by the client's needs. The world "advice" does not refer to off-the-cuff, intuitive, gratuitous or impulsive advice. "Advice" means considered judgment arrived at after careful investigation, discussion and deliberation with the principals involved. It is fully documented opinion given after all factors have been considered. It is consultation, with the reasoning spelled out in a written or oral report, and for an agreed fee.
>
> The counselor performs his work as a separate and distinct undertaking, divorced from the usual functions of real estate brokerage. He is not an agent in real estate transactions. The product he sells is the creation of his mind—his advice born of experience, blended with wisdom, tempered by judgment, and supported by facts. The counselor treats each problem individualistically. His conclusions generally cannot be applied except to a particular client or group of clients, or to a specified project or property; and the success of his endeavors is measured by the extent of acceptance and utilization of his services by his client.[1]

PROBLEMS ADDRESSED IN
REAL ESTATE COUNSELING

Counseling may be thought of as answering the client's question "What should I do?" when the question is related to a real estate problem. Some typical property owners' questions are

[1]American Society of Real Estate Counselors, *What Is Real Estate Counseling?* (Chicago: American Society of Real Estate Counselors, 1962), pp.14–15.

What is the property worth to me?

Should I keep it, sell it, or rent it?

How should I go about disposing of it?

How can I improve the benefits of ownership?

How should I develop the property?

What events are likely to affect my property,and how will they affect it?

Who are the prospective users or purchasers of the property?

How long should I plan to hold the property?

How can I best finance or refinance it?

How well are my agents performing?

Should the property be subdivided? If so, how?

How can I get permission to use or develop the property in accordance with my plans?

What can I do about a threatened or actual condemnation action?

How should a community area or public facility be used?

What impact will my proposed use have on the community?

What impact will a pending change in the community have on my property?

What costs and benefits will result from a specific decision concerning the property?

How should I deal with a conflict involving the property?

Issues Involving Risk and Conflict

Similar questions might be asked by lenders, buyers, and others, who will, of course, see the problems from different perspectives. Numerous other questions are implicit in each of the questions listed. In a situation involving conflict, for example, the client might want answers to the following questions:

What result can I expect?

What is the worst that can happen?

What risks are involved?

How can those risks be minimized?

Who are the experts in the field?

How should my team be organized?

What kind of schedule should I adopt?

Who are the likely opponents?

How can those opponents be neutralized?

How should I handle community relations during the conflict?

Examples of Counseling Problems

The following examples suggest some of the real estate problems that often confront property owners, tenants, lenders, and community leaders. Each example is based on an actual situation. In almost every instance, the client is asking the counselor, "What should I do?"

1. *Mortgage foreclosure.* A mortgage lender has foreclosed on a partially completed residential condominium project. The following questions are troubling the lender: Should the project be completed? If so, who should complete it and

under what contractual arrangements? Should the project be modified prior to completion to improve its marketability? If so, how? Finally, what marketing strategy is likely to produce the most sales revenue in the shortest possible time?

2. *Liquidation.* The trust department of a small bank is required to dispose of an estate that includes several large properties. The staff of the trust department is insufficiently familiar with the properties to judge their value, develop a marketing campaign, and negotiate the sale of the properties, so it asks for help.

3. *Development planning.* An investor contemplating the purchase of a large tract is concerned about how the property should be developed, what use or uses should be contemplated, how development should be timed, and how the finished product should be marketed. He also wants to know the most desirable way to acquire the tract.

4. *Management planning.* A small investor has acquired an income-producing property. She is uncertain about what the rent should be or how to draw up leases. In addition, she wants to know how long the property should be held and whether it should eventually be refinanced or sold outright.

5. *Development assistance.* The owners of a vocational training center wish to convert it to a medical building. They need help in selecting the architect, builder, and management and in arranging the necessary financing.

6. *Investment advice.* A family has inherited substantial landholdings in a distant state. It wants to know whether to sell or hold the tract, what the tax consequences of a sale will be, and how to go about finding a suitable broker if it decides to sell.

7. *Conversion services.* A newly formed limited partnership is interested in acquiring a luxury apartment building for conversion into a residential condominium. It seeks guidance with regard to the value and physical soundness of the building, the tenant policies that should be adopted, the amenities that should be provided, the pricing of the converted units, and the kind of investment return that can be expected. It would also like to know what marketing strategy should be adopted, what mortgage terms will be available to the purchasers, and what documents will be required for the conversion.

8. *Impact analysis.* A municipal planning commission is considering revisions in the zoning ordinance. It wants advice regarding the economic impact of the proposed revisions, particularly with regard to property and sales tax revenues, employment, and school population.

9. *Management assistance.* An apartment development in another city is suffering from high tenant turnover. The owners ask for assistance in stabilizing the tenancy without reducing rents. They also request an evaluation of the manager's procedures and performance.

10. *Sales counseling.* The owner of a farm that is a short distance from a major city wants to know whether he should sell the farm, enter into a joint venture development program, develop the farm by himself, or exchange all or part of the farm for another property. The owner of an adjacent property wants to buy the back forty acres, and our client wants to know whether selling them is a good idea.

11. *Use study*. The owners of a downtown loft building that has been vacated by its principal tenant need to know whether the building should be demolished, left vacant, or rented on a temporary basis while redevelopment of the property for other uses is awaited. New office buildings are rising nearby, and a change of use may be indicated.

12. *Assessing space needs*. A bank requires new quarters. Should the building be adequate for just the bank, or should it provide additional office space for rental to other businesses? If additional space is provided, how much should there be, and how should it be designed? What provisions should be included in tenant leases to permit the bank to expand into the space at a later date?

13. *Conflict resolution*. A property owner and a tenant cannot agree on the rental to be paid over the next ten years of a long-term lease that contains a series of options requiring the parties to agree on the renewal rent every ten years. The property owner and tenant seek a counselor acceptable to both of them who will help them to ascertain the fair market rent by agreement or, failing that, who will establish a procedure by which they can reach a rental figure without going to court.

14. *Needs assessment*. A growing law firm requires larger offices. Each of its ten partners seems to have a different opinion about what would be the best office location. The firm retains a counselor to study its needs, to investigate all of the available facilities within the firm's area of practice, and to recommend an acceptable location.

15. *Location analysis*. A carpet distributor wants to know where to locate a distribution center in relation to the total expected market area. This will entail a study of all the choices realistically available to the client and for each of these choices, an assessment of driving times, toll bridge costs, expected growth patterns within the market area, freight costs, and the tax structures of adjacent competing communities.

16. *Property taxes*. A lessee who is in the eighteenth year of a twenty-year lease is required to pay all of the real estate taxes. He wants professional assistance to determine whether the taxes being charged are excessive. If so, he will need help in reducing the taxes over the remainder of the lease term.

17. *Neighborhood analysis*. The owner of an apartment complex is concerned about undesirable changes in the neighborhood. She wants to know whether she should keep or sell the property and whether it should be sold as an apartment complex or converted into condominium units and then sold.

18. *Evaluation*. An investor has been offered an income-producing property and wishes to know what risks are involved, what aftertax cash flow is to be expected, how sound the property is, how the purchase should be financed, and what advantages and disadvantages would be associated with rehabilitation.

19. *Facilities planning*. An industrial company needs to expand a plant and wants to know what it can expect to get for the plant in the market, what it would have to pay for a suitable existing facility at another location, how much it would cost to acquire a site and build a new building, what its moving costs are likely to be, where suitable sites are likely to be available, where a suitable facility might

be rented, and what the aftertax implications of these various possibilities would be.

20. *Use study*. A developer has optioned a parcel of land suitable for development and wants advice on the type of development best suited to the parcel, the likely pricing of the units built, the probable rate of sales, and trends that are likely to affect the success or failure of the project.

21. *Redevelopment planning*. A group of investors wants to consolidate streets and sites in an old downtown warehouse district in order to create a high-rise office and hotel site. All of the investors agree that a plan should be worked out to close the streets, create larger parcels, and subdivide the more usable properties after demolishing the buildings. Some of the investors wish to sell; others wish to enter into joint ventures. The city is willing to close the streets if it receives its fair share of the newly created land. A plan and an assessment of the project's chances are necessary.

22. *Portfolio review*. The owners of a large collection of office buildings, hotels, apartment complexes, and industrial properties want to know what changes they should make in their portfolio to improve its overall performance without increasing investment risks. The apartment complexes have not been performing well. Should the owners sell off some or all of these complexes?

23. *Cost-benefit studies*. A community that is contemplating the offer of a property tax abatement in order to attract a new downtown hotel wants to know whether the anticipated benefits justify the revenue sacrifice being contemplated. It wonders just how much the hotel is likely to produce in the way of sales and room taxes, jobs, and indirect benefits.

24. *Forecasting*. The owners of a downtown office building wonder what effects current trends in office building construction, office space design, local business patterns, and area population characteristics will have on their investment. They want to know how long they should hold the property and what will eventually become of it.

HOW COUNSELORS
ASSIST CLIENTS

The solutions that real estate counselors present and the methods by which they reach those solutions are just as diverse as the problems that confront real estate owners and users. Each problem requires individualized treatment. To be really helpful, counselors may need special knowledge and skills—perhaps in such fields as investment analysis, operations research, statistics, construction management, real estate finance, and income tax planning. But it is the broad experience and good judgment of real estate counselors that focus such special knowledge and skills on the client's problem.

Clients can benefit from the counselor's ability to

Analyze property values
Conduct research
Evaluate management performance
Forecast investment outcomes
Formulate plans to achieve objectives
Identify and define problems and opportunities
Investigate markets
Model investment scenarios
Negotiate and arbitrate between parties
Orchestrate transactions
Persuade individuals to take action
Plan developments
Provide expert testimony
Train others to provide real estate services
Understand complex situations

THE ETHICS OF
COUNSELING

No profession can survive without ethical behavior. The client of a professional must feel satisfied that they are in good hands and that the professional will not abuse the trust implicit in their relationship. The conduct of a professional person must meet higher standards than those required of other practitioners and must reflect a sense of responsibility to both the client and the community. Professional codes of ethics identify proper relationships with clients, fellow practitioners, and the public in general.

Real estate counselors accept a special responsibility because they present themselves to the public as qualified and objective professionals whose duty is to put the client's interest ahead of the counselor's and to seek no financial gain in connection with the assignment beyond the agreed fee. They invite the client's trust, and they may not abuse that trust without violating the client's expectations as well as their own code of ethics.

The cornerstones of counseling are independence of action, objectivity in analysis, respect for one's colleagues and for the public interest, and a fiduciary relationship with the client. These cornerstones, embraced in the code of ethics of the American Society of Real Estate Counselors, have certain practical implications. As set forth in the Society's Standards of Professional Practice, they are

Standard No. 1:   The Counselor must not accept any assignment involving a conflict of interest, and must withdraw from any assignment if an unavoidable conflict of interest arises after the assignment has been accepted, unless such conflict is fully disclosed in writing to all parties and all parties agree that the assignment may be accepted or continued.

Standard No. 2:   The Counselor must not accept any assignment or engage in any practice involving a violation of the law or of his specific ethical responsibilities, and must immediately withdraw from an assignment if such violation is perceived.

Standard No. 3:   The Counselor must not accept any assignment if the terms or conditions of such assignment do not permit complete freedom and objectivity in performing the assignment and rendering his advice thereon. Specifically,
1.   The Counselor must not accept any assignment which makes his fee contingent on the substance of the advice or counsel given.
2.   The Counselor must not accept any assignment in which he is called upon solely to lend his professional reputation or signature as a Counselor to predetermined opinions or positions.
3.   The Counselor must not accept any assignment which precludes or limits his ability to develop factual and supportable opinions, findings or conclusions.
4.   The Counselor must not accept any assignment which is beyond the scope of competence, knowledge and expertise when he is prevented from obtaining the needed knowledge or expertise from other sources.

Standard No. 4:   The Counselor must not accept any counseling assignment which involves no function other than the determination of the value of real estate. However, the Counselor may, in connection with other counseling services, render value opinions provided they are clearly qualified as preliminary, informal or approximate and with a definite understanding that such opinions are not to be construed as appraisals.

Standard No. 5:   The Counselor must not accept any assignment which requires him as an individual to perform concurrently and for compensation other real estate services relevant to the counseling assignment for the same client, unless such other real estate services are agreed upon at the time the counseling assignment is accepted, or are requested by the client on his own initiative.

Standard No. 6:   The Counselor must not accept any assignment which may require him to testify under oath unless his client understands that such oath supersedes the Counselor's obligation to preserve the confidential relationship between them.

Standard No. 7:   The Counselor shall not testify in any proceedings regarding any assignment except with the written consent of his client or in response to legal process, and will cooperate in any efforts by his client to quash such process.

·   The value of counseling services depends on the personal integrity of the counselor. No amount of trade knowledge, technical expertise, or communications skill can offset a lack of honesty, courage, and fairness in the counselor. Thus, the first decision facing the prospective client is the selection of a counselor whose character is as sound as his or her professional competence.

CHAPTER TWO
THE COUNSELING
FUNCTION

This chapter deals in a general way with what the counselor does in the conduct of his or her counseling practice. The chapter emphasizes the activities performed in the real estate counseling profession and gives particular attention to the counselor's responsibility to the client and to the client's obligation to cooperate fully with the counselor.

A counselor is often a member of a real estate brokerage firm, but his counseling practice is distinct from the firm's brokerage function. A counselor does not act as an agent in real estate transactions. His professional service is sound advice that is the distillation of years of experience used in the judicious analysis of pertinent factual data.

The relationship between the counselor and his client is similar to the relationship between the lawyer and his client.

A counselor translates his knowledge of the past into projections of the future. His broad experience equips him to comprehend the most sophisticated problems in the real estate field, which may involve the conservation of property as well as analysis of its diversified uses and potentials. In his studies of the many complex and challenging problems encountered in real estate, his perspective, professional objectivity, and detachment enable him to recognize and select the courses of action most beneficial to his clients. His skills in communicating his findings and recommendations to his clients render his services valuable in the most practical sense.

EVOLUTION OF REAL ESTATE COUNSELING

In the United States many outstanding real estate advisers are members of the American Society of Real Estate Counselors. ASREC is an affiliate of the National Association of Realtors and is thus restricted to Realtors. A group of Realtors with long and varied experience joined together to promote the growth and improve the quality of real estate counseling by adopting and enforcing standards of professional practice for this real estate service. In November 1953 this group founded the Society, which became affiliated with the National Association of Realtors in February 1954. ASREC was founded for the purpose of meeting the public need for competent, disinterested, and independent real estate advice and guidance rendered by qualified experts on a fee basis.

In discharging its obligations to the general public, the Society takes careful measures to invite into its membership only Realtors who have demonstrated their integrity and are qualified by experience, training, and knowledge to develop and express sound judgments on diversified problems in the real estate field. Membership in ASREC is by invitation only.

An individual's membership in the Society indicates that he or she is considered qualified to render competent professional advice in matters relating to real estate and is qualified and authorized to use the designation CRE (Counselor of Real Estate). Members of ASREC subscribe to and pledge themselves to abide by the Society's code of professional ethics and standards of professional practice.

COUNSELING DISTINGUISHED FROM OTHER REAL ESTATE FUNCTIONS

Advice based on the experience and judgment of the real estate professional is one of his most important products. Such advice should not be given away or buried in other legitimate real estate services. Neither should it be overshadowed by conventional fee or commission arrangements. The real estate counselor's relationship with a client justifies both specific and adequate fees, but it also obligates the counselor to avoid possible conflicts of interest.

It is important to understand at the outset that counseling is not so much a separate body of knowledge as a relationship with the client. The real estate counselor as such is not in competition with the appraiser, the broker, the property manager, or the expert in any specific real estate field. Usually he has already identified himself as an expert in one or more such fields, but he recognizes that his relationship with the client as a broker working for a commission, as an appraiser bound to an objective judgment of value, or as a property manager interested in retaining management of the client's property might conflict with the client's need for objective, unbiased advice pertinent to his problems. The counselor's relationship with the client tends to be more confidential, even more personal, than that of the real estate expert.

Under some circumstances a counselor may function as an advocate for his client, in which case he might disqualify himself as an appraiser of market value in a particular assignment. It becomes very important, therefore, that the client's relationship with real estate experts be carefully identified and clearly defined. The prospective client should recognize that there can be both practical and philosophical distinctions between the exclusive agent, the appraiser, the broker, and the counselor.

Real estate counseling should be limited to those persons who are willing to approach the service on a professional basis. Very rarely is a real estate practitioner thanked or given credit for free advice that ultimately proves to be sound. However, free advice that is hastily or improperly developed or proves to be unsound can be a source of constant irritation to a client, if not a basis for adverse publicity or loss of goodwill. To say that "free counseling is not cheap" is an understatement. Such counseling can be very costly to both parties.

Counseling, therefore, is the giving of only one's best advice, thoroughly researched, thought out, and checked, even to the extent of consulting other specialists. Frequently, if not always, counseling is needed most *before* decisions are made, not for confirmation. Unfortunately, counseling is sometimes sought after it is too late.

FIGURE 2–1   The Counselor working with a client. Courtesy of L. W. Ellwood and company and Manufactures Hanover Trust Company.

IDEAL BACKGROUND FOR COUNSELING

Educational

The counselor should be a mature and analytical individual with intellectual curiosity and an ability to recognize and understand a wide variety of cultural matters. He must be able to quickly grasp the problems associated with the production, financing, marketing, and management of real estate. He must have a good knowledge of where the answers to these problems may be found, if he does not have ready answers from his own education and experience. The counselor's basic background should generally include an undergraduate college education, with a graduate becoming increasingly common. The ability to think, write, and speak well and the ability to appreciate a wide variety of cultural subjects and many fundamental issues outside the real estate business itself are obviously important assets. Familiarity with business and economic concepts is also of considerable importance to the prospective counselor.

Having laid a firm, broad-based educational foundation, the counselor is better prepared to undertake a program of continuing education throughout the rest of his professional career. The courses given by the various affiliates of the National Association of Realtors, as well as postgraduate work at universities, help the counselor to keep up with the changes that take place in the developing, financing, marketing, managing, and analyzing of the many types of real estate. It must be realized, however, that most real estate problems are intellectual rather than "bricks and mortar" oriented. This is not to say that the physical elements of real estate are unimportant. But more often than not it is the personal and intellectual relationships that are most difficult to understand or resolve.

Experience

Obviously, a good grounding in fundamentals is important for counseling and, in fact, for any career in real estate. But experience in such areas as the building, marketing, operating, financing, appraising, and insuring of real property is all-important. It may not be necessary to draw on all of this experience to solve a particular counseling assignment. However, since each assignment differs to some degree from all other assignments, this broad-based background is essential. Also, familiarity with the different functions of real estate enables the counselor to bring a more knowledgeable and comprehensive point of view to bear on the client's problems. A breadth of educational background and pertinent business experience are important even though the expertise of most counselors falls within an identifiable specialty. An individual's education, experience, and track record can produce the kind of visibility in the business community that will lead to the enhancement of his or her status and to a wider clientele.

COUNSELOR-CLIENT RELATIONSHIP

As was stated earlier, counseling is not so much a separate body of knowledge as a relationship with the client. That relationship requires not only a thorough appreciation by the counselor of his responsibility to the client but also the client's understanding of what the counselor needs and expects from the client.

Counselor's Responsibility to Client

Obviously, one of the counselor's responsibilities to the client is to thoroughly know his business. Counseling is such a broad term that its direct application to the real estate business is often misunderstood, misused, and misinterpreted. A real estate counselor's first function may often be to "clear the cobwebs" or "open the eyes" of the client as to the general nature of his problem and the relevant real estate phenomena before performing such specific services as appraising, managing, or brokerage. The complexity of today's many real estate markets requires analysis of the effects of freeways, urban renewal, zoning, airports, financing, and taxes, to mention only a few of the areas in which the professional counselor must be knowledgeable. Performance in these areas requires specialized professional experience and judgment. It is the counselor's responsibility to guide his client in defining the issues involved in the problem, to suggest alternatives, and to advance solutions after adequate research, study, and perhaps consultation with other real estate specialists.

Counselor's Expectations of Client

Among the things that the counselor should expect from his client are

1. *Client screening.* The counselor should determine as early as possible whether the prospective client is ready, willing, and able to seek and accept professional advice. The counselor should promptly discern whether the prospective client reveals indications of some ulterior motive for using the counselor's function. If the counselor discovers any motive of this kind, he is well advised to promptly withdraw from what might become an uncomfortable, unprofessional, or improper business relationship.

2. *Maximum amount of factual information.* The prospective client must be made to realize that in order to develop the appropriate questions and to outline the nature of the problem and its possible solutions, the counselor requires a maximum amount of pertinent factual information. Thus, the client must be made to realize that any such information in his possession should be disclosed to the counselor as soon as possible, if only to reduce the time and expense necessary to obtain the same information from other sources.

3. *Complete honesty.* It is extremely important that the relationship between the counselor and his client be based on complete honesty on both sides. If the

client is not prepared to provide the counselor with all of the facts in a straightforward and thoroughly sincere manner, both parties may be wasting their time. The quality of the counselor's ultimate service to the client is in direct relation to the completeness of the germane factual data provided by the client. A counselor should never have to play "guessing games" with his client.

4. *Confidentiality of the report.* The entire staff of both the client and the counselor should fully understand that the results of a study (presented in a written or verbal report) are confidential. Although the completed report may be treated as belonging to the client after it has been paid for, it should be made plain to the client that any distribution of the report should be discussed with the counselor. The counselor, in turn, should be given the opportunity to suggest that it might be mutually beneficial to maintain the confidentiality of the report. For instance, the interests of both the client and the counselor might best be served by postponing the disclosure of a report whose results could become the subject of future litigation.

Determining Client's Needs

In determining the client's needs, it is important to distinguish between his immediate problem and his long-range goals. Although considerable effort may be needed to distinguish between these two areas, examples might include

1. *Immediate problem.* This hurdle must be overcome before a concentrated effort can be made to work toward accomplishing the long-range goals. The nature of the long-range goals should be carefully considered as the immediate problem is solved. Otherwise, the short-term solution could make the achievement of the long-range goals unnecessarily difficult. Also, immediate problems and long-term goals entail two quite different time horizons.

2. *Long-range goals.* More complex steps are usually involved in long-range goals than in immediate problems. For example, long-range goals might involve solving collateral problems such as making zoning changes, bringing in utilities, or building for a future change in the highest and best use. Again, it is essential that the solution of the immediate problem not militate against the successful consummation of the long-range goals.

It might be advisable for the client to take immediate steps to improve cash flow (if this is a problem) while awaiting a change of zoning or use (over which the counselor may have limited control at best). Alternatively, if cash flow is not a problem and capital gain is the obvious objective, the counselor might focus his preliminary advice to the client and his study of long-range goals and their implementation accordingly. Certainly, the counselor's final conclusions would be meaningless unless the counselor is adequately cognizant of his client's needs. It is not inconceivable, however, that a client's plans might not match the highest and best use of the property or the estate. It may even be that the property in question should be sold as a first of several steps in solving the client's problem.

The counselor's relationship with the client should enable him to recommend and select engineers, attorneys, tax experts, real estate professionals, and other persons with specialized experience, particularly experience with certain types of real estate such as airports, office buildings, railroads, steel mills, or churches. The counselor should interpret the requested advice provided by such experts in a manner that will provide the maximum benefits to the client.

The counselor must be dedicated to a high level of both professionalism and social responsibility. Consequently, the counselor must present the various alternatives to his client, not only from a financial standpoint, but also from a legal and ethical standpoint. The counselor should have the courage to withdraw from a situation in which he judges that the client's lack of social responsibility and integrity will be harmful to the community. The respect of the community and a reputation for integrity are cornerstones of the counselor's practice.

PROFESSIONAL FEE ARRANGEMENTS

There are a variety of professional fee arrangements. These are influenced to some degree by the nature of the assignment, the client relationship, the expertise of the counselor in general as well as in relation to the particular problem involved, the amount of time required, the complexity of the problem, and the importance of the problem. Not only the number of hours or days that the counselor spends on solving the particular problem but also the number of years of his accumulated knowledge, experience, and judgment must be factored into the fee. Recent experiences tend to be of greater importance when a counselor tackles an assignment. However, his exposure to diverse experiences, even in the distant past, affects both his worth and his present analytical ability. One element that is important to the success of any counselor is to have made mistakes. By "having been there," he can more ably recognize current problems and contribute to their solution. Although there are almost as many fee arrangements as there are counselors in this field, such arrangements do have certain characteristics, including, but not limited to, the following:

1. *The straight or fixed fee.* This fee arrangement usually applies whenever the scope of an assignment is clearly measurable. Here the fee tends to be a lump-sum amount. In many cases, however, the estimation of such a fee must include certain firm assumptions with regard to the data available, the expertise required, and the amount of time necessary to complete the assignment. Further, the client's needs remain unchanged during the assignment, and generally any changes in conditions will not affect the fairness of the fixed fee.

2. *Modified fee.* In many cases, some modification of a lump sum or fixed fee is necessary to provide for changes during the course of the assignment or for factors that must be considered for the proper execution of the counselor's responsibility. In such cases, it is extremely unlikely that a fixed fee would be equally fair to both sides. Although the modified fee has many variations, it generally provides for a minimum and maximum range that is satisfactory to both parties.

Frequently, the fee may be based on a specific time and expense arrangement, which may be coupled with a retainer. In some assignments it is often found satisfactory to work on a time and expense basis, with estimated minimum or maximum fees, or both. It is sometimes found that a compromise between the estimated and fixed maximum fee may provide for an estimated maximum, not to be exceeded without further authority from the client.

3. *Performance fees.* Some counselors hold that they must work for a fee on a noncontingent basis and without the prospect that any future contingency will influence their compensation. Other counselors feel that some type of bonus or incentive payment, which bears no relationship to a commission payment, is fair and proper, especially in a sale or financing transaction.

The counselor never accepts an engagement on a wholly contingent basis, nor does he ever share fees with a broker. He may list a property for sale with brokers, but only with the promise of a locally prevailing full commission to the successful broker. Sometimes he will work on a flat fee or hourly basis and will be paid without regard to the outcome of the transaction. Such fees are very modest when compared to a wholly contingent commission. Of late, the counselor has increasingly altered his method of charging, in order to retain and attract the highest-quality personnel. A system of minimum fees, payable whether the transaction occurs or not, plus or against a performance fee, is now very much in vogue. For example, a highly marketable property is to be sold for $10 million. Let us say that the counselor feels that a 2 percent performance fee, or $200,000, is reasonable. He feels that an investment analysis, the premarketing preparation of a brochure and other sales materials, and the time of personnel and the sales effort would cost him $50,000. He therefore suggests a minimum fee of $50,000, with two months' preparation time and six months for the sales effort. If the sale occurs, he receives the $200,000, from which he subtracts the $50,000 paid in advance. If no sale occurs, he has received the $50,000 for his efforts and he may have recovered his costs.

Whenever the scope of an assignment is clearly measurable, some counselors will set a fixed fee. Many situations, however, do not permit a precise predetermination of the amount of proper compensation. In such cases, a minimum and maximum range may be established, with both parties jointly determining the final amount. Incentive compensation is occasionally provided where the nature of an assignment warrants it. Such compensation is usually in addition to a noncontingent minimum fee.

A counselor may base his charges on the following considerations: the intricacy of the problem, the urgency of the assignment, the professional skills required, the savings effected, the time expended, the personnel employed, and the results obtained.[1]

---

[1]John R. White, "The Distinction between a Broker/Agent and a Counselor in a Sale or Financing Transaction," speech, March 12, 1982.

It would seem that some differences of opinion regarding fees relate to different types of assignments. It should again be emphasized that in the final analysis the counseling profession is more a relationship to a client than a separate body of knowledge. If the assignment of the individual Realtor is to act as a broker, there is nothing improper about charging like a broker, provided that the understanding with the client is based on a full disclosure of all the facts and intentions. In some states, in fact, counselors are required to hold a broker's license. Thus, the wearing of the counselor's hat really depends on the client relationship and not on the discipline or body of knowledge that appears to be, at least superficially, the principal activity involved.

Hence, it would appear that, in considering fees of all types, including fixed, performance, compensation, and contingency fees, it is important to have a relationship with the client that fully discloses all of the facts, so that the relationship avoids not only all conflicts of interest but any appearance to others of a conflict.

SELECTED REFERENCES

CHURCH, BYRON. "Evolution and Relationship of the Real Estate Appraisal and Consulting Professions." Speech given to Southern Colorado Chapter, Society of Real Estate Appraisers, October 11, 1976. Mimeographed.

DOLMAN, JOHN P. "Real Estate Counseling—Some Distinctions from and Relationships with Real Estate Valuations." *The Appraisal Journal*, October 1973, pp. 453–63.

NICHOLS, RICHARD E. "Appraising or Counseling—Is There a Difference?" *The Real Estate Appraiser*, September–October 1970, pp. 47–48.

PETERSON, GERALD L, and LEE W. FREDERICKSBURG. "Counseling vs. Selling." *The Real Estate Agent*, November–December 1979, pp. 24–28.

"The Problem Solvers: Commissioned Brokers List and Sell, Consultants Solve Problems for a Fee—Is That Really the Way It Works?" *Real Estate Today*, July 1978, pp. 22–29.

RANDALL, ROLAND RODROCK. "Real Estate Counseling Field Dates Back to 1913." *Real Property News*, March 6, 1975, pp. 1–2.

"Realty Consulting: A Blend of Talent and Experience." *Real Estate Forum*, November 12, 1972, pp. 42–43.

"Should You Counsel for a Fee?" *Real Estate Today*, May–June, 1975, pp. 42–48.

STRUNG, JOSEPH. "Consultant/Client Relationships—Be Prepared." *AIM*, July 1977, pp. 36–37.

CHAPTER THREE
THE COUNSELING PROCESS

In Chapter 2 counseling was discussed from the perspective of what the counselor does. Building on that base, we are now ready to concentrate on *how* real estate counselors carry out their work and on the method that has generally been devised by counselors in resolving problems brought to them by clients.

It might be remembered that although a broad, flexible format is described herein, in practice each individual assignment calls for variations from this generalized methodology. That is, the counseling process, as presented, is a guide to systematizing an individual service in order to improve its quality. This process might be thought of as a road map used to reach a financial destination, which in this case is solving a client's problem. Just as there are different ways to reach physical destinations, so too the counselor will depart from the counseling process at times in order to reach his client's destination or objective.

The counseling process might well be defined as an orderly way of solving a problem in real estate or helping a client to reach a decision involving real estate. The steps involved in this process are set forth in Figure 3–1.

DEFINITION OF THE PROBLEM

The counseling process generally begins with the definition of the problem, and in some cases it ends with the presentation of the report. In other cases, the counseling

FIGURE 3–1   The counseling process.

Define the Problem in Terms of:					
Purpose	Client	Property	Time Schedule	Resources Needed	Report Form

Establish the Counseling Relationship			
Agree on Defined Problem	Establish Fee Arrangement	Establish Budget	Enter into Contract

Develop the Plan of Execution			
Set Deadlines	Review Business Files	Identify Personnel and Assign Tasks	Set Critique Points

Perform the Assignment		
Compile Required Data	Analyze Data	Formulate Conclusions and Recommendations

Prepare the Report with Conclusions and Recommendations Consistent with:			
Definition of Problem	Contractual Obligations	Data Analyzed	Agreed-Upon Report Form

Review the Report	
Check Accuracy of Computations	Check Logic and Reasonableness of Conclusions and Recommendations

Present the Report		
Verbally	Written	Ongoing Dialogue

Note: A number of the items presented in this chart are found in the article "The Counseling Process" by Jared B. Shlaes, which appeared in the January 1975 edition of *The Appraisal Journal.*

process continues beyond the presentation of the initial report and may very well extend from the initial counseling with the architect and the developer through the completed building project, the lease-up period, and the establishment of a well-managed real estate project.

Defining the problem begins with determining the purpose for which the counseling assignment is to be carried out. In the beginning the counselor, together with the client, must determine as completely as possible exactly what questions the counselor is to raise, what problems he is to solve, and what ultimate goals he is to achieve.

An early interview of the client by the counselor is essential to determine as many of the client's objectives and acceptable alternatives as can be uncovered. It is important to discover the client's attitude toward the project or the problem: Is the client's attitude generally positive, or does the client have some doubts and questions about the entire matter? What long-term or short-term goals is the client attempting to achieve, and what priorities should be considered? For example, the assignment may be to find a location for a project. If a location has been found, the assignment may be to help the client decide what kind of building should be put on the site. Perhaps help must be provided to assist the client in deciding about the probable market and the prospective tenants for the proposed project. Finally, the counselor may assist in the planning of an entire proposed project.

Another assignment might involve a client who is considering whether to renew a lease, which would be a relatively short-term decision, or exercise an option to purchase, which would be a long-term decision.

FINANCIAL CONSTRAINTS

It is important in the beginning to discuss with the client the financial status of the project and whether adequate financing is available from either the equity or mortgage position in the property. Will there be equity partners, will there be participation of both equity and debt investors, or will the entire project be sold to a limited partnership or syndication and proceed on a cash basis?

Should it be determined in the beginning that the financing has not yet been arranged, a part of the counselor's assignment might be to assist in locating mortgage capital. If there are equity partners, the counselor may need to consider the aftertax impact for partners in various tax brackets. In the case of limited partnerships, syndications, or institutional investors on a cash basis, the counselor's concern becomes one of cash flow to property rather than cash flow to equity. These matters relate directly to the time involvement of the counselor as well as to his ultimate recommendations.

AESTHETIC AND ETHICAL CONSTRAINTS

Another important matter that must be taken into account in considering the objectives, goals, and priorities of the client is the client's possible relationship to the property and to the people it will ultimately affect. A real etate project can affect many people adjacent to the property who do not ever occupy space in the project. Will a proposed project have any effect on the client's relationship to the community surrounding the property, and if so, will that relationship eventually have an adverse effect on either the client or the project?

The client's relationship to existing properties can be explored on the basis of whether the client has a long-term commitment to the project and whether he intends to dispose of, enlarge, or otherwise alter the property. Thus, in such situations time becomes the deciding influence in the counselor's advice to the client.

PHYSICAL CONSIDERATIONS

When considering the basic nature of the property itself, it is necessary that the counselor determine at the outset what kind of property he is dealing with. Is it proposed construction; is it an existing project; is it a project that is about to be expanded, demolished, or altered; or is it some other course of action?

An assignment involving proposed construction or property that is to be altered or expanded may very well involve a long-term time commitment on the part of the counselor. An existing project may involve no more than an investment analysis to determine whether or not the financial goals of the client can be achieved in the project.

Any special or unusual features of the property might influence the questions to be answered and the problems to be solved.

TIME CONSTRAINTS

Another important step in defining the problem has to do with the determination of the time schedule involved. First, consideration should be given to the schedule imposed by the client. Second, the ability of the counselor and his staff to meet that schedule should be considered. Finally, consideration should be given to the timing or phasing of various parts of the report. The counselor must ascertain whether the entire project will be completed as a single operation or as a series of intermediate steps.

A major project to be constructed in phases over a period of three, four, five, or more years would involve detailed analysis of the initial phase and consideration of the potential impact of the later phases. The counselor may be called upon for analysis of the timing of the later phases.

THE COUNSELOR
AS A COORDINATOR

In proposed construction it is often highly advisable to schedule an initial meeting of the client, the architect, and the counselor in the earliest stages of preliminary drawings. The eventual success of a project may depend on close liaison of these three parties through the entire construction and lease-up program. This ongoing relationship is an extremely important part of the definition of the problem and strongly influences the total fee to be charged by the counselor.

The initial phase of a counseling assignment also includes consideration of the resources and the personnel that will be needed to complete the job. The personnel required for the job may very well include both the staff of the counselor and outside people with additional skills. In certain situations, the counselor will find it advisable to include such specialists as architects, attorneys, accountants, engineers, contractors, management personnel, landscape architects, surveyors, demographers, ecologists, sociologists, and money managers.

It is critical in the beginning to have an understanding of exactly what data the client will furnish and what data the counselor must generate. The counselor must have a comprehensive set of plans and specifications on proposed projects or on projects to be altered or expanded, though a final set of working drawings may not be required. The counselor should determine whether engineering studies, cost estimates, or surveys are available or needed. Copies of all leases are essential to the counselor's work, and the client should also provide copies of contracts between the client and third parties that might affect the work or decisions of the counselor.

COMMUNICATING
WITH THE CLIENT

Defining the problem includes considering the type or types of reports that will be needed to complete the assignment. Some simple counseling assignments and some of the more complex counseling assignments involve only a verbal report. This frequently takes the form of a meeting with the client, but in some instances verbal reports are made at meetings with the client together with a board of directors and other people involved in the project.

Periodic reports and the final verbal report may call for charts, slides, photographs, and other visual aids that enhance the presentation of the counselor's findings, conclusions, and recommendations.

Other report forms include very brief memorandums, letters, and the ultimate formal written report with complete documentation and exhibits. Often the counseling assignment will include both verbal and written reports.

PLANNING AND BUDGETING
THE ASSIGNMENT

A budget for the project should be established at this point in the counseling process and developed in detail with the involved personnel, both in-house and outside. Specific tasks should be assigned to individuals, and a job plan and flowchart should be prepared. An example of such a chart is illustrated in Figure 3–2.

FIGURE 3-2 Job Plan—Fee Analysis, Office Building Feasibility.

WORK REQUIRED	PERSONNEL	STAFF DAYS			ELAPSED TIME (DAYS)	FEE ALLOCATION
		START	FINISH	NO. DAYS		
Client, builder, architect interview; contract, job plan, work assignments	W.D.H.	1-5	1-12	2.5	7	$ 2,500
Tenant profile of office buildings in market area	K.D.	1-8	1-18	6	10	900
Plan study and cost analysis	W.A.L.	1-8	1-11	3	3	750
Office rent study	K.D.	1-8	1-18	3	10	450
Operating expense study	M.B.C.	1-8	1-10	2	2	1,000
Demographics and market area analysis	M.B.C.	1-11	1-13	2	2	1,000
Exhibits	J.R.	1-20	1-30	3	10	600
Coordinate work, computer runs, analysis, interim reports to client, etc.	W.D.H.	1-15	2-5	5	20	5,000
Write and review report; deliver report and review report with client	W.D.H.	2-8	2-15	3	7	3,000
Totals				29.5	40	$15,200
						2,280
						$17,480
						$17,500

Allowance for contingencies (15%)

Most counselors who have been in business for some time will have ample data files on similar types of projects. Generally, the counselor will check these files for demographic information, data on the construction costs of similar projects, income and expense data for comparative analysis, and information on public utilities. The in-house data files provide the basis for the eventual compilation of supplementary data for the job.

ESTABLISHING THE
COUNSELING RELATIONSHIP

Once the problem has been fully defined, it is important to establish firmly the counseling relationship between the counselor and the client. A firm agreement should be reached as to exactly what services the counselor will provide, in what form, and at what time. The key to this understanding is clearly spelling out the client's responsibility to the counselor. Once there is a mutually acceptable agreement on these issues, the counseling assignment is likely to progress satisfactorily.

At this phase in the counseling process it is important to establish the fee arrangement so that there will be no misunderstanding on the part of the counselor or the client. The type and amount of the fee and the timing for payment of the fee should be agreed upon. The fee may be paid in a lump sum or set up on a per diem or hourly arrangement. In some instances, a retainer might be appropriate. Retainers are important in major assignments involving long-term commitments of time and expenditure by the counselor. They can also be important in situations where the client's credit or financial stability is unknown or questionable.

The timing of the fee payment is an important part of a counseling agreement. Some counselors prefer to receive a retainer as a part of their total compensation, complemented by periodic payments as the job progresses. In assignments with well-established clients or in smaller assignments the entire fee may be paid after completion of the job.

In most instances, counseling agreements should be put into contract form. A typical counseling contract will specify the name of the parties, the property type and location, the scope of the assignments, the amount of the fee, and the completion date of the work. The contract should further specify what information is to be furnished by the client and what information is to be provided by the counselor. Any special arrangements for payment should be clearly spelled out, and if there is a possibility that additional services will be rendered after the completion of the initial report, the contract should stipulate what types of additional services are anticipated and how payment for those services will be made. If specialized services are required to complete the assignment, the contract should make clear how payment for such services is to be provided.

Figure 3-3 illustrates a fairly comprehensive contract agreement that can be used for many types of assignments. In some cases, special contracts need to be prepared by an attorney to fit the individual situation.

FIGURE 3–3   Contract For Professional Services.

DATE: January 8, 1983

BETWEEN: HAGOOD & ASSOCIATES, INC.   AND: Hulen Development Corp.
           Real Estate Counselors   1915 South Adams
           800 North Freeway   Fort Worth, Texas 76105
           Fort Worth, Texas 76102

hereinafter called the Counselors: hereinafter called the Client:

whereby the Client intends to have prepared a feasibility study on a proposed twelve (12) story office tower to be located on five acres at the southwest corner of Hulen and Bryan in Fort Worth, Texas,

and toward execution of this intent, the Client desires to retain the Counselors for professional services; each agreeing to the following conditions.

1. SCOPE OF SERVICES: Counselors will confer with Client, his architects, engineers, et al. to obtain a complete understanding of the project and timing of construction. A narrative report will be prepared to include a project cost analysis, delineation and tenant profile of the market area, income and expense analysis, and ten-year cash flow analysis which includes before and after tax returns and reversions. Any problems discovered during the analysis will be immediately reported to Client with suggestions for possible solutions. The report and all work will be in conformance with the Code of Ethics of the American Society of Real Estate Counselors.

2. BASIC FEE shall be: Seventeen Thousand Five Hundred Dollars ($17,500.00)

   unless additional charges are authorized as extensions thereof by the Client, his Attorney, or his Agent.

   In return for said services, Client agrees to compensate Counselors in the amount of $ 8,750.00   as retainer upon signing of this agreement, and the remainder upon completion of ten (10)   copies of the report. Except for unforeseen and unavoidable circumstances, Counselors anticipate completion of the report on or before seven (7) weeks   from receipt of this signed contract and retainer in office of Counselors.

3. ADDITIONAL SERVICES, should they be requested by the Client, his Attorney, his Agent, or a Court, such as conferences, court preparation, and court apearances, the Client agrees to compensate the Counselors at the rate of $ 1,000.00   per day, provided such additional services are performed within six months after delivery of said report. In the event that such services shall be required more than six months after delivery of said report, the compensation shall be at the customary per diem rate charged by the Counselors as of that date.

4. It is further understood that neither the employment to make this study or appraisal nor the compensation therefor is contingent upon the amount of any valuation or other conclusion(s).

5. Client shall cooperate by furnishing appropriate data to facilitate the report and help assure its completeness, accuracy, and integrity. In addition to furnishing further items that may be later determined to be needed, Client agrees to initially supply the following items enumerated in Paragraph 5a below.

(1)	(2)	(4)	(5)	(6)	(8)	(9)

5a. Client shall have a duty to advise the Counselors at the commencement of and during the study relative to the following items of which he may have knowledge, which may have a bearing on the factors being researched and the conclusion(s) being formulated by the Counselors. The Counselors shall be the final judge of their appropriateness or inclusion in the study for the purposes intended, nor shall failure to ask for any item be considered an act of omission.
    (1) An accurate Legal Description.
    (2) Leases; immediately past, present, and pending.
    (3) Income and expense statements, preferably for the last three (3) years.
    (4) Proposed future rents and projected expenses.
    (5) Master Plan and/or Construction Plans.
    (6) Surveys which may be pertinent, i.e., Boundary, Topographical, Aerial, Soils, Subsoil, etc.
    (7) Structural, Pest Control, and other conditions surveys.
    (8) Client's cost breakdown and copies of bids as received.
    (9) The last 3 years' income and expense statements on Client's two adjacent office buildings.

6. This contract is subject to our usual terms and conditions enumerated below.

TERMS AND CONDITIONS

A. Payment for all services shall be due and payable on the date said services are performed. If said sum is not paid within thirty (30) days after the services have been performed, an additional charge based on the maximum charge legally permissible will be added each month until paid in full. No relationship shall exist between any payments to or due from other parties and payments due for services rendered by Hagood & Associates, Inc.

B. In the event the sums due by the terms of this agreement are not paid when due, and suit is commenced for the collection of the sums due, the Client agrees to pay all costs of said suit, including the fees of any experts hired to testify in such suit, and such sum for attorney's fees as may be set by the court.

C. Extra production costs at standard rates and approved extra expenses shall be billed on a monthly basis and they become due upon receipt of statement. Also, the cost of preparing exhibits for court, photo enlargements, maps, special telephone or travel costs, etc., shall be borne by Client, and the Counselors shall, in addition to their basic compensation, be reimbursed by the Client for such costs advanced by the Counselors.

D. Abandonment or suspension of the Study shall not relieve the Client of monies due. The Counselors shall be paid for their services performed; and all work and such extra work caused or on account of it shall be paid for at no less than usual daily charges plus expenses computed in our usual manner.

E. Ownership of all file copies of calculations, photographs, and texts of reports, as instruments of service, under all circumstances is that of the Counselors.

F. Client assumes full responsibility for damages awarded to third parties due to misuse of the report, in addition to any damages arising to Counselors from said misuse. Counselors will not unreasonably withhold complete, in-context disclosures of the report in prospectuses of limited circulation, provided that Counselors shall approve the proofs of each such use and shall have final authority as to the meaning conveyed by said use.

G. Client understands that delays are frequently encountered beyond the control of Counselors due to temporary unavailability of data sources, because of illness, absence due to travel, or the need to obtain information from public and private sources where impending events make it more appropriate to obtain the new input than proceed without it.

H. The Client and the Counselors each bind themselves, their partners, successors, executors, administrators, and assigns to the other party of this agreement, and to the partners, successors, executors, administrators, and assigns of such other party in respect to all covenants of this agreement. Except as above, neither party shall assign, sublet, or transfer any interest in this agreement which purports to vary, transfer, or diminish his obligation hereunder, without the written consent of the other party hereto.

I. Client specifically agrees to the assumptions and limiting conditions attached hereto regarding use of the report.

ASSUMPTIONS AND LIMITING CONDITIONS

The legal description to be furnished by the Client will be assumed to be correct. No responsibility is assumed by the Counselors for matters of a legal nature, and the Counselors will render no opinion of the title, which will be assumed to be good and merchantable.

All information to be contained within the report prepared by the Counselors which will be furnished by others will be assumed to be true, correct, and reliable. The Counselors will make a reasonable effort to verify such information; however, no responsibility will be assumed for its accuracy.

All mortgages, liens, encumbrances, leases, and servitudes will be disregarded unless so specified within the report. It is recognized, however, that purchasers in the market will likely take advantage of the best available financing, and the effects of such financing on the value of the property will be considered.

The Counselors do not assume any responsibility for hidden or unapparent conditions of the property, subsoil, or structures, or the correction of any defects now existing or that may develop in the future.

The sketches to be used in the report are to assist the reader in visualizing the property. The Counselors will make no survey of the property and assume no liability in connection with such matters. It will be assumed that there is no encroachment or trespass unless noted within the report.

Possession of the report or a copy thereof does not carry with it the right of publication, nor may it be reproduced in whole or in part, in any manner, by any person without the written consent of the Counselors. Neither all nor any part of the contents of the report shall be conveyed to the public through advertising, public relations, news, sales, or other media without the written consent and approval of the Counselors, particularly as to value conclusions, the identity of the Counselors, or the firm with which they are connected.

Any distribution of total value between land and improvements will apply only under the existing or specified program of utilization. Separate valuation for land and buildings must not be used in conjunction with any other study or appraisal and is invalid if so used.

Should any part or parts of this contract be held invalid by a Court of Law, all other parts shall remain in full force and effect.

Mutually agreed that this shall form a contract, subject to acceptance by Client within thirty (30) days from the date hereon.

HAGOOD & ASSOCIATES, INC.   CLIENT
Real Estate Counselors

_____   _____
                                    _____
                                    DATE:_____

DEVELOPING THE PLAN OF EXECUTION

Once the client-counselor relationship has been firmly established, the counselor is ready to plan the execution of the assignment. A good way to begin is to set deadlines and to coordinate the efforts of the staff and outside services. It is highly desirable to set critique points to determine whether or not the work is on schedule and then to check the quality of the work that has been completed to date. Sometimes mid-project changes are needed to produce the desired results on time.

The actual performance of an assignment should proceed as nearly as possible in accordance with the established plan of execution. Unanticipated influences will frequently appear, and such influences may require a change in the basic plan of execution or in the entire consultation effort.

PERFORMING THE ASSIGNMENT

Completion of the assignment involves the compilation of all required data from pertinent sources, both internal and external to the operation of the counselor's office. When all of the necessary data have been compiled, the analysis portion of the assignment becomes the prime consideration. The data must be analyzed from the standpoint of quality, quantity, and appropriateness to the assignment.

The processing of the data will frequently involve computer analysis. In many cases, a specific program must be developed to fit the assignment. Where real estate appraisers tend to follow a fairly standardized format, counseling assignments are rarely identical with other counseling assignments performed in the past. Although there may be a considerable degree of similarity among counseling assignments, a particular problem will require the development of a specific program of data analysis.

The final step in the processing of data is the formulation of conclusions and recommendations. For example, if the assignment involves a feasibility study and the data indicate that the present worth of the anticipated cash flows does not equal or exceed the cost of the project, then clearly something must be done to either increase the cash flows or reduce the costs. An interim conference with the client may be called for at this point.

If the assignment is to make an investment analysis involving the purchase of an existing property at a particular price, and if the costs of operation and financing are firmly established, and, further, if the investor's required yield and anticipated holding period are known, the processing and analysis of the data should lead the counselor to a conclusion regarding the amount of gross rent necessary to produce the desired return and a determination of whether that gross rent is obtainable in the market.

PREPARING THE REPORT

Preparation of the actual report sometimes begins early in the plan of execution with the preparation of exhibits and other illustrative materials. At other times no part of the report will be prepared until all of the data processing and conclusions have been completed.

The actual report, whether verbal or written, should be carefully prepared to be certain that it addresses the problem and that it presents a conclusion which will assist the client in solving the problem.

The report should conform with all the contractual obligations pertaining to timing, the solution to the client's problem, and the form of presentation. The amount of data analysis included in the report is dependent in most cases on the nature of the problem and the type of report agreed upon.

A verbal report may contain little data but considerable explanation of the kinds of data used and the method of analysis. It may also be accompanied by graphs, charts, photographs, and other visual aids.

The complete formal report may include much or even all of the relevant data, together with detailed analysis and conclusions.

REVIEWING THE REPORT

Once the report has been completed, all computations should be carefully checked for accuracy. A last and final check of the logic and reasonableness of the conclusions and recommendations should be made to be certain that the report and all its findings have considered the purpose of the assignment, the nature of the property, and the nature of the problem.

PRESENTING THE REPORT

If the report is to be presented verbally, a firm appointment with the client should be established, the report given in a complete and concise manner, and adequate time allowed to consider and answer any questions raised by the client.

A written report should, in all instances, adequately convey the findings in accordance with the definition of the problem and should always reflect the professional integrity of the counselor.

The assignment generally culminates with delivery of the report, and perhaps with one or two additional conferences. There are situations, however, in which the nature of the assignment, the type of development, changing conditions, and other matters may require ongoing dialogue between the client and the counselor. Usually such situations will have been contemplated in preparing the contract with the client. Sometimes, however, it is necessary to meet with the client, define the additional problems, and recommence the counseling process.

SELECTED REFERENCES

DOLMAN, JOHN P.   "Real Estate Counseling: Some Distinctions from and Relationships with Real Estate Valuation." *The Appraisal Journal,* October 1973, pp. 453–63.

GRAASKAMP, JAMES A.   "A Guide to Feasibility Analysis." Chicago: Society of Real Estate Appraisers, 1970.

HALL, ROBERT W.   "The Counseling Process: In Answer to the Client's Problem." *Real Estate Appraiser and Analyst,* May–June 1979, pp. 39–41.

MIDDLETON, NORMAN G.   "Guidelines for Counseling." *Real Estate Today,* April 1976, pp. 15–17.

SHLAES, JARED B.   "The Counseling Process." *The Appraisal Journal,* January 1975, pp. 62–70.

CHAPTER FOUR
THE COUNSELOR'S ROLE IN DECISION MAKING

The role of the real estate counselor is unique. Unlike others who operate in the real estate market in an intermediary or advisory capacity, the counselor actually develops and enters into the client's decision-making framework. Client objectives and criteria are applied (altered, modified, or restated) to this framework, and a decision is made. In essence, the counselor simulates the decision-making process for the client. On the basis of client reaction and response to the plan, as well as the possible modification of original objectives and criteria, an ultimate decision is made, with continuing guidance and advice to the client by the counselor. The more significant aspects of the counselor's assignment are to ensure that the client's "problem" is well defined (that is, objectives are clearly stated and alternative strategies or solutions are offered and analyzed) and that a course of action is selected.

The counselor is both a specialist and a generalist. Although the counselor brings his own special expertise to the client's decision-making process, he also recognizes the potential need for capabilities beyond his own in acting on or implementing a decision on behalf of the client. This may require obtaining input or advice from a wide range of professionals regarding their particular specialties as these pertain to the questions at hand. Such professional advice might include that of attorneys, accountants, architects, engineers, economists, leasing agents, brokers, appraisers, financial analysts, or others whose knowledge is pertinent and beyond the counselor's own expertise in any of these areas or disciplines. It is the counselor's responsibility in the use of any or all of these specialists to orchestrate their collective efforts as well as his own on behalf of the client and to interpret the contribution of each specialist to the client's decision-making process and ultimately to the implementation of a decision.

Often the counselor's area of expertise will be limited to some real estate function in the general areas of marketing, management, or finance. The counselor who is highly specialized in a single area may require (in addition to legal, accounting, design, or other like expertise) the services of other counselors with other real estate–oriented skills. With the advances in decision theory, counselors may find the need for modest retooling in their particular specialty, as well as others, if only to be better able to understand and interpret for the client the analysis of others and their contribution to the client's decision-making process.

PRELIMINARY ANALYSIS OF CLIENT "PROBLEMS"

A problem is defined as "a situation in which something has gone wrong without explanation."[1] This definition provides a differentiation between problem solving and decision making. Problems are historical in nature, and problem solving involves finding the cause of an aberration from a normal state. As such, a problem in the strict sense of the word may not actually exist; rather, the client's "difficulty" may be one of making a decision from among alternative courses of action (that is, selecting from among alternative investment opportunities or making a decision to buy, sell, lease, etc.). The counselor's role, therefore, is more often that of aiding the client in decision making rather than problem solving. Thus, it is important for the counselor to make this distinction between problem solving and decision making at the outset in order to serve the client's needs best. Historically, emphasis has been placed on identifying and solving "problems" for clients when the ultimate need to make a decision has been the paramount issue. Probably more emphasis should be placed on decision making and on decision-making tools. Client "problems" are not problems at all. It is client objectives (and the articulation, refinement, and ordering thereof) that are central to the counselor's role and represent the foundation upon which the analysis of the alternative courses of action and ultimate decisions are based.

[1]Charles H. Kepner and Benjamin B. Tregoe, *The New Rational Manager* (Princeton, N.J.: Kepner-Tregoe, Inc., 1981), p. 25.

The Questioning Process

Most critical to the client's decision-making process is the need to identify as precisely as possible the client's goals or objectives. Often clients have only some vague notion of just what they wish to achieve in their investment decisions. It may also be that clients have conflicting objectives that require articulation and resolution prior to the formation of a decision process or the analysis of that process. The counselor acquires this information through inquiry in an initial information-gathering conversation with the client. The goals or objectives elicited from conversation with the client may require either broadening or narrowing; they may also need to be refined or restated in a more precise manner; and they will require ordering on the basis of their relative importance to the client as well as to minimize or eliminate conflict.

As the initial step in the decision-making process, it is imperative that the counselor understand the true nature of the client's "difficulty" (that is, what his real objectives are and how those objectives can best be achieved within the context of specific investment opportunities). The major concern of the counselor at this stage is to distinguish between the client's perceived and real needs and to translate those needs into weighted options for decision making.

Articulation

The ability of clients to articulate their objectives in precise terms may be limited. Therefore, it is incumbent upon the counselor to add precision to clients' statements regarding their goals. For example, return requirements may be stated in the form of cash flow or yield. Further, cash flow return requirements may be in the form of rates or of dollars. The counselor, in discussion with the client, provides the desired precision by separating the concepts and applying specific dollar and/or percentage terms to each. The counselor has a continuing obligation to resolve any conflicts that result from a more precise articulation of client goals. For example, the client may state that cash flow is relatively unimportant but that a high yield is required. That statement implies staying power, a possible need for tax shelter, and an emphasis on capital gain. All of this needs to be restated by the counselor as specifically as possible and reviewed (possibly revised) by the client before alternative courses of action may be considered and analyzed.

Categories of Client Objectives

Certain attributes of an investment position are difficult, if not impossible, to quantify. Features such as pride of ownership, specific location, number of stories, design, and accessibility are all important client criteria which, although perhaps easily articulated, are not readily measurable. The impact of such nonquantifiable features may influence the level of cash flow or return, but often this is a judgment call to be made by the counselor.

The more measurable aspects of client objectives are those which are perhaps less well expressed by the client but which can be specifically formulated and analyzed by the counselor. These aspects would include such objectives as levels of cash flow in either dollar amounts or rates, level of investment by the client, capital recovery, shelter, leverage, wealth accumulation, profitability versus liquidity requirements, and risk versus return. These more measurable and quantifiable objectives need to be refined and ordered as a result of discussion between client and counselor. Having structured the client's objectives in this way, the counselor can proceed with the decision plan, utilizing these objectives as criteria against which alternative courses of action may be tested for fit.

Alternative Courses of Action

Once the client's objectives have been stated and ordered, the counselor needs to identify alternative courses of action (strategies) that are necessary to achieve those objectives. Courses of action or strategies emanate from client objectives and involve identification of data needs and tools of analysis and decision making that might be applicable, assessment of the resources available to carry out the assignment, and identification of the time and money constraints imposed on the entire process. In hypothesizing alternative strategies or courses of action, the counselor sets the framework for establishing an action plan and implementing the decision. Based on the counselor's knowledge, experience, and judgment as well as the fit of the action plan to the stated objectives of the client, the decision may range from no action at all to a complete change of the client's investment position.

STEPS INVOLVED IN DECISION-MAKING

The scientific method of decision making suggests that a client has a problem that needs definition and solution. Problem solving and decision making represent two entirely separate processes. As such, each process represents different perspectives to the client and the counselor, and although they may utilize similar tools of analysis, they will utilize those tools differently, providing different forms of input and information into the process. Problem solving requires finding a means for overcoming a barrier to an objective. Decision making is action oriented and need not deal with a "problem" in the strict sense of the word. To reiterate, entirely too much emphasis has been placed on problem solving when, in fact, clients have needed counselor assistance in their decision-making process.

The accompanying diagram represents a synopsis (schematic) of the decision-making process incorporating the modification regarding definition of the problem.[2]

Decision Making in Practice

Well-stated and well-defined goals may be specified in ratios and relationships between investments and estimated returns to those investments. The relationships may be relatively unsophisticated inferences from first-period projections, or they may result from more rigorous forecasting techniques and models. It is possible that the sophistication in data collection and analysis suggested here is neither necessary nor warranted in all (or even most) instances. In fact, some decisions and decision-making processes may even be hindered by data collection and analysis if, for example, a timely decision is required in order to take advantage of a market opportunity. In these and other circumstances the hunch, intuition, judgment, and logic of the experienced counselor may be all that is necessary for decision-making purposes. However, even though much of the counselor's decision making may not require the sophistication of the tools suggested here, this does not preclude the counselor's knowledge of data collection and analytical tools and techniques.

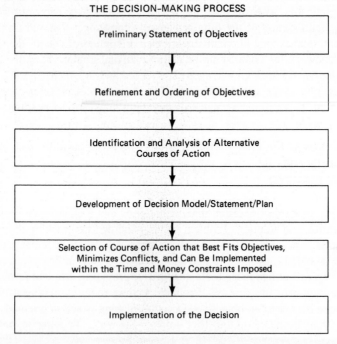

THE DECISION-MAKING PROCESS

Preliminary Statement of Objectives

↓

Refinement and Ordering of Objectives

↓

Identification and Analysis of Alternative Courses of Action

↓

Development of Decision Model/Statement/Plan

↓

Selection of Course of Action that Best Fits Objectives, Minimizes Conflicts, and Can Be Implemented within the Time and Money Constraints Imposed

↓

Implementation of the Decision

[2]This decision-making process differs from the counseling process shown in Figure 3–1. Although there are some similarities, the decision-making process focuses on a decision being reached, whereas the counseling process is concerned with other functions such as report preparation and review.

Less sophisticated thought processes (hunch, intuition, and the like) may be formalized by the use of such tools. Further, and perhaps more important, the use of more sophisticated techniques by others may be understood and countered by the counselor if this is necessary and appropriate.

DECISION-MAKING TOOLS

Decision tools make it possible, among other things, to express complex relationships in simpler terms, to reduce or represent large data sets in more manageable proportions for mathematical manipulation and analysis (modeling), and to verify or question the hunch, intuition, or judgment of the counselor or the client regarding the decision to be made or implemented. Three forms of decision tools will be considered in this chapter: statistical decision tools, financial decision tools, and operations research. The subsequent discussion is not meant to suggest that the listing of these decision tools is all-inclusive or that applications other than those indicated cannot be made. The decision tools considered, however, are major tools with whose prime areas of application and use counselors should be familiar.

Statistical Decision Tools

Statistical analysis involves the collection, classification, and interpretation of data and ultimately making a decision on the basis of the analysis. The ultimate purpose of such analysis in a statistical sense is to identify and explain variability in data sets. On the basis of that identification and explanation, judgments and decisions can be made about the data sets. The rules and procedures of statistical analysis are very formal and precise, and if followed closely by the counselor, they identify the limitations and the applications of the statistical measures that evolve from the analysis. Often statistical analysis falls short (particularly in real estate decision making), with the analyst calculating only statistics (central tendency, dispersion, regression models, and the like) without the attendant measures of reliability and significance. Without the latter, forecasts regarding a particular phenomenon are at best suspect and represent a misuse and abuse of statistical analysis.

A simple distinction needs to be made at the outset between a statistical population and a sample. A statistical population consists of the census or enumeration of all items or objects within a given area or category. The characteristics of a population are called parameters and include measures of central tendency and dispersion. Obviously, an enumeration or census is not possible in many instances due to the constraints of time, effort, and money that are placed on the analyst. As a result and to economize on time, effort, and money, the counselor will almost always be working with a sample from which he will derive characteristics (statistics) that will be the basis for decisions. The sample, then, is simply a set of observations drawn from a population, and it is used to represent that population as a basis for analysis.

Statistical techniques and analysis, as has been noted, involve data collection at the outset and then data analysis and the identification of sample characteristics (statistics). They also involve the presentation of data in summary, tabular, or chart form so as to make the larger data sets more manageable and understandable. This form of data collection and statistical analysis is referred to as descriptive statistics. It includes techniques for measuring central tendency and dispersion. These are necessary first steps in almost any form of statistical analysis.

Although descriptive statistics are important to the counselor's analysis and interpretation of data sets, inferential statistics make possible a more powerful application of statistics in decision making. Inferential statistics involve the estimation of parameters of a larger data set (population) from sample characteristics (statistics). Inferential statistics may be used for forecasting or predicting as well as hypothesis testing. Obviously, the decision-making capabilities of the counselor are enhanced by a general understanding of statistical analysis, particularly by an understanding of inferential statistics.

Statistics and statistical analysis are and have been fundamentally important tools in business and economic decision making. Statistics and statistical analysis aid in determining what types of data are necessary to meet the purposes of an analysis; what data should be collected and how it should be manipulated; and how the results of the analysis are to be interpreted and utilized for purposes of decision making. Statistics, therefore, provide the basis for collecting, analyzing, and interpreting quantitative information for decision-making purposes.

Measures of central tendency.   A set of data regarding a singular phenomenon (price, rate of return, age, income, population, employment, and the like) may be described, at least in part, with measures of central tendency. The most commonly used measure of central tendency in a data set is the average. The average is calculated by summing the values of any series of data and then dividing the sum by the number of observations within the data set. The basic formula for a sample mean (ungrouped data) is as follows:

$$\overline{X} = \frac{\sum\limits_{i=1}^{n} X_i}{n}$$

where

n = number of observations

X_i = a specific value of variable X

$\sum\limits_{i=1}^{n} X_i$ = sum of *all* values of variable X

The mean average is the most important and popular summary measure in this area of statistics. It is not only the statistic most representative of the data set, but it may also be used along with a measure of dispersion for inferential purposes. Two other measures of central tendency may provide insights into the data not fully represented by the arithmetic average or mean. The first is the median, which is a positional average and represents the middle observation in a series of observations arranged according to magnitude. In essence, it is the item that divides the data set exactly in half. Since position is the determining factor, the actual values of the observations within the sample have no effect on the value of this measure. Such is not the case, of course, with the mean since the mean takes each value in the entire series into account.

The final measure of central tendency, the mode, is also a position average. It is the value that appears more frequently than any other in a data set. The mode thus represents the most probable outcome within a data set. The mode is useful in many real estate decisions since such decisions are keyed to the most probable user or investor and not necessarily to the characteristics calculated through the median or the mean. There are some obvious problems with the modal value, particularly if it is not unique to the data set (that is, more than one value may be repeated an equal number of times). At the other extreme, a modal value may not exist; or, looking at it another way, each item within the data set may be considered the modal value by virtue of the fact that all of the items appear the same number of times (once). Such a determination has very little utility for decision-making purposes.

Measures of dispersion.   The mere calculation of the measures of central tendency does not fully describe all the values in a data set. The values in a data set nearly always differ from the measures of central tendency. If this were not so, there would be no variability in the data set and decisions would be made on the basis of measures of central tendency alone. Such a data set would be somewhat sterile, and the genuineness of its relationship to a real-world phenomenon might even be suspect. Therefore, the extent to which observations depart from the measures of central tendency (particularly the mean) constitutes another important descriptive measure of data sets. Among the measures of variability or dispersion are the range, the average deviation, and the standard deviation.

The simplest measure of dispersion is the range, which is the difference between the extreme values in a data set. The range represents a very crude measure of dispersion. For example, it tells us nothing about the intervening values between the extremes in a data set. Its use, particularly for further statistical analysis, is extremely limited. The average deviation, though also of limited use, does make possible an interpretive statement about the data. However, it is of greater importance in helping us to understand the need for and calculation of a standard deviation. The average deviation is the mean of the absolute deviations from the mean (or the median) of all observations in a data set. In essence, this suggests that a counselor takes the difference between all observations in the data set and the mean or median value, ignores their signs, adds them, and divides the total by the number of observations. Obviously, it is mathematically incorrect to ignore signs in this manner, and thus there are limits to the interpretive statements about the data set that can be based on average deviations. This mathematical inconsistency and its correction provide the basis for understanding the calculation of a standard deviation.

If the difference between the mean and the observed values is squared, the mathematical inconsistency of ignoring the signs is avoided. Squaring these differences, however, presents another problem—squared units are not comparable to the units from which they were calculated. Therefore, in order to make the standard deviation comparable to the units from which it was calculated, the square root of the average (adjusted) squared differences is taken. The formula for the standard deviation of a sample is as follows:

$$s = \sqrt{\frac{\sum\limits_{i=1}^{n}(X_i - X)^2}{n - 1}}$$

where

$$X_i = \text{values of individual observations}$$

$$X = \text{mean value of data set}$$

$$n = \text{number of observations}$$

$$\sum\limits_{i=1}^{n}(X_i - X)^2 = \text{sum of squared differences}$$

A measure of standard deviation along with the arithmetic mean provides the basis for fully describing the data set. The standard deviation is one of the most widely used measures in statistics and also the most reliable measure of dispersion. It provides a basis for comparing distributions with similar means, and it is helpful in judging the representativeness of the mean. In addition to possessing useful descriptive qualities, the standard deviation plays a key role in statistical inference, which might be considered the ultimate purpose of statistical analysis, particularly for decision making.

Statistical inference and prediction. The counselor needs to analyze and interpret market characteristics in order to make decisions on the basis of forecast market conditions and trends. The list of market conditions that need to be analyzed is almost endless. What is the market rental? What are the past trends and the likely future trends in construction costs? What financing terms are available currently, and what financing terms will be available in the near future? What are the property tax rates and tax burdens likely to be in the foreseeable future? How much space is likely to be demanded for the submarket being considered? What is the community's population and employment level likely to be in the foreseeable future?

All of these questions and others are based on a variety of forms of statistical analysis and on the inferences that can be drawn from such analysis. Statistical prediction (forecasting) is based on the assumption that causal influences in the market will continue to operate as they have operated in the past and as they operate in the present. It is to be emphasized that such analysis is not a substitute for the judgment of the counselor but rather an aid to the counselor in verifying judgments or in making better judgments.

Statistical inference and prediction are based, at least in part, on the understanding and interpretation of the normal curve and the normal distribution. The normal curve is a graphic representation of the normal distribution. The normal distribution is a probability distribution that is based on the results of large samples as well as large numbers of samples from the population of a continuous variable. The counselor should be familiar with the characteristics of the normal curve and the normal distribution and the concomitant analysis leading to statistical inference and prediction. Even though the counselor may never use statistical decision theory in daily practice, competitors and some clients use it as a basis for making decisions. Therefore, there is a need to understand these concepts if for no other reason than to intelligently respond and react to both the client and the competition.

Regression and correlation analysis.   Regression analysis is the process of describing the association in movement between two or more variables: a dependent variable (Y) and one or more independent variables (X_1, X_2, etc.). Correlation analysis, on the other hand, shows how close the association is between the movements of dependent and independent variables, and thus how good a predictor of the values of the dependent variable the values of the independent variables are.

For simple linear regression, the analyst essentially starts with two data sets (one representing the dependent variable and the other the independent variable) that are assumed to be related in some way. The pairs of dependent and independent variables are used as coordinates, and preliminary analysis consists of plotting the data on a scatter diagram to determine whether such a relationship exists. Since the concern is simple linear regression, it is presumed that the relationship is linear. If such a relationship is verified by the scatter diagram, then a regression line can be calculated to provide the "best fit" to the data in the sample. The general formula for this line of best fit is as follows:

$$Y = a + bX + e$$

where

$a = $ the Y intercept, or the value of Y where
the line crosses the Y axis

b = the slope of the line, or

$\dfrac{\Delta Y}{\Delta X}$, or the change in Y *for a given unit change in X*

e = the error term representing the
difference between the observed value of Y
and the calculated value of Y

As with central tendency and dispersion, there are a number of measures of reliability and significance that can and should be calculated before any inferences or predictions are made. The regression line represents an average, and both the intercept and the slope of that line are point estimates that are also averages. As a result, there are measures of dispersion that can be calculated about the line itself as well as point estimates that provide an opportunity for the analyst to test hypotheses. In addition, confidence intervals can be developed for the regression coefficient, the regression line, and points on the regression line as well as for individual forecasts. Correlation coefficients and coefficients of determination can and should also be calculated from the data to measure relationships between data sets and to explain variations in the dependent variable.

Multiple regression involves the use of two or more independent variables to explain the behavior of a dependent variable. If the assumption of linearity with respect to the regression parameters is maintained, the regression equation would be as follows:

$$Y = a + b_1X_1 + b_2X_2 + \ldots b_nX_n + e$$

Most statistics derived from the multiple regression model are analogous to the statistics in simple regression. Multiple regression shows, measures, and tests the combined effect of all the independent variables on the value of the dependent variables.

Multiple regression requires substantially greater computational capacity for development of the model (intercept and coefficients) than is required by simple linear regression. The latter can be accomplished very effectively on many hand-held calculators. Multiple regression, on the other hand, requires, at the very least, the capacity of a microcomputer programmed for such analysis to provide the attendant statistical measures as well as measures of reliability and significance. Although there are some hazards in multiple regression such as colinearity between and among the independent variables that can adversely affect the predictive quality of the equation, multiple regression analysis, unlike other forms of analysis, permits specific study of the variables considered so that they may be identified, analyzed, and properly handled within the model. This seeming weakness of the technique turns out to be a strength in comparison to the characteristics of other models or forms of data analysis. However, the analysis, use, and interpretation of a multiple regression model require substantially greater sophistication than is required for simple linear regression.

Financial Decision Tools

In any investment decision a basic choice has to be made between profitability and liquidity; for most investors, this means that a balance has to be struck between the level of risk and the required rate of return. Financial decision tools provide the basis for achieving such a balance and for making selections from among alternative investment opportunities. Some of the decision tools discussed in this section have been criticized for either simplicity or complexity, for inconsistencies among some of these tools in ranking investment alternatives, for wide-ranging investment return calculations, and for internal inconsistencies brought about by different levels of investment, differences in the timing and direction of cash flows, different derivations of rates to be used in the analysis, and the like. It is not the purpose of this chapter to reiterate the problems and criticisms associated with the array of financial decision tools discussed; however, the reader should be aware of these problems and criticisms and should be prepared to deal with them in any analytical context. The subsequent discussion of financial decision tools is general, and it should be noted that all of the tools can be applied in both aftertax analysis and before-tax analysis. For most investments and for most investors, the aftertax implications are more meaningful for decision-making purposes. This implies that the counselor requires some understanding of these implications or has access to a person or a source with this capability or information. Further, the subsequent discussion is devoid of any mathematical examples, as the discussion centers on the conceptual aspects of financial decision tools.

Ratio models versus yield models. In the discussion of profitability measures (rates of return), a distinction needs to be made at the outset between cash flow rates and yield rates and between the models associated with each of these. The model for cash flow rates is the basic investment model, where investment value is a function of income capitalized at a cash flow rate. The basic model is $V = I/R$. Within this model (for rate derivation purposes), V represents investment dollars and income is represented by first-period cash flow (in the case of average rate of return, it is an average cash flow based on a summation of all cash flows to the investment position less recapture of the investment divided by the anticipated holding period). In the basic cash flow model, time is only implicitly included and no specific reversion is estimated or forecast. In the average rate of return model, the holding period is explicitly included and a reversion is forecast. However, the time value of money is ignored in the calculation of the average rate of return.

Yield models or discounted cash flow models, on the other hand, explicitly incorporate time into the calculation. This is specifically identified as the investor's holding period. Further, the timing and pattern of cash flows are significant to the model and a forecast reversion is required. As would be expected, the model is slightly more complicated than the basic cash flow model. It is generally defined as follows:

$$V = \sum_{t=1}^{n} \frac{CF_t}{(1 + i)^t}$$

where

V = amount invested

CF_t = cash flows (both periodic and lump-sum)

$\dfrac{1}{(1 + i)^t}$ = reversion factor (for each period of the investment holding period)

i = yield rate

$\displaystyle\sum_{t=1}^{n} \frac{CF_t}{(1 + i)^t}$ = present worth of cash flows

Profitability measures.   Fundamental to every investment decision is the investor's desire to retain the investment capital intact or to recover that investment capital by the end of the holding period, if not before. In addition to seeking the recovery of the investment capital, the investor is seeking a return on the investment.

In both the net present value model and the profitability index model, the present worth estimates are compared to the amount of the proposed or required capital outlay in an effort to rank the proposals for investment purposes. The forecast cash flow (both periodic and reversionary) is discounted at a rate (referred to variously as the discount rate, the cost of capital, or the hurdle rate) acceptable to the investor to produce the present worth estimate.

The net present value model compares the present worth of cash flows discounted at an acceptable rate with the investor's cash outlay. The decision rule is to select the investment opportunity that produces the highest net present value.

The profitability index model operates like the net present value model except that the relationship between the present worth of cash flows and the cash outlay is expressed as a ratio or index (the present worth of cash flows divided by the cash outlay). As with the net present value model, the decision rule is to accept the investment opportunity that produces the highest positive index, that is, greater than one.

Where the profitability index is equal to one or the net present value is equal to zero, the interpretation usually given is that the investment proposal is minimally acceptable. It is important to note, however, that under these conditions the rate used to discount the cash flows is exactly equal to the internal rate of return.

Among a number of rates of return that might be calculated for a particular investment proposal or alternative, the internal rate of return (IRR) has received particular emphasis in recent years in real estate investment and analysis. The internal rate of return is defined as that rate at which the present worth of forecast future net cash flows (PWCF) exactly equals the amount of the original investment or capital outlay (CO). In other words, the internal rate of return is the yield rate on an investment of a given amount, assuming that the future net income forecasts are realized.

The internal rate of return is more specifically defined as:

The annualized rate of return on capital which is generated or is capable of being generated within an investment during the period of ownership. It may be the effective mortgage interest rate on a mortgage loan; it may be the Discount Rate on total property investments; or it may be the Equity Yield Rate on an equity investment. It is that rate which discounts all returns to equal the original investment. The IRR is generally considered to be the result of calculation rather than a specified or desired (given) rate of return.[3]

The mathematical representation for the calculation of IRR follows:[4]

$$\text{IRR} = i, \text{ where } \sum_{t=1}^{n} \frac{CF_t}{(1+i)^t} = \text{CO}$$

In order to calculate IRR, it is necessary to have data on (1) the amount of net cash flows to the investment (both annual flows and reversion), (2) the timing of those cash flows, (3) the income forecasting period, and (4) the initial amount of the investment.

The internal rate of return has not been without its detractors or its problems. Both the detractors and the problems center on similar issues, and the discussion here will be oriented specifically to the problems.

A number of disadvantages of the internal rate of return concept have been discussed and analyzed in a variety of publications. The problems of multiple yields, size-time disparity, magnitude (extremes) of yield, and reinvestment assumption have been dealt with in both the financial literature and the real estate literature. Some of the problems associated with the concept can be handled internally within the model if these problems are known or anticipated. More specifically, the model can be altered slightly (as noted below) to accommodate these recognized problems.

The problem of multiple yields occurs when a series of incremental cash flows includes substantial cash outlays (negative flows). The problem is not so much the negative cash flows (though magnitude is important) as the multiple changes in the direction of cash flows—from positive to negative, or vice versa. Since the like-

[3]Byrl N. Boyce, ed., *Real Estate Appraisal Terminology*, rev. ed. (Cambridge, Mass.: Ballinger Publishing Co., 1981), p. 138.
[4]This is the same mathematical representation presented earlier as a discounted cash flow (DCF) model.

lihood of sizable negative cash flows exists in many (if not most) real estate developments and investments at various times during the investment holding period, the problem of multiple yields often rears its ugly head. Obviously, there is some inconsistency within the model if it generates multiple yields, since the concept of internal rate of return suggests a unique solution to a specific investment problem.

Calculations of the internal rate of return that reflect low yields will generally understate the actual rate of return, whereas calculations that reflect high yields will generally overstate the actual rate of return. The problem in calculating the internal rate of return at extremely low or high rates occurs because of the reinvestment assumption inherent in the calculation. This issue can be resolved with slight modifications of the model.

When different capital outlays are required for two or more investment alternatives or when the income projection periods are different, direct comparisons of calculated internal rates of return are not entirely valid. The counselor must also ask this question: What can or must the investor earn from the extra capital not required by the largest capital outlay or during the extra years of the longest income projection period? The answer (which is the result of calculation) relative to opportunity costs provides the decision tool for selecting among the alternative investments.

As noted previously, slight modifications of the model may also obviate some of the disadvantages of the internal rate of return. The discussion below centers on three such modifications.[5]

The problems of multiple yields and magnitude of yield (extremely high or low) may be handled by specific treatment of both negative and positive cash flows to the investment. In effect, modification of or adjustment to the IRR concept is a direct function of the counselor's ability to forecast cash flows and calculate yield. If, in fact, negative cash flows are forecast or the yield calculation is considered unreasonably high or low, then provision can be made within the model to accommodate these problems.

For example, the IRR may be adjusted by considering all negative cash flows to be part of the initial outlay (that is, part of the original investment). Because of the different time periods at which negative flows occur, a discounting process (typically at a safe rate) must be implemented in order to add those flows to the initial investment. Positive cash flows are then carried forward (typically at a market rate) to the end of the investment holding period and accumulated to a terminal value. The yield calculation (AIRR—adjusted internal rate of return) is then a function of the adjusted initial investment, the terminal value, and the investment holding period.

A modification of the foregoing (MIRR—modified internal rate of return) holds that only those negative cash flows up to the first positive cash flow are to be added (through discounting) to the initial investment. All subsequent cash flows (both negative and positive) are then discounted at a rate such that they exactly

[5]This discussion is adapted from Boyce, *Real Estate Appraisal Terminology*, pp. 4–5, 104, and 167.

equal the adjusted initial investment. That rate is the modified internal rate of return.

A further modification of the IRR model is the financial management rate of return (FMRR). This model, which is based on the terminal value rate of return concept, derives from the assumption that long-run wealth maximization is the primary goal of the investor. The FMRR model is structured to include as many of the unique characteristics of the real estate market as possible. It addresses directly such deficiencies in the IRR model as multiple yields and implicit assumptions with regard to the discounting outflows and the reinvestment of inflows.

The internal rate of return can be partitioned to give the counselor some insight as to the balance between the level of risk and the required rate of return. Partitioning the internal rate of return requires the identification, by source, of the investor's yield by breaking up that yield into its component parts (for example, cash flow, tax shelter, equity buildup from mortgage amortization, and capital gain). The concern, therefore, is not only with the magnitude of the internal rate of return but with its composition as well and with the contributions that the individual or grouped components make to the total yield.[6]

In contrast to the yield rate, there are a number of cash flow rates that advisers and investors often use in assessing the "profitability" of investment alternatives. As noted previously, these are single-period ratios, and in a sense they provide a rule of thumb measurement for preliminary analysis. Cash flow reduces the speculative quality of investments in real estate (particularly land) and mitigates some of the risks associated with such investments. In the face of the level of yield requirement articulated by the investor, cash flows, to the extent that they exist, reduce the emphasis on producing the desired yield from the proceeds of resale. Therefore, comparing certain cash flow rates can provide the counselor with preliminary insights as to the relative risks of alternative investment opportunities. The reciprocals of cash flow rates provide multipliers that may be compared in precisely the same way as has been noted above for cash flow rates. The concept of average rate of return is also included within the context of cash flow rates. However, the reader is cautioned to recognize that in calculating the average rate of return, the method for developing (averaging) cash flows differs substantially from that employed in the more traditional cash flow rate analysis.

Liquidity measures. In the discussion of profitability measures, it was noted that capital recovery is fundamental to every investment decision. The concept of capital recovery is made much simpler if one follows the procedure of looking first at the reversion for recapture. It is imperative that provision be made for capital recovery, because without capital recovery there can be no return on investment. On the other hand, to the extent that one recovers more than the original amount invested, one has developed a positive return on the investment. Although the concept of recapture is related to the mechanical process of discounting, it should not be confused with that process.

[6]See Donald J. Valachi, "The Three Faces of IRR," *Real Estate Review,* Fall 1978, pp. 74–78; and Robert H. Zerbst, "Evaluating Risks by Partitioning the Internal Rate of Return," *Real Estate Review,* Spring 1979, pp. 80–84.

Cash flows (as opposed to cash flow rates) reduce the speculative quality of any investment. As noted in the discussion of cash flow rates, the reciprocals of those rates provide multipliers that can be utilized for analytical purposes in much the same way as the cash flow rates. Further, a slightly different view of these multipliers provides us with a measure of the concept of payback. The payback period is defined as:

> the time required for complete recovery of an investment; often used with the concept that all income is considered a return of capital until the entire investment is recaptured and that income received after complete pay-back is considered profit.[7]

The distinction between the payback concept, as it has been defined here, and the concept of capital recapture, noted above, in the calculation of rates of return is that the answer to the payback question tells us how long it will take for the investment position to be recovered (recaptured) from cash flow. The concept is viewed more as a liquidity measure than as a tool for yield calculations. It is to be reiterated that the liquidity concerns of the investor are paramount since the investor must recover the investment before earning a rate of return on it.

Operations Research

Operations research is, as the name implies, an analysis of the efficiency of operation of one or more investment vehicles to better ensure their long-term investment potential. Operations research in real estate investments considers the operations as an entity and concerns itself with the physical and fiscal aspects of that entity as they relate to performance.

In the context of decision making, the physical and fiscal analysis of the entity provides the counselor with information by which he can identify the changes necessary in proposed courses of action, the expenditures necessary to prevent physical deterioration of the property itself or deterioration in some particular aspect of its operation, and strategies for improving performance. Thus, the ultimate purpose of operations research is to improve performance and protect the long-term integrity of investments.

Operations research models.   There are several types of operations research models, but these models are usually limited to quantitative methods. As such, most of the models are mathematical in form, representing a set of equations that relate significant variables in the operation of an investment to either a proposed or an anticipated outcome. Implicit in most operations research models, therefore, is a measure of effectiveness that is used to determine the extent to which the operation of the investment is achieving explicit goals. These goals are objectives that the client-investor has expressed as precisely as possible. Consistency in the statement of goals is essential to the logic of the operations research model that is

---

[7]Boyce, *Real Estate Appraisal Terminology,* p. 182.

to be utilized to analyze the efficiency of the operation. Operations research models and techniques often bring to light inconsistencies in stated goals. The recognition and resolution of such inconsistencies provides a guide to more efficient and effective decision making. Thus, operations research clarifies the relationships among various courses of action, determines their outcomes, and indicates which course of action will best fit the stated goals of the client-investor.

The various types of operations research models are far too numerous and complicated to be dealt with in detail in this chapter. Therefore, only a partial listing and treatment are attempted here.

Linear programming. Linear programming represents one of the most widely used quantitative tools available in operations research. The primary function of linear programming is to determine the best allocation of scarce resources, though there are many applications in scheduling and distribution. Linear programming represents but one technique in the general area of mathematical programming that is concerned with the development of modeling and solution procedures to maximize the realization of the decision maker's objectives. Specifically, linear programming is the planning of operations in terms of maximized linear functions of a number of variables that are subject to certain constraints. The term *programming* is related to planning, and linear programming refers to modeling a problem and subsequently solving it by mathematical techniques (setting up and solving a system of linear equations). Specific application of linear programming in a real estate context include environmental protection, urban development, and facilities location.

Monte Carlo simulation. Computer simulation represents a descriptive rather than an optimization technique. Simulation involves developing a model of some real-world phenomena and performing experiments on that model. In essence, computer simulation allows for a more sophisticated form of sensitivity analysis than traditional tools would provide. Through the estimation of probability distributions, the counselor (or the client) attempts to assess the combined influence of variables which affect decision outcomes but about which some degree of uncertainty prevails. The possible combinations of values of each such variable are simulated in the Monte Carlo model to determine the range of likely outcomes and the probability associated with each. Monte Carlo simulation generates information that enables the counselor or client to analyze various combinations of risk and return and thus make more profitable decisions over the long run.

Bayesian analysis. In this form of statistical analysis, subjective probabilities (referred to as prior probabilities) are assigned to the occurrence of some real-world phenomena. The events to which the probabilities are assigned are mutually exclusive and exhaustive. Subjective probabilities are assigned on the basis of whatever information is currently available. Should additional evidence be obtained (for example, via sampling), prior probabilities are revised on the basis of this evidence by means of Bayes' theorem. Bayesian analysis formalizes the thinking processes of the counselor and/or client regarding decisions to be made about real estate investments. The potential application of Bayesian analysis to real estate investments is substantial. As an operations research model, Bayesian analysis allows for periodic revision of the probabilities of achieving stated objectives in light of new information and experience, thus producing better management of the investments.

Game theory. Gaming, in contrast to some of the more sophisticated simulation models, abstracts a limited range of the more important aspects of real-world phenomena for decision-making purposes. Gaming ranges from simplified risk and reward decision models in matrix form to highly elaborate heuristic models of the urban process. The purpose of game theory (regardless of model) is to force participants to make a series of interrelated goal-oriented decisions regarding the disposition and development of aspects abstracted from real-world phenomena. Game theory allows participants to experiment with decisions related to real-world phenomena without suffering potential detrimental and possibly devastating effects of bad decisions. The ultimate utility of game theory models depends on a tolerable degree of abstraction and on the extent to which the models manage to incorporate realistic bodies of data and theory corresponding to real-world phenomena and constraints.

SUMMARY

The real estate counselor aids the client in decision making by entering into the client's decision-making framework. Client objectives (stated as precisely as possible) are essential; however, it is important for the counselor to distinguish between the client's real and perceived needs, to rank goals, to resolve conflicts, and to quantify where possible. With client objectives articulated and goal priorities established, the counselor needs to identify alternative courses of action and select from among them to achieve client objectives.

The available decision-making tools enable the counselor to formalize thought processes and to express complex relationships in simpler terms. Whether the counselor uses formalized decision tools or mathematical models in his counseling practice, he needs to be familiar with their real or potential application and use by others. In particular, the counselor must be alert to and must guard against the misspecification of decision tools or models and thus their misuse in application.

Three general categories of decision tools have been discussed in this chapter: statistical decision tools, financial decision tools, and operations research models.

Statistical decision tools provide the counselor with a formal means of classifying, analyzing, and interpreting quantities of data for decision-making purposes. Statistical analysis rules and procedures are very formal and precise. Followed closely, they identify limitations and applications of the statistical measures that evolve from the analysis.

Financial decision tools and investment decision making aid the counselor in choosing between profitability and liquidity and in achieving a balance between an acceptable level of risk to the client and the rate of return required. Financial decision tools also enable the counselor to make selections from among alternative investment opportunities consistent with client objectives.

Operations research models enable the counselor or client to analyze the operating efficiency of the investment with the ultimate purpose of improving performance and thus protecting the investment's long-term integrity. Operations research models are mostly mathematical in form, relating significant variables in the operation of an investment to a proposed or anticipated outcome.

In many decision-making circumstances, immediate action is often called for in order to take advantage of a market opportunity. In such circumstances, the benefits of a lengthy period of analysis or the application of more sophisticated decision tools may be precluded. Counselors and clients are not precluded, however, from understanding the principles and concepts of the decision tools discussed in this chapter and their potential for increasing the decision maker's ability to base decisions on more than hunch, intuition, and judgment.

SELECTED REFERENCES

AKERSON, CHARLES B. *The Internal Rate of Return in Real Estate Investments*. Research Monograph. Chicago: American Society of Real Estate Counselors and American Institute of Real Estate Appraisers, 1976.

BENEDICT, NORMAN R. *Forecasting with Linear and Curvilinear Regression*. Research Monograph for Statistical Library: Part II. Chicago: American Society of Real Estate Counselors and National Association of Realtors, 1974.

———. *Graphic Statistical Presentations*. Research Monograph for Statistical Library: Part III. Chicago: American Society of Real Estate Counselors and National Association of Realtors, 1975.

———. *Market Analysis and the Real Estate Counselor*. Research Monograph for Statistical Library: Part IV. Chicago: American Society of Real Estate Counselors and National Association of Realtors, 1977.

———. *Mean and Standard Deviation*. Research Monograph for Statistical Library: Part I. Chicago: American Society of Real Estate Counselors and National Association of Realtors, 1973.

BOYCE, BYRL N., ed. *Real Estate Appraisal Terminology* (rev. ed.). Cambridge, Mass.: Ballinger Publishing Co., 1981.

COOK, THOMAS M., and ROBERT A. RUSSELL. *Contemporary Operations Management: Text and Cases*. Englewood Cliffs, N.J.: Prentice-Hall, Inc., 1980.

DRAPER, NORMAN, and HARRY SMITH, JR. *Applied Regression Analysis* (2nd ed.). New York: John Wiley & Sons, Inc., 1981.

EPLEY, DONALD R., and JAMES H. BOYKIN. *Basic Income Property Appraisal*. Reading, Mass.: Addison-Wesley Publishing Co., Inc., 1983.

JAFFE, AUSTIN J., and C. F. SIRMANS. *Real Estate Investment Decision Making*. Englewood Cliffs, N.J.: Prentice-Hall, Inc., 1982.

KAU, JAMES B., and C. F. SIRMANS. *Tax Planning for Real Estate Investors* (2nd ed.). Englewood Cliffs, N.J.: Prentice-Hall, Inc., 1982.

KEPNER, CHARLES H., and BENJAMIN B. TREGOE. *The New Rational Manager*. Princeton, N.J.: Princeton Research Press, 1981.

MESSNER, STEPHEN D., et al. *Marketing Investment Real Estate: Finance, Taxation Techniques* (2nd ed.). Chicago: Realtors National Marketing Institute, 1982.

PYHRR, STEPHEN A., and JAMES R. COOPER. *Real Estate Investment: Strategy, Analysis, Decisions*. Boston: Warren, Gorham & Lamont, 1982.

SPURR, WILLIAM A., and CHARLES P. BONINI. *Statistical Analysis for Business Decisions* (rev. ed.). Homewood, Ill.: Richard D. Irwin, Inc., 1973.

CHAPTER FIVE
LOCATION ANALYSIS

Location, location, location. Everyone interested in real estate has heard some speaker refer to the three prime ingredients for successful real estate ventures. What is a location, and how can a counselor's analysis of a location benefit his or her client? Location to most people is the physical property rather than the set of economic factors that influence the property built on the site. The term *location* in real estate literature refers to and is defined as "an economic characteristic of real estate composed of immobility, constant change, dependence, and elements of special distribution. Location is an economic concept even though a particular location [a site] may be described in physical and legal terms."[1]

A location is often regarded as a site, although the two terms are not synonymous. A site is a specific land parcel upon which a real estate activity may take place. A site is defined as "a parcel of land which is improved to the extent that it is ready for use for the purpose for which it is intended."[2]

In much of the real estate literature and in everyday practice, the distinction between the economic location and the physical site is blurred. One of the objectives of this chapter is to assist the reader in understanding how the analysis of a location

---

[1]Byrl N. Boyce, ed., *Real Estate Appraisal Terminology* (Cambridge, Mass.: Ballinger Publishing Co., 1981), p. 155.

[2]Ibid., p. 221.

may be helpful in the selection of both a location and a site for real estate development. The reasons for undertaking a location analysis are to find a site within a location upon which to place an economic enterprise, to make an investment, or to dispose of a parcel of owned property at the highest possible selling price.

Location analysis is important in real estate activities because the economic factors affecting a location are virtually uncontrollable by the developer, investor, lender, or other participant in the real estate development process. The real estate decision-making process studies alternative locations in order to select the best available alternative, in the knowledge that once a decision has been made, the factors beyond the property boundaries will have a significant influence on the property for its entire economic life. As times change, the owner could remodel the property to better adapt it to new market conditions. However, the location will not yield to the developer's designs and location remains one of the least controllable factors in the operation of real estate.

REGIONAL ANALYSIS

Although the product of an enterprise may vary from selling houses to selling hamburgers, each enterprise has the objective of being a successful venture. The developer, builder, entrepreneur, manager, or promoter wants to produce a product or service for which there is a sustained market and effective purchasing power.

Since a commitment to pay a fixed cost (such as the cost of real estate) must be made before—and sometimes a long time before—sales begin, sustained effective purchasing power in the market is important. The effective purchasing power study begins at the regional level because many factors that will ultimately influence the success or failure of an enterprise are determined by regional economics. The health of an enterprise is directly related to the economic well-being of its region. Thus, it is necessary to analyze the components of a region.

Major Employers

An important aspect of a region's "health" is its major employers. Employment is the single most important economic factor in valuing a region. In analyzing regional employment, the counselor's first step is to identify the major employers and to determine whether they hire a significant percentage of the total employed. An employer that hires as little as 5 percent of the total work force can be a significant factor in both the direct employment and the indirect job creation of a region. It is thus important to understand the characteristics of both that particular employer and its industry. An indication of the financial health of a given industry can be found in corporate financial statements and industry publications and studies. The attitude of important industrial firms toward a particular region is revealed in their employment trends and in their recent capital expenditures in that region. Once the major employers have been identified and their economic base and attitude are understood, it is important to review the products produced or the services provided and the general trends that affect such products or services.

For example, if the regional economic base is largely heavy manufacturing, and particularly if such manufacturing is limited to a single manufacturer, a single industry, or a group of related industries, then the current strength and the projected future of that manufacturer, industry, or group of industries is critical.

Even if employment is well diversified, it is still necessary to understand the general employment trends of a region. Trends in the number of people employed are the key to regional viability, for example, blue-collar employees versus office employees, manufacturing jobs versus service jobs. Trends are often known to the counselor through living in the region and following local events, although a report will likely require documentation of data and trends. Regional employment and unemployment trends should be compared with state and national trends as a measure of the economic health of a region. The counselor also should discern the reasons for any variance.

Economic Changes

Few things are constant except change. Challanges today are faced from the heaviest manufacturing to the highest technological industries. Historic dominance in capital or skilled labor intense industries has given way to high cost and aged equipment. Changes in autos, steel and heavy equipment are well documented and understood. Where the next significant changes will occur and what impact these changes will have on the subject of an analysis, require skilled observation and understanding of economics that may reach far beyond an immediate location.

The counselor uses economic trends to assist in the identification and analysis of the impacts of such changes on the value of the property under study. The impacts may be positive as well as negative. The emergence of high tech and its concentration in certain east or west coast locations have indeed created positive value benefits in those areas. Conversely the loss of heavy industry has a negative impact on the "steel belt".

Today the basic industry of a region may be medical care facilities in a specialized field and a host of related suppliers of services. Potential or actual consumers and suppliers may locate in the region to take advantage of, or be near enough to reach, such facilities should a need for them arise. An establishment's decision to be near its customers is tempered by the rent (or price) of optimum locations. Sometimes a slightly less desirable but an affordable and viable location is selected over the optimum site. Location analysis will rarely disclose a single clearly identifiable generator of economic activity. "The mine" or "the plant" has given way, as has "the company store," to a host of suppliers and users existing in intertwined relationships.

Economic Boundaries

In the analysis of a region, a neighborhood, or a specific site, it is necessary for the counselor or analyst to identify both the economic and the physical boundaries applicable to the subject at hand. These boundaries are important in both data collection and data analysis. Physical boundaries such as rivers, highways, and railroads are more easily identified than economic boundaries, which are often more subjective, though equally important. Most observers perceive a railroad as both a physical and an economic boundary. School districts, subdivisions, and suburbs are perceived as being more or less desirable, and thus have economic boundaries that are as real as the river or the "tracks." In addition to comprising natural features such as rivers, ports, lakes, and natural resources, a region is a complex of employers and employees, providers and users, producers and consumers. Enterprises within a region, whether they are manufacturing, medicine, education, distribution, banking, government, or a host of other types, generate the paychecks from which other economic activities flow. Each major enterprise has an impact on the economy of the region, the area, or the neighborhood, and the extent to which that impact is significant establishes the economic boundaries for the analysis.

The nature of an enterprise is less critical than its economic impact on a region. If the major regional enterprises are suppliers to older steel mills or automotive-related manufacturers, their impact will be perceived as different from that of high-technology, computer, or service-related enterprises. Whatever the regional characteristics, the major employers or employment centers, historical and projected employment trends, salary levels, and skills needed are of primary concern in any regional analysis.

We almost always look to the past before preparing estimates for the future. It has been said that those who fail to learn from history are destined to repeat it, which implies that a failure to understand the past interaction of economic and other forces will probably lead to unfortunate present and future decisions. The role of the counselor includes using historical data with modern interpretation and analysis in order to formulate plans that will assist his or her client in optimizing investment returns.

Population Changes

Population changes are usually directly related to employment changes, though certain retirement areas are notable exceptions. The size of a region's population may determine whether there are enough people to support an enterprise. Likewise, the presence or absence of major employment opportunities may determine whether a region is attractive for relocation. Employment and population changes may not always be on the same cycle; however, trends in population should assist in formulating projections for the future course of an enterprise. Regional population trends, like regional employment trends, should be compared with state and national trends for a comparative perspective.

Usually employment opportunities foster growth in population within an area, and the greater the employment opportunities, the more likely, and the more rapid, will be the in-migration of population. The relationship between employment and population trends should be helpful to the counselor in analyzing in-migration or out-migration within the study area. It is quite possible that within a region one area could be growing in population and another area declining in population. Population shifts for the region as a whole, as well as for its components, can be a significant influence in determining the proper location for a successful enterprise.

Census Data

Demography, the study of social and vital statistics and the science of charting the movement of population, is based largely on the study of census data. Census data offer an abundant source of information on population characteristics, including such features as age, family size, income, and education levels. However, the published census data state what existed at some time in the past. Through the analysis of census data, certain predictions may be made about the future, but such predictions must always remain suspect. Census data, like much of the information we deal with in appraising, development, or retail sales, are subject to interpretation as these data relate to the site and user in question. For example, a clearly defined population growth trend in an area tells us little about the one successful local industry that was built on the availability of inexpensive coal from a single mine that has exhausted its vein of coal and is now closing.

Census data, with its numerous groupings of population characteristics, age levels, and income levels, may tell us a good deal about the potential of a particular enterprise. Income levels may be very important for the success of a business. Some employers and retailers may look for locations with high income levels, whereas others may prefer lower income levels because these are beneficial to their particular manufacturing or retailing enterprise. Age grouping or family size may be a key factor in a location decision. Clearly, a younger, family-oriented population is interested in different products than is a population over 65 years in age.

The accumulation of data should always generate these questions: (1) Is the future likely to be a mirror of the past? (2) Are there available substitutes for the basic industries or service enterprises upon which growth has depended? (3) As changes occur, what will their consequences be for a given location?

Transportation

Whether by jet, rail, bus, auto, truck, birchbark canoe, or foot, transportation has been, and continues to be, a critical element in the development of successful locations. The counselor's analysis of transportation will consider many factors, including the areas from which materials are drawn, products distributed, and employees and customers attracted. In choosing a location for a commercial enterprise, the cost and convenience of transportation are significant considerations. Several factors involved in transportation need to be understood and analyzed as a given location and site are considered.

The differential costs of transportation between sites being considered may be critical in a site selection, though there are times when transportation costs are not especially important. Maine lobsters are served in California, and the cost of transporting them is high—but that cost is absorbed as a part of the cost of dinner. If the item to be transported is large, heavy, and fungible, then the cost of transportation is critical. Cement may be transported long distances, but wet concrete is trucked relatively short distances because the cost of transportation is high in ratio to the cost of the product.

If an enterprise manufactures expensive lightweight calculators that are sold worldwide and we are studying its distribution of finished products, our concern is with a convenient airport with regular service to a large number of destinations. For otherwise equal sites, the final selection may weigh heavily on their distances from suppliers, favorable trucking zones, and reasonable accessibility to residential areas from which we hope to attract employees. If the client employs a large but relatively low-paid work force in a major metropolitan area, public transportation is a major consideration. From either an economic or a geographic perspective, the price of a site will probably reflect the desirability of its neighborhood.

If the objective of the study is to determine a viable location for the construction of a new fast-food franchise, the counselor might focus the study on a set of factors diffferent from those used to locate other real estate enterprises. Distances to established residential areas, the location of other retail and food outlets, and the purchasing patterns of the local and transient patrons would all be important. In such an analysis, the speed of the traffic, the number of traffic lanes, distances from stop signs, cross streets, and the location of existing competition would influence the relative desirability of the sites that might be available for a particular enterprise. In the site selection the critical transportation element would focus more on the capacity to service the consumer than on raw materials, employees, or finished goods. If convenient transportation is available to the consumer, then the other transportation demands of the business can probably be adapted to the site.

When the focus of the counselor's study is to assist in the location of new retail outlets, whether freestanding stores or regional shopping centers, the analysis would focus on the transportation patterns of the potential customers that could be attracted to the new facility. The transportation of materials (inventory) and employees would be less critical than the ability of the shopping center or the store to accommodate the transportation needs and demands of the consumer. Downtown retail stores once dominated the retail market largely because of the availability of public transportation. Dependence on public transportation has diminished significantly during the past thirty years, as the importance of the suburban shopping center has risen. Changing public attitudes toward transportation are obviously a crucial element in this pattern of change from downtown to suburban shopping dominance. Therefore, a pertinent question is whether the transportation patterns in the areas under study are likely to change.

One method that may be used to rank several probable locations for a particular site use is to prepare a chart listing the key locational factors. In the example presented in Figure 5–1, each item is weighted according to its importance. The weightings range from 1 to 10, with 10 being the highest weighting. By means of this weighting system, it has been determined that property A is the most desirable for the use being considered.

The weighting is assigned to each feature after consultation with the client. It should reflect his or her needs and desires as well as the expectations and judgement of the counselor. Where the features can be grouped, a weighting should be assigned to each group. If this is not done, each feature carries equal importance.

Public Services

Not long ago, cities were competing for the distinction of having the largest land area in the United States. If the top ranking in population was not possible, perhaps there could be a top ranking in total land area. In almost any city developed since World War II, one could find passed-over parcels of land as developers sought sites that were inexpensive to acquire and develop. Extension of utilities to outlying areas was common and expected, and it mattered little that utilities were being extended through vacant parcels at some considerable distance to reach the new "hot area." Utilities were like the automobiles necessary to reach the suburbs. If you needed more—build more.

Today, however, we have different attitudes. Environmental concerns have raised the standards and, along with general inflation, increased the cost of constructing and operating sewer treatment plants and other utilities. Water in many areas is difficult and expensive to reach, in short supply, and perhaps affected by weather, interstate agreements, pollution of varying sorts, and aging and soil-infiltrated reservoirs and distribution systems with rising maintenance costs.

Although sewer capacity may be abundant in a region, it may not be adequate in a particular area or at a specific site. Sewer bans, moratoriums on new taps, or limitations on flowage are concerns. In a developing area the impact of future development on sewer capacity should be considered. Regional planning, water, and sewer department personnel who deal with these problems daily are excellent sources of information. The sewer system must not only be in the ground but must also be of a size that can service the property and be connected to a public utility

FIGURE 5-1 Location Feature Analysis.

FEATURE	WEIGHT OF FEATURE (1–10)	PROPERTY							
		A		B		C		D	
		RANK	RANK × WEIGHTING	RANK	RANK × WEIGHTING	RANK	RANK × WEIGHTING	RANK	RANK × WEIGHTING
Close to shopping	8	3	24	4	32	3	24	1	8
Close to public transportation	9	3	27	4	36	3	27	2	18
Effect on cost of occupancy	5	3	15	1	5	2	10	4	20
Relative to vehicle and pedestrian congestion	7	3	21	1	7	2	14	4	28
Relative to competition	8	4	32	4	32	3	24	2	16
Totals			119		112		99		90

Source: Malcolm L. S. Bryce, CRE, Bryce, Kipp & Company, Ltd., Calgary, Alberta, Canada.

with excess capacity. If the object of the analysis is to bring the system to or near its maximum capacity, the counselor should consider the consequences. A system that reaches capacity after the client's project is completed may significantly reduce competition for a period of time. Occasionally, on-site utility systems are found to have been installed in such a manner as to require relocation in order to proceed with a desirable construction or development project. Therefore, care should be taken to locate any on-site utility easements or installations.

An often overlooked public service is mass transit. The use of rail mass transit tends to be an older, large-city, eastern phenomenon, although there are a few exceptions. In San Francisco the original mass transit system, the cable car, survives both as a means of transportation and as a tourist attraction. The principal means of transportation reflects in part the time during which a city was developed. The newer western cities are almost totally dependent on the individually owned automobile to transport their citizens. The patterns of development of these cities reflect commuting times to major employment, business, retail, and service centers. Buses may be an option in such areas, but the buses occupy the same roadways as autos and trucks and do little to speed the flow of riders, though they are obviously more energy efficient than autos and, if widely used, would reduce the number of autos, congestion, and perhaps employee transportation costs.

If the enterprise seeking a site has the option of locating in an area totally dependent on private autos where land costs are relatively low or in an area also served by public transit where land costs are higher, a higher site purchase price might be well justified in the long run if public transportation is popular. Mass transit is very expensive and difficult to install in new city construction and is substantially more expensive and difficult to retrofit in older cities. Most urban areas are confronted by increasing demands on the existing tax base and by more programs and needs than can usually be funded from current taxes. This means that the possibility of installing new light rail or other mass transit systems will become increasingly remote. The federal push to construct more mass transit facilities appears to have diminished for the foreseeable future. Therefore, a location with existing transportation options would be preferable to a location with promised future mass transit.

The maintenance of the utility systems in most major urban areas will become more expensive and difficult with the passage of time, and accordingly the long-range implications of growth in the study area should be carefully considered from this standpoint. The extension of utility systems and the increase in the capacity of existing systems must be carefully analyzed to assure that the location being studied will have the utilities that are necessary for intended land uses.

Police and fire protection, telephone systems, public and private education, cultural opportunities, and religious facilities could each be a part of the location analysis. Although every city provides some, most, or all of these human services, the quality and cost of each service might vary greatly between cities. The cost-benefit ratio between competing cities should be understood. The funding of such services by local real estate, income, inventory, or sales taxes may have a direct bearing on the viability of a specific site or location.

Zoning

Although there are some exceptions, Houston being the best known, urban areas are generally zoned. Since the early 1900s zoning has been the most commonly accepted legal tool for regulating municipal land use in the United States. Zoning typically separates residential, retail, and industrial land use activities for the presumed protection of each activity. Ideally, zoning achieves compatibility of property uses within an area or a neighborhood, which in turn should produce desirable economic results.

If the purpose of the counselor's study is to select the best available site with specific characteristics, a desired zoning classification will usually be specified. The counselor may be aware of the willingness of local officials to grant variances or to allow zoning changes and, accordingly, may suggest sites that might be rezoned to fit the desired enterprise. Although zoning administration has often been used as a tool for encouraging municipal development, it is frequently used today as a means of curbing, directing, or controlling growth.

In addition to the restrictions that zoning ordinances place on a site, there may be further restrictions in recorded deeds, subdivision covenants, and licensing or occupancy permits. Real estate taxes, special assessments, building permits, occupancy permits, and fees, as well as the possibility that the site might be taken by eminent domain, are other possible restrictions on a site. Although zoning and other restrictions are generally imposed for purposes of control, they may also be used to induce a particular industry or user to locate in a municipality.

A site zoned for an intended use with utilities in place of sufficient capacity to serve the proposed need would be preferable to a less costly site whose zoning, utilities, or approvals have not yet been obtained. Delays can create added costs and contribute to lost opportunities. Going too far beyond existing developed areas increases the chances that intercepting and competing sites will become better sites within the location chosen for the project.

Special Objectives

Although the analysis that the counselor is called on to perform is usually broad in scope, occasionally the client needs answers to limited and direct questions. In such a case, the analysis may only involve answering the specific questions of the client and the particular concerns of the client will focus the analysis on certain areas. The requirements of a high-technology engineering and design firm will be quite different from the requirements of the claims office of a major insurance carrier even though both need 100,000 square feet of office space. Therefore the counselor's focus would be quite different in the studies conducted for these clients.

Not all locational analyses require the study of a region or even of a broad neighborhood. A dry cleaner wanting to establish another outlet in a city where his business is well established may only be interested in "the best location on South Broadway." The needs of the client in such a case will most definitely narrow the counselor's scope of analysis.

FIGURE 5–2   Site Selection Checklist.

Site address
Site dimensions
Site topography
Soil conditions
Site size
Percentage of site usable
Asking price
Price per unit (e.g., total apartment units permitted on the site)
Zoning
Utilities
  Sewer location
  Sewer size
    Restriction, capacity, cost
  Water location
  Water supply pipe size(s)
    Capacity, cost
  Electricity location, capacity, cost
  Heating
    Natural gas
      Location, size of supply pipes
      Availability, cost
    Steam
      Location, size of supply pipes
      Source, capacity, cost
    Other (in certain areas processing gases, hot water, or oil may also be distributed)
  Telephone
    Capacity to handle increased usage
    Current capacity to handle computers and other telecommunication devices
    Cost
School district
Police district
Fire protection
Tax valuation
Tax rates
Easements

A checklist that might be used for a particular site selection is provided in Figure 5–2.

MARKET IDENTIFICATION

The delineation of a market is a process that identifies a location for a use or uses and the area that the use or uses will serve. It either implies a known location as a starting point or provides the means by which to determine the most effective location in light of existing or proposed competition.[3] For the dry cleaner who wants to locate on South Broadway, the most advantageous location will be the site where the greatest potential traffic can be captured. Usually considerable description and study is required in order to identify the market that the client is trying to serve.

If the client plans to sell pizza or lease warehouse space and it has been determined that an area can support this additional service, then a market study to quantify the existing and potential demand in the area would be appropriate. The existing competition would be located geographically and ranked by appropriate comparative features—number of square feet available or potentially available, price of the space, physical features, amenities, traffic flow, age, curb appeal, and other features that would be important to a potential user of the space or service. The list would obviously be quite different for various classes of real estate or proposed services. The features identified for the comparison could be ranked by the counselor and the client in order of importance, and the ranking could then be used to compare the properties or services. The proposed new product, property, or service should be ranked along with the competition.

Surveys, interviews, and questionnaires may be used to measure the pricing, physical features, amenities, and services that are a part of the unsatisfied market potential in the area. The counselor may call on other professionals to conduct the marketing studies while he concentrates on the real estate–related analysis. If the product is the real estate itself, the counselor might conduct the entire study with his own staff.

One aspect that should be recognized in the analysis is the sophistication of the competition. Both the location analysis and the market study may determine that demand exists for 100 additional two-bedroom apartments with physical features and amenities similar to those of the apartments found in the present market. It may be further determined that the present competition consists of dozens of ten-unit apartment buildings owned by diverse individuals who manage their own buildings and are more concerned with maintaining a low vacancy rate than with increasing rents. Thus, a developer considering building 100 units whose cost of construction would require a rental rate of perhaps 150 percent of the present rates might decide that the project is nonviable because the competition is too diverse and too unsophisticated. To compete at rates 150 percent of the present market with apartments having no unique features would be financially unsound even if a market with adequate effective purchasing power existed. Under these circumstances an additional study would be used to determine what features might attract the segment of the market willing to pay a premium rent for unique features even at a price per square foot or per apartment unit considerably higher than that now paid for the typical unit in the same area.

---

[3]Stephen D. Messner et al., *Analyzing Real Estate Opportunities: Market and Feasibility Studies* (Chicago: Realtors National Marketing Institute, 1977), p. 67.

In the midst of sophisticated competition, one would expect rents to be increasing rapidly with low vacancies when strong demand is present. Once the unique features have been identified and it has been determined that the enterprise is economically justified, then attention should turn to market penetration.

MARKET PENETRATION

Since real estate development is a slow process, it is rare for one enterprise to "scoop" the market. While planning is proceeding, the potential for competing development should be considered. If there are only three logical sites upon which the enterprise could be successfully carried out, it might be possible to option all three sites for a period of time to ensure that the client's project is on-stream well ahead of any competing enterprise and that it occupies, at least for the option term, a unique market position. Because real estate development is often discussed at public meetings and plans must be submitted to public officials for approvals, it is very difficult to keep a proposed project secret for long. Uniqueness, except for location, may not be long-lived.

It has been said that the prime ingredient of a successful real estate operation is location. In this context, the term *location* includes physical as well as economic attributes. Location is the one element in a real estate enterprise that cannot be duplicated exactly by the competition. Earlier the impact of location and timing was mentioned as one of the factors over which the developer or manager had the least control and which was subject to the greatest constraints. These outside limitations apply to the competition as well. Far too often in the development process, a concession is made to the price of a site because the site is the first substantial cash item in the development process. A cheap but inferior site is no bargain. If a secondary site is chosen because of price, the competition is left with the better site upon which to take advantage of the market interest generated by the original entrepreneur. The competition then has the market advantage because of the unique feature—location. Only institutions and very good restaurants are able to overcome the handicap of location constraints, and sometimes restaurants fail to overcome this handicap.

SELECTION OF THE OPTIMUM SITE

The optimum site for one enterprise may be totally unworkable for another. Particular types of enterprises tend to seek sites within defined locations that support their activities in order to maximize benefits and reduce collective costs. There is a tendency for like or related enterprises to seek sites in the same area. We find manufacturing concerns in industrial parks, major retailers in shopping centers, service suppliers along major traffic arteries, and professionals in downtown office buildings. In each instance, the site is selected on the basis of its desirability for the individual enterprise. Agglomerations of similar enterprises create economies as distances between suppliers of materials, products, and services are reduced. Such agglomeration effects and external economies may be found in an industrial park, a central business district, a city (gambling in Las Vegas), an area (computer component construction in the "Silicon Valley"), or a region (oil and gas or other mineral exploration). The location of major new automobile sales facilities on the same street (automobile row) or in the same area is a long-established practice. Shopping centers enable retailers to benefit from the close proximity of their competition and of major traffic generators such as department stores.

The objective of the location analysis is to determine whether the client's specific project or program can be profitable in an area and on a specific site. Sites are compared on the basis of a matrix of details, including physical, geographic, political, economic, and even emotional elements. Life cycles and emotional evaluations are important but highly subjective aspects of the location analysis. Local guidance is always beneficial, no matter how skilled the analyst. If local residents avoid an area because of perceived problems, their attitude to the area might not be reflected in the other aspects of the analysis. Failure to recognize such influences on business patronage could doom a proposed enterprise to failure.

The optimum site should be selected on the basis of the best set of present and perceived future measures of these multiple influences. Which factors receive the greatest weight in the analysis will be established in part by the specifications for the assignment that are developed between the counselor and the client. The client selects the criteria important to his enterprise, and the counselor interprets the real estate information and recommends specific alternatives. The counselor will usually base his recommendations on his analysis of such topics as

1. Physical characteristics, including terrain, topographic, and subsoil characteristics determined from maps, inspections, and soil borings.
2. Utility features, including the location of pipes or wires, the cost of service, and available capacity from utility suppliers.
3. Zoning features, including the local government's attitude toward business in general and the specific enterprise in particular, as determined from public records and interviews with government representatives, particularly where rezoning, variances, or special permits are required.
4. Economic factors, as determined from the counselor's direct knowledge of the area and from a variety of sources such as demographics, regional or local planning studies, and utility use and market studies. The sources for specific economic information are varied, and their selection will depend in part on the thrust of the analysis.

Other chapters will deal with the site selection process as it pertains to specific types of enterprises such as office, retail, industrial, and other special purpose real estate activities. Depending on the activity, the location (or the site) may have a significant impact on the cost of the enterprise or only a nominal impact. Since diverse enterprises maximize their returns and reduce costs through different objectives, the optimum site will be selected not only on the basis of its specific physical merits but also on the basis of its potential contribution to the overall profitability of the enterprise.

SELECTED REFERENCES

APPLEBAUM, WILLIAM, et al.   *Guide to Store Location Research with Emphasis on Super Markets.* Reading, Mass.: Addison-Wesley Publishing Co., Inc., 1968.

BOYCE, BYRL N., ed.   *Real Estate Appraisal Terminology* (rev. ed.). Cambridge, Mass.: Ballinger Publishing Co., 1981.

BROWNING, JON E.   *How to Select a Business Site: The Executive's Location Guide.* New York: McGraw-Hill Book Company, 1980.

ERICKSON, RODNEY A.   "Firm Relocation and Site Selection in Suburban Municipalities." *Journal of Urban Economics,* July 1980, pp. 69–85.

FREED, SHERVIN, and WILLIAM BEST.   "Future Challenges to the Site Selection Expert." *Industrial Development,* July–August 1981, pp. 9–13.

GIBBONS, JAMES E.   "Apartment Feasibility Studies." *The Appraisal Journal,* July 1968, pp. 325–32.

———   "Mortgage Equity Capitalization and After Tax Equity Yield." *The Appraisal Journal,* January 1967, pp. 31–49.

GRAASKAMP, JAMES A.   *Fundamentals of Real Estate Development.* Development Component Series. Washington, D.C.: Urban Land Institute, 1981.

———   *Guide to Feasibility Analysis* (3rd ed.). Chicago: Society of Real Estate Appraisers, 1970.

GROSS, SHELDON A.   "A Model for Effective Site Selection." *Real Estate Today,* May–June 1975, pp. 56–63.

HUBBARD, ELBERT W.   "A Commentary on Site Selection: Is Quality of Life a Criterion?" *Atlanta Economic Review,* March–April 1978, pp. 52–53.

MESSNER, STEPHEN D., et al.   *Analyzing Real Estate Opportunities: Market and Feasibility Studies.* Chicago: Realtors National Marketing Institute, 1977.

NELSON, RICHARD L.   *The Selection of Retail Locations.* New York: F. W. Dodge Corporation, 1958.

RAMS, EDWIN M.   *Analysis and Valuation of Retail Locations.* Reston, Va.: Reston Publishing Company, Inc., 1976.

RATCLIFF, RICHARD U.   *Real Estate Analysis,* chap. 4. New York: McGraw-Hill Book Company, 1961.

STAFFORD, HOWARD A.   *Principles of Industrial Facility Location.* Atlanta: Conway Publications, Inc., 1980.

CHAPTER SIX
INVESTMENT ANALYSIS FOR PROPOSED PROJECTS

Proposed developments are among the most interesting and challenging assignments for the real estate counselor. Depending on the counselor's experience and specialized field of activity, such assignments can cover a wide range of real estate endeavors, including residential tracts, condominiums, shopping centers, hotels, and office buildings. Due to the complexity of some of these endeavors, the counselor will frequently enlist the collaboration of other specialists, coordinating a team effort. Opinions and recommendations resulting from the analysis are often decisive in determining whether a project will be implemented as planned, modified, deferred, or even abandoned.

The need for independent and competent analysis of proposed developments arises from numerous sources. These include corporations, financial institutions, joint venture partners, and landowners. Experienced developers frequently prepare their own feasibility studies, but they may seek a critique or an independent study from a knowledgeable outsider.

In a typical investment-type situation, the crucial question is "Will it fly?" Will the market value of the complete development justify its costs, including all hard and soft costs plus carrying charges, and provide a reasonable entrepreneurial profit? In making this determination, the counselor must have a full understanding of the relationship between the economics of the proposed development and the anticipated cost. Although construction costs can generally be determined within a narrow range, conditions affecting ultimate rent levels, space absorption, availability, and cost of financing are difficult to predict.

SITE ANALYSIS

Site Acquisition

Usually the site will have been acquired before the counselor received the assignment. It may have been in the same ownership for many years, or it may require a more intensive use in view of increased land values. It may have come under the control of more aggressive new owners as a result of a corporate merger. Finally, the site may have been purchased recently for the specific purpose of developing it in the near future.

Should the counselor be involved in the site acquisition, it is imperative that he or she be fully up-to-date on the terms of sale and the developments proposed for the most recent comparable sales, including pending transactions. Being fully attuned to prevailing conditions is particularly important in a rapidly changing market. Also needed is thorough knowledge of land use controls, including height and density limitations, parking requirements, and the provisions of a specific plan or of limitations and requirements imposed by a local redevelopment agency and their relation to zoning regulations.

Prior to site acquisition the counselor's function is to advise the client of the market value of the land sought based on an analysis of benchmark transactions. Since the targeted site frequently involves multiple ownerships and parts of the site may be under lease, the counselor may have to assist the client in negotiating lease modifications or buy-outs and relocations of tenants. In the site assembly process, premiums may have to be paid for certain key parcels. This is justified as long as the average site cost is reasonably consistent with prevailing land values.

Legal Matters

Where land use is regulated by a zoning ordinance clearly defining the development possibilities, problems concerning the permitted land use tend to be minimized. Even in such circumstances, however, it is necessary to check into the following matters and to analyze their impact on the subject property.

1. Street or alley widening dedication requirements
2. Setback requirements
3. Controls relating to access (for example, the location of garage ingress and egress)
4. Land use regulations established by redevelopment agencies
5. Land uses proposed under a general plan
6. Effect of environmental impact studies

7. The situation regarding the transfer of development rights
8. Deed restrictions (restrictive covenants)

In jurisdictions where development is subject to the granting of a conditional use permit or similar procedures, interviews with members of the staff of the local planning department and discussions with architectural or planning firms familiar with the policies and philosophies of the individuals involved in the permit process are necessary in order to find out what type of development is most likely to be approved. Frequently, the developer's objective will be to obtain approval for the most intensive use of the land, though this may not coincide with the optimum utilization in view of the realities of the marketplace.

PHYSICAL CHARACTERISTICS

Size and Shape

The configuration of the site will determine its suitability for the proposed development. Particular emphasis will be placed on the suitability of the site for a building with efficient and competitive floor sizes and layout, adequate cost-effective parking, and good accessibility and on-site vehicular circulation.

Topography and Soil

Certain terrain features can be advantageous for specific types of development; for example, a sloping topography can provide convenient access to different garage levels. More frequently, irregular terrain adds to the construction cost because it increases the expenditures for excavation and retaining walls.

Soil conditions will be examined by soils engineers. Any construction costs above the norm for special foundations and any related costs resulting from an extended construction time and increased carrying charges will have to be recognized. Sometimes it is advisable to insert a provision in the option for a site that allows the purchaser to decline purchase if soil conditions are unacceptable for the intended uses.

Utilities and Other Public Services

The availability and cost of water and sewer service of sufficient capacity will have to be checked by a qualified engineer. The costs of street widening, median strip improvements, installation of traffic signals, and related matters will also have to be examined. Adequate public transit is lacking in most of the major cities of the United States. However, neither the shortcomings of such facilities nor heavy traffic congestion has had any serious detrimental impact on new development.

BUILDING DESIGN

The real estate counselor can provide valuable input in the development of the conceptual design and the preparation of preliminary architectural drawings. Frequently, serious deficiencies in planning and layout could have been avoided if the services of a qualified real estate expert had been secured. This observation is not intended in any way to depreciate the ability or know-how of the architectural profession, but there exist numerous examples of poorly conceived developments that can be traced to the developer or the architect, or both. Often the problem has been a product built without proper regard to prospective users' reactions to it.

The "Right" Building

"Highest and best use" is a vastly overworked phrase, deeply embedded in the vocabulary of the real estate analyst. Frequently glossed over or merely given lip service, it is truly the cornerstone in the study of a proposed development. It covers the entire spectrum of type, size, and quality of building together with appurtenant parking and amenities. It is the real estate counselor's function to carefully sort out and "try on" various development plans and finally to identify the type of project that holds the greatest promise in terms of return on investment and other objectives of the developer.

Initial screening consists of selecting the basic type of utilization most suitable for the location. Initially, the site may appear to be adapted for retail, office, or hotel use. Several studies will have to be made in order to determine the most feasible type of use or combination of uses.

Once this analysis has been accomplished, the basic guidelines concerning size, height, type of construction, and other matters will have to be established and preliminary cost and economic studies will have to be made. This phase will be followed by the formulation of more specific guidelines for the developer. In connection with office buildings, for instance, the counselor should have an understanding of the floor sizes required in specific locations. These sizes will be influenced by the types of tenancies identified with the area, floor ratio efficiency, and elevator service and parking needs. In certain jurisdictions building safety requirements are much more stringent for structures exceeding a certain number of floors, substantially increasing construction costs. These requirements must be considered in the determination of the most logical and economically appropriate development plan. Anyone familiar with the real estate scene is aware of numerous situations where major developments were financed and constructed and ultimately failed, not just because of poor timing but because of poor judgment in the type of development or because of inherent design deficiencies.

The landscape is littered with buildings that turned out to be financial nightmares for the developers. The examples include single-family residences too costly for their location or of bizarre architecture, luxury high-rise condominium projects in overbuilt markets, office buildings placed in unproven locations in a "pioneering" effort, and shopping centers in areas already oversaturated with retail facilities. Ironically, virtually every one of these failures was preceded by some type of "feasibility study."

It is recommended that the counselor be involved from the start in the basic design concept and have sufficient contact with the architect to establish certain basic features. Architects specializing in particular types of facilities obviously have the ability to design an attractive, well-functioning building that will receive good market response. On the other hand, an architectural firm may not have adequate experience in, say, high-rise luxury condominiums, lacking the capability of designing a building that meets the demand of the market in terms of unit mix, apartment areas, and even floor plans. Occasionally, the architect may be overly influenced by the client's wishes and perceptions. The real estate consultant, through his market research, is in an excellent position to help the architect and the client to avoid pitfalls and prevent costly mistakes.

Some real estate consultants have a broad background in real estate development. This enables them not only to analyze proposed construction from an economic and design standpoint but also to make recommendations concerning building construction, equipment, energy-efficient features, and interior appointments that will result in substantial cost savings without diminishing the integrity of the building or its financial performance. These savings will involve a review of working drawings and specifications as well as the construction contract.

FINANCIAL FEASIBILITY

Financial feasibility involves the following major steps:

1. Analysis of demand and supply situation
2. Cost study
3. Income and expense projection
4. Examination of the cost to economic value relationship

Analysis of Demand and Supply Situation

The methods applied and the statistical data used in forming an opinion concerning the economic outlook for a proposed development will depend on the type of property. It should be pointed out at the outset that any forecast will be affected by unforeseeable conditions and the impact of economic cycles.

In connection with retail projects, for instance, a regional shopping center, the process consists of delineating the trade area, identifying existing and proposed competitive facilities, analyzing the trend of population and per capita retail sales, and forecasting the business volume to be captured by the proposed project. Ample and reliable statistical data are available to project the annual sales per square foot

FIGURE 6–1   Nicholson Centre—a mixed use development planned for the future Washington Metro Area Transit Authority White Flint station in Rockville, Maryland. Courtesy of Perkins & Will, Architects, Chicago, New York, Washington.

of the gross leasable area of the proposed development and thus to ascertain with a reasonable degree of certainty the probability of its financial success.

The task of projecting the effective demand for most other types of real estate facilities is a great deal more difficult, as the decisions of the potential consumer are frequently affected by extraneous conditions that cannot be foreseen at the time the analysis is prepared. For instance, high mortgage interest rates can dry up the market for condominiums because would-be buyers are unable to qualify for loans and because other would-be buyers who were planning to switch from their single-family dwellings to condominiums cannot sell their houses.

A comprehensive study of existing and proposed facilities together with a tracking of past absorption, rental, and occupancy levels is fundamental to the demand-supply analysis of various types of real estate development. The underlying principle is that past performance is the best indicator of what lies ahead. It was once a tenet of urban land economics that a demand for virtually all types of urban real estate facilities is created in direct relationship to population growth. Actually, the demand for space does not fit that neatly into this pattern. This is clearly demonstrated by the vast amounts of new office space that have been absorbed in New York City and, to a lesser degree, San Francisco while there has been an actual decline in population.

In connection with office buildings, it is not feasible to quantify future demand by segmenting the market and pinpointing how much of the demand for space will be generated by certain types of users—for example, attorneys, accountants, and financial institutions. Nevertheless, it is imperative to assemble information on past absorption, to thoroughly investigate the leasing status of recently completed buildings, and to obtain information on buildings that are planned or under construction. A thorough examination of the rental market is likely to disclose the potential demand of major corporations or financial institutions for large blocks of space as a result of expansion requirements or relocation. Thus, the consultant will be thoroughly familiar with the extent of existing and proposed competitive development. Moreover, as a by-product of the market survey, a better understanding of the positioning of the subject vis-à-vis competitive products will emerge.

Based on the result of the market analysis, the consultant will prepare a forecast concerning rental rates, preleasing, and absorption, that is, the time required subsequent to the completion of the building to reach a "normal" occupancy status. There is a tendency to base absorption estimates on the experience of previous years. This approach is essentially logical, as absorption patterns reflect the economic growth and viability, or the lack thereof, of a given area. However, this type of thinking can be misleading since real estate development is cyclical in nature and overbuilt conditions are usually followed by an absence of new construction, which in turn results in scarcity and the rapid absorption of new development that subsequently comes on the market. It is fallacious to adopt this rapid absorption pattern for the purpose of future projection as the pattern is greatly influenced by scarcity that had been building up when construction was down. Strong demand and rising rents trigger another construction boom, putting more space on the market than can be absorbed during a tolerable time frame. Keen competition for tenants results in a softening of the rental structure and giveaways.

Another factor that can adversely affect absorption is the emergence of outlying competitive developments that siphon off the "backroom" activities of large corporate and financial tenants into suburban locations with substantially lower occupancy costs. The trend away from high-rise buildings in central business districts to low-density projects in suburban locations will most likely continue and gain momentum, as it enables business to efficiently operate support activities by taking advantage of computerized communication systems.

Since absorption projections are inexact by their very nature, it is advisable to make a series of assumptions illustrating a range of possibilities and thereby to highlight the risk element connected with the project. Upon the conclusion of these studies a decision will have to be made to go ahead with construction or to explore modifications of the project such as a downscaling or phasing. The final commitment will be influenced by several factors, perhaps the most important of which are the cost and terms of financing, the requirements relating to preleasing, and the personal guarantees to be provided by the borrower.

The developer's ability and inclination to assume the financial risk resulting from a lengthy lease-up period will also play an important role. By making the owner-developer fully aware, not only of the profit potential under optimistic assumptions, but also of the additional capital requirements under adverse conditions, the real estate counselor is providing sufficient background information on which to base a carefully weighed determination.

Cost Study

To function effectively, the consultant should be conversant with construction costs or have access to reliable sources of building cost information. In the analysis of the cost of the project, it is necessary to include all items connected with its development. The principal classifications are as follows:

1. *Direct costs.* These are the costs of construction (labor, materials, overhead, and contractor's profit), including site work, parking, and tenant improvements.
2. *Indirect costs.* These costs can be broken down into the following two major categories:
   a. *Construction related*
      Architectural and engineering fees
      Consultants' fees
      Soil tests, permits, and testing
      Taxes and insurance during construction
      Cost of obtaining financing (interim and permanent)
      Interest during construction
      Land carry during construction (interest accruing on current market value of land during construction period)
   b. *Development related* (start-up costs)
      Advertising and promotion
      Leasing commissions
      Revenue deficiency during rent-up period
3. *Developer's profit.* Although not a cost item as such, developer's profit is customarily provided for in a financial feasibility study. Unless there are other considerations, a major objective in going ahead with a real estate development is to make a profit. The targeted profit margin will generally be in the range of 10 percent to 20 percent of all costs, depending on the risk connected with the project.

Income and Expense Projection

Two basic methods for evaluating the economics of a proposed development are available to the analyst. For the purposes of this discussion, they are identified as (a) the cash flow method and (b) adjusted stabilized capital value analysis. A brief outline of both methods follows.

Cash flow method. The starting point in this analysis is the time of completion of the building, usually the date the certificate of occupancy is issued. The study will typically cover a ten-year time frame requiring the following inputs:

   Related to income
      Preleasing status at the date of completion
      Rental rates applicable to preleased space and to space leased upon completion of the building
      Rate of absorption
      Pattern of future rental growth

Related to expenses
Developer's expense exposure
Expense structure during the rent-up period (certain categories of expenses will be lower for a partially occupied building)
Future expenses

Related to investment characteristics
Debt service requirements, including the lender's participation in net or gross income
Discount rate to be applied to cash flow
Capitalization rate to be used in estimating the market value of the property upon sale at the end of the cash flow projection
Adjustments to be made for sale commissions and the lender's participation in profit

Related to other matters
Provisions for leasing commissions concerning leases made subsequent to the start of the cash flow projection
Allowance for the cost of finishing off space (for instance, the installation of tenant improvements following the initial preleasing)

The cash flow method, which typically requires computer assistance, will result in an indication of the economic value of the project. That value will then be related to the cost of the development up to the start of the cash flow study, including all applicable direct and indirect costs that have been incurred. Those costs will include loan charges, interest up to the commencement of the cash flow study, leasing commissions connected with the preleasing of space, and interest on land value or ground lease rental. It is of vital importance not to double up on these charges or to omit any of them. It may be advisable to conduct a series of sensitivity analyses, using a spectrum of assumptions concerning rental levels and growth, absorption rates, and return requirements.

Unless there is an adequate positive margin between the estimated economic value and the projected cost, the proposed development would not be justified and other options should be explored.

Adjusted stabilized capital value analysis. As shown in the following case study, adjusted stabilized capital value analysis also relates the total cost of the project to its economic value. It is simplified in that the cash flow phase is limited to the rent-up period from the date of completion until a stabilized occupancy level has been achieved. In essence, the analysis consists of evaluating the economic feasibility of the project by relating its total cost, consisting of direct construction costs, indirect costs (construction and development related), and land value, to the investment value of the property. The investment value takes into account direct and indirect costs to be absorbed by the developer subsequent to the completion of construction, particularly the income deficiency (rental shortfall) until the building has reached its projected level of stabilized occupancy. In this example, prevailing income and expense levels are assumed to be constant during the three-year fill-up period, but a growth factor could be applied. The case study could be broadened by making a series of assumptions relating to income and expense projections and absorption periods.

CASE STUDY

The following study relates to a proposed office building in a suburban location of a major city. Basic items concerning the project are:

Type:	Twenty-one-story office building
Gross building area:	330,000 square feet
Rentable area:	300,000 square feet
Parking:	Nine-level structure—930 cars
Construction period:	Twenty-four months
Absorption period:	Three years subsequent to completion of building

Cost Estimate
Estimated Direct Costs
Office building shell
   330,000 square feet @ $65.00 .... $21,450,000
Tenant improvements
   60,000 square feet @ $17.00 (initial increment) 1,000,000
Parking structure
   326,000 square feet @ $21.50 7,009,000
On-site and off-site work 600,000
Total estimated direct costs $30,059,000

Indirect Costs
Construction related

Architectural and engineering fees (3.5%)	$1,052,000	
Financing and interest during construction*	7,500,000	
Legal, title, miscellaneous	500,000	
Insurance and taxes during construction	850,000	
Subtotal		9,902,000

Development related

Preleasing expense	$ 150,000	
Land carry†	2,940,000	
Subtotal		3,090,000

Total indirect costs
   (excluding income deficiency during rent-up period) 12,992,000
Total construction and indirect costs $43,051,000
Land Value
   80,000 square feet @ $175/sq ft 14,000,000
Total cost estimate $57,051,000
Note: The foregoing cost estimate excludes developer's profit.

*Based on $50 million loan at 13 percent plus two points, 50 percent draw, and 24-month construction period.

†Land value of $14,000,000 × 10.5%—two years.

Stabilized Income and Expense Analysis

Revenues

Office tower...	$8,900,000	
Parking income (net)	850,000	
Total estimated revenue		$ 9,750,000
Less vacancy reserve		487,000
Effective gross income................................		$ 9,263,000

Expenses*

300,000 square feet @ $7.55/sq ft......................		2,265,000
Net operating income		$ 6,998,000

Capitalization

$6,998,000 ÷ 10.5%		$66,647,000

*Includes operating expenses, decorating and alterations, insurance, and taxes.

Income and Expense Projection: Initial Lease-up Period

	YEAR 1	YEAR 2	YEAR 3
Revenue			
Ground floor	$ 196,000	$ 196,000	$ 196,000
Office floors...........................	3,480,000	5,323,000	7,166,000
Net parking revenue	350,000	525,000	700,000
Total annual revenue	$4,026,000	$6,044,000	$ 8,062,000
Expenses			
Cleaning/janitorial	$ 180,000	$ 253,000	$ 320,000
Heating, ventilating, air conditioning	30,000	46,000	62,000
Elevator	37,000	57,000	68,000
General................................	90,000	126,000	160,000
Administrative	130,000	176,000	219,000
Energy.................................	240,000	337,000	427,000
Insurance	40,000	42,000	44,000
Real estate taxes	500,000	683,000	734,000
Total expenses	$1,247,000	$1,720,000	$ 2,034,000
Subtotal	$2,779,000	$4,324,000	$ 6,028,000
Deductions			
Leasing commissions....................	$ 250,000	$ 165,000	$ 235,000
Tenant improvements	1,550,000	1,000,000	1,550,000
Total deductions	$1,800,000	$1,165,000	$ 1,785,000
Net operating income	$ 979,000	$3,159,000	$ 4,243,000

Computation of Adjusted Capital Value Estimate

Stabilized capital value	$66,650,000
Less present value of rental shortfall (discounted at 10.5%)	
Year 1: $6,998,000 − $ 979,000 = $6,019,000 × 0.904	$ 5,441,000
Year 2: $6,998,000 − $3,159,000 = $3,839,000 × 0.819	3,144,000
Year 3: $6,998,000 − $4,243,000 = $2,755,000 × 0.741	2,041,000
Total rental shortfall (including tenant improvements)	$10,626,000
Adjusted capital value	$56,024,000

Results of Analysis

The test of feasibility in both the cost estimate and the capital value analysis is related to a specific time, namely, the time when the building has been completed, some of the tenant improvements have been installed, and a portion of the leasing expense has been absorbed. The income and expense projection for the initial lease-up period includes provisions for the balance of leasing and tenant improvements. Since the cost is over $57 million, whereas the investment or capital value is only $56 million, the project is evidently economically not justified as presently designed and under prevailing market conditions. Only in connection with a more successful preleasing program would the project be more promising, and even then it would hardly generate a profit for the developer.

A somewhat more simplified method of applying the test of feasibility is to include all of the direct and indirect development costs in the cost study rather than carry certain items over into the initial lease-up projection. The accompanying supplemental study illustrates this approach.

Cost estimate		$57,051,000
Add: Leasing commissions	$ 650,000	
Tenant improvements..........................	4,100,000	4,750,000
Total costs		$61,801,000
Economic estimate		
Stabilized capital value		$66,650,000
Less income deficiency		
Year 1: $6,998,000 − $2,799,000 = $4,199,000 × 0.904		$ 3,796,000
Year 2: $6,998,000 − $4,324,000 = $2,674,000 × 0.819		2,190,000
Year 3: $6,998,000 − $6,028,000 = $ 970,000 × 0.741		719,000
		$ 6,705,000
Adjusted capital value		$59,945,000

There is a greater negative margin in connection with the second analysis as it assumes that all the costs relating to tenant improvements and leasing commissions are incurred at the completion of construction rather than phased over the leasing of the building. The result, however, is the same—the project as proposed is not feasible.

MAJOR DISTINCTIONS BETWEEN SALE AND RENTAL PROJECTS

Counseling takes on a different aspect when it is related to noninvestment properties to be sold primarily to owner occupants. Included in this category are single-family dwellings, most often in residential tracts, and various types of commercial and residential condominium developments. The counselor's function is to conduct a comprehensive market survey to identify sources of demand and to investigate the track record of competitive developments, including price trends and absorption. The counselor will also make an analysis and recommendations concerning design features, floor plans, siting, adequacy of parking, and availability of financing. In addition, the counselor will participate in the pricing and marketing strategy.

Another dimension of real estate counseling pertains to the speculative builder of investment-type properties such as apartment buildings, shopping centers, office buildings, and industrial facilities. Frequently, a developer will de-emphasize the quality of construction in order to meet competitive rent levels and to achieve a profit upon sale. Under these circumstances the consultant's input will not consist of any of the development-related functions previously outlined in this chapter but will be directed primarily toward an analysis of rent levels and rate of absorption and the price obtainable for the completed and occupied building.

DEVELOPMENT AND MARKETING

If the investment feasibility analysis resulted in a positive outlook for the project, indicating an area of risk acceptable to the developer, the real estate counselor may then be engaged to participate in the development process. This will involve organization and planning, project supervision, leasing or sales, and postconstruction services. It may entail some or all of the following activities.

1. The counselor will participate in the selection of the architect and review preliminary and final plans, outlines, and detailed specifications. In addition, the counselor will analyze budget estimates, contractors' bids, and construction schedules and assist in the selection of the general contractor. A significant contribution can be made by eliminating costly building design features that do not proportionately contribute to the value of the project. Similarly, in choosing equipment items and finish materials, substantial savings can sometimes be accomplished without affecting the competitive edge of the end product.

2. Following final approval of the project a team will be organized. Depending on the complexity and type of project, it may include an attorney experienced in real estate development, a real estate brokerage or leasing company, and a space planner.

3. Concurrently with these activities, loan negotiations will be under way. The counselor, being familiar with financial markets, will be in a position to assist the client in obtaining loans (construction and permanent) on the most favorable terms available. Moreover, the counselor can analyze and explain to the client the probable financial impact of the mortgage financing providing for the lender's participation in revenue and profit upon sale and provide the advice needed in making a determination to secure the best loan package.

4. Upon approval of the plans and specifications and confirmation of the funding arrangements, construction documents will be prepared, final cost estimates submitted, and a final construction schedule established.

5. Depending on the counselor's experience, he or she may be involved in the supervision of construction.

6. In conjunction with the real estate brokerage firm, the counselor will, in the case of a rental project, develop a price schedule at which the units will be sold, develop the standard form lease, and establish rental rates, tenant allowances, and an overall leasing strategy.

7. Again, depending on the type of project, the counselor may be instrumental in choosing a property management firm and may assist in the staffing of permanent building personnel and the appointment of service companies.

It is quite obvious that in order to render the entire spectrum of development-oriented consulting services, a broad range of experience and capabilities is needed, typically requiring the services of an organization rather than an individual.

CONCLUSION

Analysis of proposed investment properties imposes a heavy responsibility on the real estate counselor. It requires broad experience and a thorough knowledge of prevailing market conditions. The assignment must be undertaken conscientiously. It has to be approached with an evenhanded independent attitude. One cannot be influenced by a developer's desire that a project be implemented or by the fact that substantial expenditures were made prior to the counselor's involvement and that a negative recommendation will not be readily accepted. On the other hand, the tendency to be overly cautious or negative, motivated perhaps by the desire to protect the investment of a client, will result in advice that is not attuned to the marketplace. Frequently, such advice will be counterproductive as the client will miss out on the opportunity to make a profitable investment.

Real estate activity runs in a cyclical pattern. Enthusiasm abounds when the market is strong, and gloom pervades when it is sluggish. The experienced counselor who has observed the vicissitudes of the real estate business will keep abreast of economic trends, assemble and analyze pertinent data, and prepare a carefully balanced forecast or series of projections leading to recommendations of the most feasible and logical course of action that can be pursued.

SELECTED REFERENCES

ABBOUD, SAMIR. "An Analytical Process of Real Estate Projects." *Appraisal Institute Magazine,* February 1979, pp. 33–41.

BARRETT, G. VINCENT, and JOHN P. BLAIR. *How to Conduct and Analyze Real Estate Market and Feasibility Studies.* New York: Van Nostrand Reinhold Company, 1982.

BROWN, ROBERT KEVIN. "The Investment Counselor's Role in the Development Process." *The Appraisal Journal,* July 1971, pp. 374–80.

BROWN, WILLIAM J.   "Cooperation between Architects and Real Estate Appraisers in Planning and Developing New Projects." *Real Estate Appraiser,* September–October 1971, p. 30.

GRAASKAMP, JAMES A.   "A Rational Approach to Feasibility Analysis." In *Real Estate Counseling.* Chicago: American Society of Real Estate Counselors, 1976.

HANFORD, LLOYD D., SR.   *Development and Management of Investment Property.* Chicago: Institute of Real Estate Management, 1964.

"Problem Solving: Development Financing, Marketing, Management."   *Real Estate Forum,* April 1977, pp. 18–21, 24, 26–32.

ROSS, THURSTON H.   "The Counselor and Investment Feasibility." *The Appraisal Journal,* January 1976, pp. 44–54.

SIMPKIN, JOHN G., and GORDON C. NIELSEN.   "The Rise of Project/Construction Management." *Real Estate Review,* Winter 1977, pp. 47–53.

CHAPTER SEVEN
INVESTMENT ANALYSIS
FOR EXISTING PROJECTS

This chapter differs from the previous chapter which deals with proposed real estate projects. In the case of a proposed development, the counselor must look to the future in analyzing an investment. The *future* is equally important when investment in an existing property is being considered. In addition, however, the counselor needs to carefully review the *present* condition of the property and its leases and to study the *past* operating performance of the property.

CASH FLOW REQUIREMENTS

Investors' cash flow requirements vary from case to case, depending on the amount of risk they are willing to assume. For instance, with a high-risk property such as a restaurant, relatively high cash flows may be demanded. On the other hand, with a net leased property which has tenants with good credit and from which high net resale proceeds are anticipated within the reasonably near future, investors may be content with a modest current cash flow and look more to the future sale of the property than to current cash flows for the desired overall return.

The alternatives available to investors are another factor that will influence their need for cash flow from a real estate investment. For example, when money market accounts are attracting capital from all forms of investments, the cash flow from real estate investments must be better than it would have to be at times when the alternatives are less attractive.

In a somewhat related vein, the cost of money is relevant to cash flow requirements. Obviously, to maintain a significant cash flow with high debt service, it is necessary to achieve high rental rates. However, high rental rates in turn imply certain risks since it is possible that they cannot be achieved over the investment projection period.

The mix and timing of cash flows are of critical importance. The time value of money cannot be ignored. For instance, consider the following two competitive properties:

EXAMPLE 1

Property: An existing convenience shopping center that is paying average rents; well located with little threat of future competition.

Income: The current cash flow of $100,000 per year is expected to grow at the rate of inflation, which is estimated at 5 percent per year.

Resale: Assumed to occur at the end of the fifth year; cost of sale is expected to be $164,000; basis of value at the sale is the sixth-year projected cash flow capitalized at 10 percent.

Capitalization: Investigation indicates that a 15 percent cash flow return is required.

Capital value estimated:

| | YEAR | | | | | |
	1	2	3	4	5	TOTAL
Cash flow	$100,000	$105,000	$110,250	$115,763	$1,233,830*	$1,664,843
PW factor @ 15%	0.869565	0.756144	0.657516	0.571753	0.497177	
	$ 86,957	$ 79,395	$ 72,491	$ 66,188	$ 613,432	$ 918,463

*$121,551 + [($121,551 × 1.05)/0.10] − $164,000.

EXAMPLE 2

Property: An existing office building net leased to a major corporation; lease
                expires at end of five years.

Income: The current cash flow is $120,000 per year.

Resale: Corporation has an option to buy the property at the end of five years
                for $750,000.

Capitalization: Investigation indicates that a return of 15 percent is required.

Capital value estimated:

YEAR					
1	2	3	4	5	TOTAL
Cash flow $120,000	$120,000	$120,000	$120,000	$870,000*	$1,350,000
PW factor 0.869565	0.756144	0.657516	0.571753	0.497177	
$104,348	$ 90,737	$ 78,902	$ 68,610	$432,544	$ 755,141

*$120,000 + $750,000.

The examples show that although the office building starts off with 20 percent
more cash flow than the shopping center and the cash flow of the shopping center
does not equal that of the office building until the fifth year, the more favorable
resale of the shopping center more than offsets its cash flow disadvantage. The
certainty of future sales prices should be given serious attention. The shopping
center turns out to be the superior investment.

Although perhaps obvious, it cannot be overstated that cash flow is the principal standard by which investment properties are equated. Therefore, it is a very
significant part of investment analysis and deserves in-depth attention in the counseling process.

DESIRED EQUITY CAPITAL
APPRECIATION

The impact of appreciation on total yield has become critically important in recent
years. Investors have looked increasingly to real estate because it appreciates and
thus provides a hedge against inflation.

The equity yield concept in real estate which takes into account projected
cash flow, the benefits of mortgage amortization, and appreciation or depreciation
is identified with the late L. W. Ellwood. Although Ellwood had to first develop
the basic formula that is used in solving for the overall rate, $R_o - MC +$ Depr.
$1/s_n$, the most relevant application was to test for the prospects for equity yield
performance by use of the derived formula,

$$\frac{r - R_o}{1/s_n} = \text{Depr./Appr.}$$

where R_o = Overall yield Depr. (Appr.) = Total property value change
Y_E = Equity yield $1/S_n$ = Sinking fund factor at equity yield rate

M = Mortgage to value ratio C = Mortgage coefficient
$r = Y_E - MC$
I = Interest rate

This latter formula tests various equity yields for the amount of appreciation or depreciation required to produce the desired equity yield.

EXAMPLE 3
R_o (overall capitalization rate) = 10%
Y_E (equity yield being tested for) = 15%, 16%, 18%
Mortgage = 12% interest, 75% of value, thirty-year term, monthly installments

TEN-YEAR PROJECTION

Y	r	R	÷	$1/S_n$	Appr.(+)/Depr.(−)1
14%	0.125022	0.10		0.051713	0.483863
16%	0.130263	0.10		0.046901	0.645253
18%	0.130263	0.10		0.042514	0.834596

The analysis indicates that to achieve a 14 percent equity yield, the property must appreciate 48.39 percent in ten years, which is a compound rate of growth of 4.03 percent. To achieve a 16 percent equity yield, it must appreciate 64.53 percent, or 5.10 percent per year compounded. To achieve an 18 percent yield, it must increase in value by 83.46 percent, or 6.26 percent per year.

The above computations in effect are an internal rate of return analysis for real estate equity yield. The analysis is limited in that it assumes a stable (level) income stream. However, this shortcoming can be overcome to a large extent by modifying the analysis by providing for an increasing or decreasing income stream and value change. One way of allowing for these changes is through use of the *J* factor or any of several other techniques that allow for forecast changes in the property value and its income stream over the holding or forecast period. The counselor is well advised to be familiar with these modeling techniques that permit analysis of a property in a manner that represents expected performance both from a historical perspective and, equally important, from the perspective of investors trading in the property. Viewed on an aftertax basis, realistically forecast future income and sales proceeds are quite helpful in investment decision making.

The desirability and value of a property can, of course, be affected by many factors that cannot be measured neatly by a formula. Among these factors are shifts in population, changes in the local economy, changes in accessibility, and changes in personnel and corporate policy relative to holding relatively illiquid assets.

DISCOUNTED CASH FLOW

An important and often used method for analyzing existing as well as proposed projects is the preparation of budgets for the projection period to provide estimated cash flows. This technique can reflect year-to-year adjustments in tenancy and rental rates, differing operating expenses, and changes in financing. Cash flows can then be converted to present worth estimates by applying the appropriate discount factor from present worth tables, as shown in the following example:

	YEAR					
	1	2	3	4	5	TOTAL
Cash flow	$100,000	$105,000	$110,250	$115,763	$121,551	$552,564
PW factor (16%)	0.862069	0.743163	0.640658	0.552291	0.476113	-0-
	$ 86,207	$ 78,032	$ 70,633	$ 63,935	$ 57,872	$356,679

With the development of cash flow budgeting for purposes of income stream analysis and with the availability of business calculators and computers that have a built-in internal rate of return capacity, discounted cash flow has found an important place in real estate investment analysis. This criterion has long been used by bond traders, portfolio managers, and corporate finance departments. The counselor should be cautioned to be realistic in his selection of both the future income and the discount rate.

INTERNAL RATE OF RETURN PROCESS

Where the previously discussed Ellwood equity yield techniques required stable or gradually changing income streams, the internal rate of return method can handle irregular cash flows, both positive and negative. Internal rate of return, of course, is used to measure past or projected investment performance. One of its greatest advantages is that it permits investment in real estate to be compared directly on a yield basis with other forms of investment such as stocks and bonds, loans, and annuities.

The internal rate of return is a trial-and-error process. To find the proper discount factors (present worth factors) that will reduce a given set of cash flows to a present worth equivalent to the initial investment, different rates must be tested that will produce present values bracketing the initial investment. The next step is to interpolate the initial investment value and its related internal rate of return between the high and low trial estimates and their related internal rates of return. Many financial calculators can quickly compute the precise internal rate of return. Using the previous example as a trial analysis and further assuming that the actual investment was $375,000 instead of the $356,679 estimated in the example, the following example will illustrate the process.

EXAMPLE 4

Since the initial investment is higher than the estimated value ($375,000 versus $356,679) at 16 percent, the discount rate would have to be lower as the discount rate has an inverse relationship to the value. Therefore, a trial rate of 13 percent would appear to be appropriate.

	YEAR					
	1	2	3	4	5	TOTAL
Cash flow	$100,000	$105,000	$110,250	$115,763	$121,551	$552,564
PW factor (13%)	.869565	.756144	.657516	.571753	.497177	-0-
	$ 88,496	$ 82,230	$ 76,409	$ 71,000	$ 65,973	$384,108

By interpolation:

	VALUE	
IRR		
13%	$384,108	$384,108
	375,000	
16%		356,679
3%	$ 9,108	$ 27,429

and

13% + (3% × $9,108/$27,429) = 0.139962, say, 14%

Proof:

	YEAR					
	1	2	3	4	5	TOTAL
Cash flow	$100,000	$105,000	$110,250	$115,763	$121,551	$552,564
PW factor	0.877222	0.769519	0.675039	0.592159	0.519455	-0-
(13.9962%)	$ 87,722	$ 80,799	$ 74,423	$ 68,550	$ 63,140	$374,634
						say, $375,000

Inflation and the prospect of continuing inflation play a critical role in the investors' perception of how much appreciation will be required to produce a required yield. Investors seek returns that exceed their cost of capital, so that in times of high money cost and inflation, investors' expectations rise accordingly. As stability sets in and the cost of capital declines, investors' expectations are likewise lowered. In equity markets the end result of this process is the price level, which may be reflected by gross rental multipliers, overall rates, pretax cash flow rates, or internal rates of return.

Land that is purchased with favorable seller financing and that possesses a true growth potential probably represents one of the highest forms of leverage and appreciation potential for equity capital. Land, however, probably also carries the highest amount of risk. At the other end of the spectrum are fixed-rate investments such as ground leases and long-term bond-type leased properties. There are investors who are willing to give up appreciation potential if they think the current yield is sufficiently attractive. The critical point is where the optimum risk-reward levels equate. This point differs from investor to investor, depending on preferences.

Regardless of the rate of inflation or the state of the economy, it is important to determine the investor's goals and aspirations because these vary from case to case. They must be known if the counselor is to adequately serve the client.

Internal Rate of Return Considerations

In recent years internal rate of return (IRR) studies have become a very popular tool for testing the yield potential of real estate investments. Internal rate of return has been used in the analysis of other types of investments for many years. Its use in real estate enables the analyst to compare all the benefits of real estate investment, before or after taxes, with the benefits of other investments such as stocks, bonds, and money market instruments. If the IRR yields are competitive and do not reflect undue risk, then a property may qualify for investment.

The question of acceptable risk is very crucial to investors. As mentioned earlier, acceptable risk varies from investor to investor. In general, there is some level of return that will motivate an investor to commit to an opportunity and the analyst must understand the investor's attitude toward risk.

Because IRR analysis deals with cash flow projections, it is obvious that the assumptions employed in estimating the growth of cash flow must be realistic or the whole study will be misleading. The conventional wisdom is to "grow" the rents that are free of lease or that will be subject to releasing at market levels at the rate of inflation. Of course, any projection should be as well supported in the market as possible, but when the future is being projected, there generally is little to look to for guidance.

The term of the projection, although important, is less critical than the rate of growth of the income stream. The value of the reversion at resale has a significant bearing on the IRR. It is important that the resale assumption be in keeping with market behavior. Typically, the projection periods are for ten years, but they may be as short as five years or as long as the life of the underlying mortgage.

Other assumptions used in estimating future cash flows can also be of critical importance. As with all valuation estimates, the fixed and operating expenses must be accurate and must be projected to grow at realistic rates. Because the periods concerned are lengthy and it is assumed that turnover will occur, the possibility of tenant alterations and improvements should be considered. Leasing commissions are another expense that must be accounted for in the cash flow projections. The sales commission and selling expense should be deducted from the proceeds of the projected resale. Finally, the resale amount should be based on a reasonable forecast. Frequently, the net operating income for the year prior to the last one in the projection is capitalized into a residual value estimate at a relatively high rate to reflect the risk of error in projecting several years into the future.

There is no reinvestment assumption for IRR; the return on and of investment is at the same rate. A sinking fund is assumed in the recapture portion. It is possible to use a different sinking fund rate rather than the interest rate on the investment. When this is done, the internal rate of return is called a financial management rate of return (FMRR). The FMRR has its advocates; it is appropriately applied under the above-stated conditions of differential rates.

TAX SHELTER

One of the important investment features of real estate is the tax shelter that it can provide. The most common tax shelter application of real estate is the deduction of mortgage interest and depreciation from net operating income. In the early years of an investment this may provide a paper loss. The negative or positive tax liability is added to or subtracted from the cash flow to provide an "aftertax" cash flow. When this is projected on an annual basis and discounted to present worth at the appropriate rate and combined with the present worth of the aftertax proceeds of a resale, the investor's value can be estimated. This value will vary among investors in different tax brackets and will also change according to the effect of rental adjustments and the timing and amount of resale proceeds. The important thing is that tax considerations can play an important role and should be considered in investment analysis.

A simple format for aftertax valuation is set forth as follows:

Income Tax Liability
  Net operating income
  Less mortgage interest
  <u>Less depreciation</u>
  Equals taxable net income
      and
  Taxable net income
  <u>Times marginal tax rate</u>
  Equals income tax liability

Aftertax Cash Flow
Net operating income
<u>Less debt service</u>
Equals pretax cash flow
   and
Pretax cash flow
<u>Less (or plus) income tax liability</u>
Equals aftertax cash flow

Resale Proceeds
Resale price
<u>Less disposition expenses</u>
Equals pretax proceeds of resale
   and
Pretax proceeds of resale
<u>Less mortgage balance</u>
Equals net pretax cash proceeds
   and
Net pretax cash proceeds
<u>Less tax liability</u>
Equals aftertax cash proceeds

Tax Liability Estimation
Acquisition price
<u>Less depreciation taken</u>
Equals tax basis
   and
Pretax proceeds of resale
<u>Less tax basis</u>
Equals gain on resale
   and
Gain on resale
<u>Less disallowed accelerated depreciation (if any)</u>
Equals capital gains
   and
Capital gains times marginal tax rate
<u>Plus disallowed accelerated depreciation times marginal tax rate</u>
Equals tax liability

Investor's Value
Present worth of aftertax cash flow
<u>Plus present worth of aftertax cash proceeds from resale</u>
Equals investor's value

    There are many other applications of tax sheltering in real estate transactions such as a partnership which can provide all of the shelter and most of the gain to one group of partners and all of the income and part of the gain to other partners.

    Under any conditions, it must be cautioned that this discussion is only general in nature and should not be regarded as authoritative. One should always counsel with his or her accountant and lawyer before proceeding with tax-related dealings.

MATCHING GOALS AND INVESTMENTS

The following sections deal with investors' objectives and the risks inherent in obtaining them.

One counselor was recently employed to advise a company engaged in the printing business. The company's problem was whether to expand its present location on land that it had owned for some time or to buy or build in another location, or perhaps in two or more other locations. The company employed a type of labor that was generally available in almost any part of the city in which it was located, in fact, in any part of the country. However, its executive staff and most of its labor force lived relatively close to the present plant. Most of these people did not want to move out of the city. About 15 percent of the people in management would be retiring in three to five years. Materials and parts supply appeared to be no problem except for some variation in transportation costs and lead time to service the market for its product, which was primarily local. The sales staff felt that having a plant and distribution facilities in a nearby city or even in another state might make such a move desirable from a marketing standpoint. There were many other considerations, but the estimated market value of the property played only a minor role in the decision concerning this property. Its value in use was the primary consideration in the decision to expand or relocate it. Thus, the counselor must understand overall business requirements as well as real estate.

AGE AND CONDITION OF THE PROPERTY

Usually investors prefer a new property to an old property and a property in good condition to one that has been neglected. However, there are many more older properties than new properties, thus leaving the investor with an imbalance of property choices.

At a minimum, the analyst should be alert to possible problems associated with older properties such as the condition of heating and air conditioning systems, plumbing and electrical systems, and elevators; code violations; upgrade requirements; and deferred maintenance. Required tenant alterations and decorating should also be considered. In recent years the life-safety provisions of building codes and problems involving asbestoes insulation have had a major impact on older buildings. All of these things can represent major costs. If they are recognized and planned for, adjustments can be made for them in a transaction or they can be handled under a program of ongoing management. If they are not addressed, the result can be a disappointing or failed investment.

Most analysts are good at making yield calculations, formulating strategy, conducting financial analyses, and the like, but it is still important to survey the physical elements of the property to be sure that they do not represent some unseen future capital cost. Apartment properties are particularly critical because of the high intensity of their utilization.

Older properties represent some of the best investment opportunities today because their acquisition basis is significantly lower than that of new development and hence they can be more competitive. In an economy whose cost consciousness is continually increasing, this represents an important consideration. Some of the greatest opportunities today involve rehabilitating, remodeling, and rebuilding existing buildings. In some cases, buildings have not been developed to the full height, bulk, and density allowed. When such buildings are situated in a key location, rebuilding them to their full potential can be very profitable and a recommended course of action for the investor. Simple upgrading and modernization of older buildings in prime locations can likewise be profitable, but the counselor must carefully analyze the development and reletting process so that no hidden elements surprise the client and adversely affect the investment.

New projects, of course, carry with them tax advantages; however, their yield potential is critically linked to the price and terms of financing.

RENTAL POTENTIAL

In recent years the potential for rental increases has played an important part in the thinking of investors. These increases are likely to continue in the future but to involve less dramatic rates of change than at some time in the past.

Forecasting has become a very important dimension in the counselor's services to his or her clientele. Because of the expensiveness of today's investments and because of the emphasis on growth in the investment, the ability to make sound, realistic, businesslike forecasts is highly important.

The following are some key questions to be answered:

What is the short- and long-term rental potential of the property?
What are the basic sources of demand?
How long will it take to rent up the project?
How will the cost of occupancy affect profitability?
What is the relationship between the value and the rental potential?
Is the value inflated by projected rising rents and using low capitalization rates?
How will competition affect the project?
What will be the trends in the rental potential?
What is the relationship between the return on cost and the market value?

OWNERSHIP

The form of ownership can influence the owner's risk exposure and the profitability of an investment. Although counselors do not usually provide detailed guidance on this subject, it is an important element in any investment from the individual's perspective and it should be addressed, either by the real estate counselor or legal counsel.

Individual Ownership

Individual ownership in this case refers to sole ownership of a property. This is a simple but unusual form for larger real property because such property is ordinarily held by more than one party due to the significant sums involved in carrying the property and the risk exposure relative to rents, expenses, and cash flows.

The goals of the individual property owner may be considerably different from those of an owner in a group. The individual's goals with respect to preservation of capital and willingness to take risk relative to return are obvious points of consideration.

Because investment analysis, in contrast to a market value appraisal, relates to a particular type of ownership, the form of ownership is of much greater interest to the analyst.

The accompanying table illustrates the sensitivity of individual ownership in contrast to that of a limited partnership.

ITEM	LIMITED PARTNERSHIP	INDIVIDUAL
Scheduled gross revenue	Very sensitive to maintaining rents at top of market	Concerned with keeping tenants pacified
Vacancy and collection loss	Will accept tolerable levels in order to keep rents at top of market	Will attempt to avoid vacancy because of rent loss risk, new tenant preparation expense, and personal involvement
Expenses	Very sensitive to holding expenses down while providing adequate service; will seek ways to be efficient	Most interested in maintaining the quality of the investment; may spend more than is necessary; often lacks economies of scale
Yield	Will pay a relatively high price and accept a lower yield based on anticipated growth in income and value	Is sensitive to immediate cash flow and is less willing to base the investment on anticipated future growth

Co-ownership

Joint tenancy.   In many states joint tenancy may speed the probate process and simplify the administration of a small estate. With today's inflated dollars it is not too hard for an investor to build an estate large enough to cause joint tenancy ownership to be a potential penalty on the estate, and therefore the analyst should be aware of the way title is held.

Tenancy in common.   This form of ownership may be very important in properly positioning the estate to most advantageously utilize the existing inheritance tax law. Tenancy in common involves a community ownership of property that, among other things, typically must pass to others through the provisions of a will.

Group Ownership

Partnership.   This is probably the most common form of real property investment ownership, and it will probably increase in importance in the future. Except for some real estate investment trust holdings and a few private and corporate ownerships, apartment investments are generally held by some form of partnership.

Partnerships have the advantage of combining financial strength with the ability to pass along tax savings to the investors. Thus, through partnerships it is possible to own larger properties, employ economies of scale, and obtain more favorable financing and tax advantages.

Developer partnerships with financial institutions and pension funds have become feasible ways of developing major new properties. This trend is expected to continue in the future with the developer's ownership share being constantly under pressure to be reduced.

In the future all of the purchase price of major investment properties may be raised through syndicated partnerships, perhaps with part being financed by debt and part being financed by equity capital.

In considering partnerships, it is very important that the counselor bear in mind the distinction between limited and general partners. The liability of limited partners in an investment is limited to the amount of their contribution, but they are able to share fully in the profits. In general, limited partners are only allowed tax deductions in relationship to the amount they have at risk. General partners have liability not only for their own investment but for the total partnership as well if for some reason the other partners cannot perform.

Corporations.   The principal advantage of the corporate form of ownership for the investor is that his potential loss is limited to the extent of his investment.

His interest is tradable in shares that may or may not be sold on an exchange. A further advantage of the corporate form of ownership is that there is continuity of ownership in a corporation; that is, a shareholder may sell a large or small interest, but the corporate entity remains intact and continues. The corporation form of ownership also offers some opportunities to exchange stock for stock in transactions that are nontaxable.

A disadvantage of the corporate form of real estate ownership is that the corporation is taxed before it can make distributions and the shareholder is taxed again on the dividends he or she receives. A further disadvantage is the time and expense required to deal with a board of directors, corporate motions, minutes, and possible Securities and Exchange Commission registration involvement.

Trusts.   Real estate investment trusts (REITs) were one of the best and worst ideas of the seventies. The idea of borrowing short and lending long in construction- and development-type loans proved fatal for some REITs. However, the equity REITs generally proved to be sound investment vehicles and many have prospered and are still around. The best REITs will probably continue to grow and prosper by raising investment capital through convertible subordinated debentures, mergers, and other innovative methods.

From the counselor's point of view, the REIT may have merit because it may be a transaction vehicle for a multiple property partnership or a stock for equity swap. These can often be good solutions to an investor's needs. In recent years entire REITs have been purchased through tender offers.

Joint ventures.   The joint venture is really a small partnership that is used for a one-time venture. From the counselor's point of view, it has been and will continue to be a very important ownership form for major new project developments. In joint ventures the partners' contributions and rewards take many forms. The joint venture is an excellent way for a landowner to join his or her asset to the skills of a developer.

In joint ventures the scales are not tilted in favor of the money partner, and this fact of life must be realized and dealt with.

MEASURING INVESTMENT PERFORMANCE

Return on Investment

The techniques for measuring return on investment range from very crude to very sophisticated. Among these techniques are number of years of cash flow needed to return an investment (some foreigners call this YP—years to payout), gross rental multiplier, overall capitalization rate, pretax cash flow return (cash on cash), pretax internal rate of return, and aftertax internal rate of return.

Years to Payout (YP)

This form of yield analysis is used commonly in the United Kingdom and to a lesser extent in the United States. It is simply the quotient obtained by dividing the annual income into the investment. It is also the reciprocal of the capitalization rate.

In the United Kingdom YP generally relates to the overall investment divided by the net operating income because there is little or no long-term mortgage money available, and therefore there are very few marginal equity positions.

Years to payout is a useful comparative guide for screening investment choices. Its usefulness is limited because it does not directly consider tax sheltering, because it assumes a stable income stream, and because it fails to account for income received once the initial outlay has been recovered.

Gross Income Multiplier (GRM)

This is a fairly crude yield-measuring tool. It is simply gross revenue divided into the price or value of the overall investment. The gross income multiplier is very helpful as a general market comparison tool and is a quick rule of thumb valuation technique. It can be accurate where alternative investments and their financing are similar and there is an active market.

The reciprocal of the gross rental multiplier is the gross capitalization rate, and when the gross capitalization rate is multiplied by the net income ratio, an overall capitalization rate results.

Gross income multiplier	6
Operating expense ratio (scheduled gross revenue less vacancy and expenses)	0.45

Therefore, the net income ratio is $(1 - 0.45)$, or 0.55, and

$$1/6 \times 0.55 = 0.0917$$

A brief example will illustrate the point. Assume that the investment has a net operating income of $100,000 and that an operating ratio of 45 percent and a gross rental multiplier of 6 are indicative of the market value.

$$\$100,000/(1/6 \times 0.55) = \text{value}$$
$$\$100,000/0.0917 = \$1,090,513$$

Proof:

$$\$100,000 \div .55 = \$181,818 \text{ (scheduled Gross Income) and}$$

$$\$181,818 \times 6 = \$1,090,908$$

The limitations of this value indicator are that it deals with effective gross revenue only and that it does not take into account expenses, financing, or tax sheltering. It has its place in an active market and as an initial screening device of several similar investment properties, especially when operating expenses are unavailable.

Overall Rate

The overall capitalization rate is arrived at by dividing the estimated net operating income by the investment value or sales price. This is also a good tool where there is an active market and the properties are similar in nature. Its principal use is to compare the total property earnings to value.

The overall rate does not directly take into account financing or tax sheltering, but it is widely used in the real estate business. It can be argued that the overall rate implicitly takes financing and tax sheltering into account because these elements exist in each property and, therefore, are reflected automatically when the sales price of a property is divided into the estimated net operating income.

Pretax Cash Flow Rate

This is a more complicated yield indicator than YP, the gross rental multiplier, or the overall rate. It is arrived at by dividing the pretax cash flow (net operating income after debt service) by the equity investment. This analysis takes into account vacancy and collection losses, operating expenses, and financing. It does not directly account for the impact of tax sheltering.

The pretax cash flow rate is most useful where there is an active market and the expected future net sale proceeds do not play a major role in the value of the property. It is also a helpful gauge of whether a property provides a sufficient return to the equity position.

Aftertax Cash Flow Rate

This is basically the same analysis as the pretax except that the effects of tax sheltering as described earlier are taken into account. The aftertax cash flow rate is a sophisticated tool, but it does not work well where tenant rollovers and the reversion play an important part in the decision.

Equity Yield

This process was described earlier in the chapter, so a lengthy discussion is not needed here. Equity yield takes into account cash flow, the effect of mortgage amortization and property appreciation or depreciation as it affects the equity position. This technique assumes either a stable income stream or one that changes.

The effect of tax sheltering can be applied in this analysis to provide an aftertax equity yield view of a prospective investment.

Internal Rate of Return

Internal rate of return is the same as equity yield except that it deals with irregular as well as regular cash flows. It is used basically as a test of the acceptability of the investment rather than as a valuation tool.

The advantages of the internal rate of return are that it can deal with irregular cash flows for various periods and that the yields can be compared to other forms of investment such as stocks and bonds. The disadvantage of the internal rate of return is that the validity of the yield projections is entirely dependent on the quality of the counselor's forecast. It is easily possible to make seemingly plausible assumptions and produce ambitious yet unlikely rates of return. This analysis should be used with care.

RECOMMENDATION BY COUNSELOR

It is critical for the counselor to understand his client's goals and objectives in order to serve them properly. Each client has special circumstances that call for an investment analysis tailored to his needs. Cash flow and equity yield requirements vary from investor to investor.

It is important to give careful consideration to the physical elements of the property because they can most certainly affect the future operating experience of the investment. Such consideration is especially necessary for older properties. The form of ownership may or may not play an important role. However, each form has its own peculiarities, and these can affect the investor's tax position or financial liability. The counselor should consider ownership alternatives—sometimes recommending the involvement of a tax accountant or an attorney.

Understanding return on investment in real estate is not a very complicated task because most of the time the market does not operate in a very complicated way. The standard measures of years to payout, gross income multiplier, overall return, pretax cash on cash return, and pretax and aftertax equity yield and internal rate of return are nearly the full spectrum of yields, and, basically, they have a common understanding by most of the investment community.

The counselor's obligation is to ask the right questions and to provide clients who invest in existing properties with answers that lead to advantageous decisions. Often follow-up is as important as the initial recommendations since clients frequently lack the understanding or the discipline to follow the counselor's original advice.

SELECTED REFERENCES

AMERICAN INSTITUTE OF REAL ESTATE APPRAISERS. *The Appraisal of Real Estate*. Chicago: American Institute of Real Estate Appraisers, 1983.

——— *Financial Tables,* ed. James J. Mason. Chicago: American Institute of Real Estate Appraisers, 1981.

BOYKIN, JAMES H. "Organizing to Finance." In *Financing Real Estate,* pp. 261–92. Lexington, Mass.: D. C. Health & Co., 1979.

ELLWOOD, L. W. *Ellwood Tables for Real Estate Appraising and Financing.* Cambridge, Mass.: Ballinger Publishing Co., 1977.

MAISEL, SHERMAN J., and STEPHEN E. ROULAC. *Real Estate Investment and Finance.* New York: McGraw Hill Book Company, 1976.

MESSNER, STEPHEN D., BYRL N. BOYCE, HAROLD G. TRIMBLE, and ROBERT L. WARD. *Analyzing Real Estate Opportunities.* Chicago: Realtors National Marketing Institute, 1977.

SELDIN, MAURY, and ARTHUR M. WEIMER. "Selecting Real Estate Investment Opportunities." In *The Real Estate Handbook,* ed. Maury Seldin, pp. 1110–21. Homewood, Ill.: Dow Jones-Irwin, 1980.

CHAPTER EIGHT
PROPERTY
MANAGEMENT
COUNSELING

In order to discuss the subject of property management counseling, we must first examine what we mean by property management. Property management is simply every aspect of the physical and fiscal operations of a building. It is not limited by the type of building, which may be residential, commercial, or industrial. Moreover, it is not limited to income-producing buildings. Many people mistakingly believe that property management can occur only in an income-producing property. However, an owner-occupied corporate headquarters facility produces no rental income, yet it does require considerable management. Since all improved real estate must be managed, it is obvious that property management is a field of considerable activity and importance.

All things having to do with the physical components of the building are covered under the physical management of a property. Whether we are talking about the roof, the parking lot, or everything in between, including the elevators, the air conditioning, and the plumbing, they are all a part of the physical management responsibility. The same goes for the fiscal responsibility. It does not concern just the collection of rents, because the payment of operating costs occurs whether we are dealing with a corporate headquarters complex or with a multifamily residential development. In both cases, appropriate accounting reports must be generated, budgets prepared, and an orderly fiscal process set up and monitored.

Property management came into being as a profession immediately after the Great Depression. In 1933 a group of property managers formed the Institute of Real Estate Management to exchange ideas and to educate themselves in improved methods of managing properties for themselves and for their clients. The many foreclosures that occurred during the depression made it necessary for property management to be more than an individual on-site caring for one building. In the intervening decades many improvements have occurred in the field. Modern technology has had a great impact on the way in which the property management business is conducted.

WHO NEEDS PROPERTY MANAGEMENT COUNSELING?

In this chapter we will discuss the counseling activity as it relates to the field of property management. A fundamental question is, How do we put counseling to work in this specialized management area? Obviously, we do not mean the hands-on activities of management on a day-to-day basis, since these are properly undertaken by the individual or company responsible for the management function. Rather, we mean the counseling service as an adjunct to, or in support of, the property management activity. First of all, who needs property management counseling services? The list is long. Some examples are:

A major corporation seeking to determine whether property management responsibilities should be handled by an appropriate in-house staff or by an outside professional property management firm

A pension fund owner of a large income-producing property requiring an evaluation of the property's net income-producing performance with suggestions as to how the property could be more efficient in its net earning capability

A trustee charged with the disposition of a property and needing to determine its highest and best use

A developer faced with the decision of creating a leasing policy for a new building and requiring an up-to-date analysis of market conditions and perhaps also assistance in the analysis of the building's plans and specifications to ensure that the building will perform efficiently

In short, there are as many opportunities for counseling in the property management area as one could imagine, with the above list offering just a few examples of the possibilities. Let us review in detail what types of counseling activities would occur in each of these examples.

ESTABLISHING THE PROPERTY MANAGEMENT FUNCTION

A corporation faced with the decision of either establishing a property management department or seeking outside services needs to examine such factors as the following:

1. Are the properties to be managed located in a small geographic area convenient to the headquarters of the company, or are they located in distant cities or states?
2. Are the properties large enough, in all cases, to command the attention of an outside firm?
3. Are the properties substantial enough to require the services of an on-site manager as well as the services of an executive-level individual to supervise the manager's activities?
4. Are the properties multitenanted, or are they occupied by a single entity?
5. Do the properties produce income, or are they occupied solely by the corporate owner?
6. Are the properties all of the same type, or are some of them commercial, some industrial, and some special use?
7. Will the corporation's ownership period be temporary or long term?
8. Are the properties leased on an absolute net basis, or is the owner required to furnish a wide range of services and utilities for the tenants?
9. Are the properties encumbered by mortgages, or are they free and clear?

It is the counselor's job to seek answers to these and many other questions while he attempts to guide his or her client through the decision-making process. It is often easy to assume that a certain number of people will be needed to accomplish this responsibility and that they will be paid certain salaries for doing so. Adding up these salaries does not give one the correct answer. Unless a corporation seeking the solution to this problem takes the time to secure the services of a professional counselor well versed in every aspect of the property management area, the decision could be not only wrong but very expensive to correct. It is best to begin this type of assignment with a checklist of questions to be answered and an outline of the process whereby the necessary information can be assembled and examined in an orderly fashion so that the conclusion reached is thoroughly supported by the assembled data. It is not the counselor's goal to complicate the decision-making process. He or she must make sure that every area has been examined to ensure that no alternative is overlooked. Counselors should not come into such an assignment with a preconceived notion as to the proper course of action. On the contrary, they should keep an open mind and be completely objective in their analysis. Even though the client may state at the outset what he or she feels the solution should be, the counselor should adopt an independent stance in examining all alternatives, regardless of the outcome.

PROPERTY PERFORMANCE
EVALUATION

In our second example, a pension fund owns a large income-producing property and wants to determine whether or not the property's performance as an investment can be enhanced. Let us assume that the property is a large office building in a medium-sized metropolitan area. Again, we need to use a checklist to carry out the assignment.

The first step is to evaluate the income derived from the property. In doing so, competitive properties within the market area are examined, utilizing a comparative analysis checklist such as that shown in Figure 8–1. A numerical rating of 1 through 10 is used, with 10 being the highest rating. This information is obtained for every competitive property in the marketplace. Then the relationship of the client's property to the market is determined, and whether or not the income of the property is acceptable in view of existing conditions. After the question of the property's income potential has been resolved, the summary of each lease in effect is addressed, using a lease summary format similar to that of Figure 8–2. The leasing summary for each tenant will provide a thorough understanding of the operating requirements imposed by the leases, including escalation provisions, options, and any other information that could affect the cost of providing services for the building and the potential rental income. The next step is to examine the previous year's actual operating costs and the subsequent year's operating budget projection. With knowledge of typical operating costs in the area, the costs of providing janitorial service, electricity, maintenance, and all of the other accounting classifications shown in Figure 8–3 are compared on a per square foot basis. This comparison will pinpoint those areas that exceed the normally accepted cost limits and will help determine why these conditions exist. This review is invaluable in preparing an estimate of what the gross rental income should be and what the total operating expenses could be if certain operating efficiencies were implemented. With the preparation of this statement, a report can be written summarizing all of the counselor's recommendations and explaining how they could improve the earning capability of the client's property.

HIGHEST AND BEST USE
ANALYSIS

Our third case involves a trustee who is charged with the disposition of a property and feels the need to determine its highest and best use. Assume that the property to be surveyed is a multistory downtown motel facility in a rapidly growing metropolitan area, that the building is more than ten years old, and that it occupies a prime corner of a downtown block. The trustee must ask, "Does the property in its present form constitute the most profitable utilization, and if not, how can we

FIGURE 8–1 Checklist for Comparison and Evaluation of Competitive Buildings.

	BUILDING 1	BUILDING 2	BUILDING 3	BUILDING 4	BUILDING 5	BUILDING 6
1. Location (including convenience to restaurants, public transportation, and shopping)						
2. Rental rates						
3. Services						
4. Parking						
5. Exterior appearance and design						
6. Interior appearance—public areas						
7. Atmosphere value						
8. Interior appearance—office areas						
9. Age of building						
10. Approximate current vacancy						
11. Number of floors						
12. Approximate total net rentable area						
13. Elevator service						
14. Floor load capacity						
15. Lighting (type of fixture)						
16. Type of electrical service						
17. Management (owner, agent, other)						
18. Amenities						
19. Flexibility of space arrangement						
20. Heating and air conditioning (including controls)						
21. Janitorial service (building staff—contract)						
22. Building's acoustical qualities—public areas						
23. Building's acoustical qualities—office areas						
24. Building security						
25. Overall building rating (excellent, good, fair, poor)						

FIGURE 8–2   Lease Summary.

Tenant:

Execution date:

Tenant space:

Lease term
  Commencement date:
  Termination date:

Annual rent: $ Monthly rent: $

Rate per square foot: $

Rentable floor area of tenant space: square feet

Total rentable floor area of the building: square feet

Tenant's proportionate share
(percentage) of tax escalation:

Tenant's security deposit: $

Commencement date notification
  120-day notice:
  30-day notice:

Attachments to lease
  Special covenants:
  Rental escalations:

This lease summary is a summary only and not part of the lease to which it refers.

determine to what use it should be put in order to realize the greatest ultimate sales price?" The trustee faced with this problem would benefit from the services of a counselor.

The counselor would first of all need operating information on income and expenses during the last three years, together with a projected operating budget for the coming year. He or she would have to determine the current market value of vacant land similarly zoned in the immediate area and the market rates for comparable motel rooms in the area. After completing this phase of the analysis, the counselor might conclude that in relation to the value of the land the income produced from the property is not adequate. If so, this question remains: To what alternative use could the property be put that would enhance the income stream to a point at which the investor would receive an adequate yield on the invested capital? Having knowledge of local market conditions, the counselor determines that medium-priced office space is scarce in the downtown area and analyzes the potential for converting the motel facility to office use. With the services of an architect, an engineer, and a general contractor, a typical floor is analyzed to determine the potential cost of

FIGURE 8–3   Operating Expense and Income Coding Lists.

Operating Expense Coding List

Accounting fees	210
Legal and audit fees	220
Management fees	230
Outside commissions	240
Insurance premiums	250
Miscellaneous general expenses	290
Janitorial services	310
Building and janitorial supplies	320
Building maintenance	330
Elevator repairs expense	331
Heating and air-conditioning expense	332
Plumbing repairs expense	333
Exterior–landscape expense	334
Electrical expense	336
Roof repairs expense	337
Miscellaneous building expense	338
Maintenance under contract	339
Extermination	340
Parking lot maintenance	345
Trash removal	360
Security salaries	370
Miscellaneous maintenance expense	390
Electrical utility	410
Gas	420
Water	430
Fuel	440
Telephone	450
Sewer	460
Music	470
Miscellaneous utilities	490
Real estate taxes	510
Licenses	520
Miscellaneous taxes	590
Redecoration of public areas	610
Redecoration of leased area	615
Renovation	630
Advertising expense	710
Dues	720
Reimbursable expenses	810
State sales tax	920
Rent expense (leasing commissions)	930
Purchase of asset	950
Capital improvement—building	952

Income Coding List

Rent income	105
Maintenance income	106

Permanent parking	115
Vending machines, telephone	120
Tenant-paid improvements	130
Deposits	140
Late charge	150
Rent escalation income	170
Miscellaneous income	190

such a change of use. Using these costs and the rental rates available for the type of space to be created, the counselor analyzes the income potential and the operating costs for the property after such a conversion and determines that the expenditures are more than offset by the increased level of income derived from the new use. The highest and best use study would also include the analysis of other alternative uses to eliminate them as feasible alternatives.

The counselor's report would also include a management plan setting forth the stages of implementation and describing and documenting the steps leading to the completion and occupancy of the new facility. This plan would also set forth a leasing policy for the new space and management standards for the building. The counselor would analyze the value of the property after the conversion as compared to the current value of the property.

An observation needs to be made regarding the scope of such an ambitious effort. The comment "That doesn't sound like much if you say it fast" is certainly appropriate here. The analysis and report described above are the product of many, many hours of effort and of a substantial level of knowledge on the part of the counselor who will undertake the assignment. Such knowledge, after all, is what the client is paying for. The client is not paying for the counselor's "on-the-job" education. In utilizing the services of the counselor, as in utilizing the services of any other professional, the client has the right to assume that the counselor possesses the necessary level of proficiency.

NEW BUILDING CONSTRUCTION

Our next property management counseling opportunity centers on a developer who is proposing the development of a new office building and needs considerable assistance in a number of areas. First, he requires a close liaison with his architects and engineers in the creation of the plans and specifications for the project. It is important that as these documents are being prepared, a counselor be retained who is well versed in evaluating the relationship between the construction cost of building components and operating cost of these components over their economic life. This procedure, known as value engineering, requires a considerable level of expertise. Years of experience in evaluating the performance of various items of equipment are necessary to make the initial judgments. Examples of such judgments include

> Whether to use a single- or dual-glazed curtain wall system
> Whether to spend additional money for the installation of economizers on the air-conditioning equipment

Certain decisions of this kind are affected by marketing considerations, such as deciding whether to use hydraulic elevators or gear-driven machines in a five-story office building. If the competitive buildings in the marketplace offer faster, smoother, gear-driven elevators, then you must provide similar equipment in order to have a competitive building even if such equipment represents a significantly higher initial cost.

In arriving at decisions on these types of alternatives, it is important to have close cooperation between the general contractor, architect, engineer, developer, and counselor. The team concept of development is a way of life today.

OPTIMUM BUILDING DESIGN

The counselor's input should relate, not only to the physical components of the building, but also to such areas as the external module of the building, that is, the distance between window mullions on the perimeter of the building, which affects the flexibility of the interior space layout. Many hours of discussion have occurred between the proponents of the four-foot module and the proponents of the five-foot module. The fact remains that the type of market being served will greatly influence this particular decision. The counselor's knowledge of the market is a key ingredient in making the right choice. Basic choices are also available with regard to the ceiling grid. Should it be a 12 in. × 12 in. concealed spline system? Should it be 2 ft. × 2 ft.? Or should it be a less expensive 2 ft. × 4 ft. exposed grid? Each of these choices represents an increase in cost when compared with the other two available.

The current rental rate per square foot for quality office space is the best gauge of how to make these kinds of decisions in an intelligent and professional manner. If comparable buildings are being constructed for $75 per square foot, it would be difficult to significantly reduce that amount and still achieve the same relative rental rate. Therefore, an in-depth knowledge of the market that can be obtained from field research in the form shown in Figure 8–4 can help a great deal in determining where your product fits with its competition.

The developer's decision on the allocation of parking, on the amenities to be provided, and on the image that he hopes to create for his product are all determinants of the perspective from which the counselor's advice is rendered.

FIGURE 8–4   Field Research—Office Building Rentals.

Project name:_____   No._____
Address_____   Page_____of_____
Directions_____   Suburb_____
   Census tract_____

Owner/agent contact:_____   Phone_____

Type of building:
( ) Downtown;   ( ) suburban;   ( ) _____   Year completed_____
( ) High-rise;   ( ) medium-rise (elevators)   Under construction_____
( ) Walk-up;   ( ) _____ _____   Completion date_____
( ) With other retail uses
( ) _____

Building size:
Gross building area_____;   net rentable (office)_____
Prime tenant/owner net rentable area_____;   commercial area_____
Off-street parking spaces:_____;   garage spaces:_____

Location data: (trend, convenience, appearance, quality, features); rated: AA AVG. BA
_____

Occupancy (rental history):
_____

Facilities provided   **Services provided by owner**
Heating   ( ) Central for building
                   ( ) Central for each unit   ( ) All utilities included in rent
Air conditioning   ( ) Central for building   ( ) All except lighting power
                                                  ( ) All except air-conditioning
                   ( ) Central for each unit   power
                   ( ) Through-the-wall units;   ( ) Cold water
                   ( ) window
Paneling   ( ) _____   ( ) Hot water
Vinyl walls   ( ) _____   ( ) Heating fuel
Drapes   ( ) _____   ( ) Air-conditioning power
                   _____
Carpeting   ( ) _____   ( ) Elevator service—none_____
                   _____   ( ) Elevator starter
Parking   ( ) Off-street;   ( ) Full cleaning service;_____
                   ratio___ : ___   days
                   ( ) Inside garage: ( ) Contract;
                   ___ : ___   ( ) Employees
                                                  ( ) Covered garage:___ space
                   ( ) No off-street parking   _____

                   ( ) Public space nearby: _____
                   yes or no
                                                  ( ) Open parking space_____
                   _____   _____

Lease required ( ) How long?_____   ( ) Security guards

FIGURE 8–4   Continued

Rental analysis (as of _____)   By:_____
 Percentage of occupancy:_____%; number of square feet vacant:_____ square feet

---

 Average rate occupied space per net rentable area: $ ____; range: $ ____ to $ ____
 Asking rate for vacant space:_____
 Terms:_____

 Computation of net rentable area: ( ); percentage of public areas included:_____
 Escalation: ( ) taxes only; ( ) all operating expenses_____
 Other comments:_____

SETTING LEASE TERMS

In creating a leasing policy for a new building, the counselor will be working with
the developer, his mortgage lender, his attorney, and representatives of the entity
responsible for leasing the space in the new project. Here we will determine, based
on the market analysis, the rental rate per square foot to be offered. This rate may
be uniform throughout the building, or it may vary with the available views, the
floor height and location, or the quantity of space to be leased. What minimum
lease term should be stipulated? And what maximum term should be allowed? What
type of escalation provision will meet the least market resistance while maintaining
the best potential revenue for the developer? Will the escalation provision be a
straight Consumer Price Index? Will it be an operating expense pass-through? Or
will it be a fixed percentage of escalation based on the gross rental on a cumulative
or a noncumulative basis? Based on these terms, what tenant improvement allowance
will be stipulated? Will that allowance be based on a combination of physical
improvements to be constructed at the developer's cost together with an alternative
per square foot cost? Or will the space be provided on a pure turnkey arrangement,
with the rate to be adjusted according to the tenant's requirements? In determining
the appropriate lease, the legal terminology can be prepared by the developer's
attorney. However, the business terms of the lease should be recommended by the
counselor, whose decisions will be reached with the aid of a lease provision checklist
such as the one shown in Figure 8–5.

The shorter the lease, the better. A twenty-three-page lease should never be
allowed to hinder a marketing program when a seven-page document is all that is
needed. Less sophisticated tenants react negatively to a lease of undue length. Many
developers have seen no reason to burden the lease agreement with "boiler plate"
language that is covered by state law. The important business terms should be
covered as early in the lease as is feasible, and the more negotiable items as well
as rules and regulations should be left for the back pages.

FIGURE 8-5   Lease Provision Checklist.

A. Fundamental
    1. Name and legal address of parties
    2. Description of property
    3. Term of agreement
    4. Rental and method of payment
B. Desirable
    1. Use—limitations and restrictions, if any
    2. Utilities
    3. Repairs
    4. Glass breakage
    5. Alterations
    6. Damages
    7. Indemnification
    8. Inspection
    9. Notices
    10. Assignment and/or subletting
    11. Ad valorem taxes
    12. Signs
    13. Fixtures
    14. Eminent domain (condemnation)
    15. Default
    16. Bankruptcy
C. Options
    1. Renewal
    2. Cancellation
    3. Purchase
D. Special and miscellaneous
    1. Inducements
    2. Postponement and/or holdover
    3. Subordination
    4. Security

5. Escalator clauses
    a. Taxes
    b. Insurance
    c. Labor cost
6. Multiple tenancy
    a. Building rules and regulations
    b. Use of common facilities
        (1) Parking
        (2) Walks
        (3) Elevators
        (4) Toilets
7. Commodity rent adjustments
    a. Wholesale price index
    b. Retail price index
    c. Cost-of-living index
8. Percentage rents
    a. Advantages—changing conditions
    b. Reliability of tenant
    c. Uses
        (1) Long-term agreement
        (2) High volume of activity
             (a) Retail stores
             (b) Hotels
             (c) Garages
             (d) Service shops
    d. Rental
        (1) Minimum/maximum
        (2) Percentage rate
        (3) Variations of rate
        (4) Reports
        (5) Audits
9. Reappraisal of rental values
10. Arbitration

ASSISTING IN LOAN NEGOTIATIONS

A number of developers have found that retaining a counselor early in the mortgage lending process allows them to improve their credibility in loan negotiations. Since counselors are able to draw on a wealth of experience and on an intimate knowledge of the marketplace, many lenders view their findings and recommendations as a material improvement of the overall development. The developer should be aware that the counselor's input can mean the difference between a project that will contain market acceptance and the necessary mortgage money and a project that ends up as just another good idea that never had the opportunity to come to fruition.

A complete feasibility study for a new development can add immeasurably to the developer's confidence and to the likelihood that the lender will approve the necessary mortgage financing. A counselor's knowledge of the relationship between the property management process and the feasibility of the overall development is extremely important. The ability to project market rents and to develop an income and expense pro forma for the project is a key element in the overall feasibility analysis.

EVALUATING THE PROPERTY MANAGEMENT FIRM

Another important area of property management counseling, not listed in the examples above, is the evaluation of the performance of a property management firm in meeting an investor-client's needs. A client retains a counselor to determine the agent's level of performance and to recommend ways for improving the client's return on investment. Both an internal operating department of a corporation and an outside property management firm can be evaluated in this way. Both of these entities assume similar responsibilities, but the internal department is only responsible for the properties of its corporation, whereas the property management firm simultaneously provides similar services to a number of clients.

In accepting such an assignment, the counselor must obtain a complete operating history of the property and must be able to compare that operating history with generally accepted standards of performance in the industry and in the local market. One of the first areas that the counselor would examine is the cost of providing the property management service. A line by line analysis of the operating statements would also give considerable insight into the cost efficiency of the property's operation. Has the manager recommended cost-saving measures? And have these recommendations included, not only the initial cost, but the payback period that is necessary to recoup through savings the initial capital expenditure required. Is the property management firm utilizing the services of a contract janitorial service when an in-house staff might be more efficient and might result in a lower cost? Or perhaps the reverse is true. How is the manager handling service calls covering maintenance items? Does the manager contact outside service companies that charge both for the service call and for the time expended? Or does the manager utilize a maintenance staff whose per hour cost of labor is passed on directly to the property owner? With the counselor's experience, evaluations of such matters can be made and the resultant savings can be substantial.

WHEN NOT TO USE A COUNSELOR

There are some areas in which one might think that a counselor should be utilized, when in fact he should not. The field of energy conservation, for example, is a highly specialized field that requires engineering expertise. A counselor should readily admit that such areas could be more properly covered by others. In every instance, the counselor should also point out to his or her client the necessity for retaining other professionals, such as architects and structural, mechanical, and electrical engineers.

BRANCH BANK COUNSELING

A property management counselor can also render invaluable service when a financial institution such as a bank or a savings and loan association owns a parcel of land on which it proposes to construct a branch. The counselor can determine whether or not it is advisable to build rental space in addition to the institution's space requirements. With his knowledge of the local market for space, the counselor would be able to determine what rental rate would be available, and by performing an economic feasibility analysis, he could determine whether the return on the additional space contemplated would be a high enough yield on the incremental difference in cost to justify the investment. Obviously, the financial institution would benefit from the stronger image created by a larger, more imposing building. Moreover, prospective tenants seem to be more attracted to the buildings of financial institutions than to the commercial office space available in speculative structures.

In addition, prospective purchasers of investment properties might utilize a counselor to review statements of income and expense for such properties. A counselor's knowledge of the operating costs and income potential in his area would be helpful in making this type of analysis. Or a condominium association might utilize a counselor to provide guidance in setting up management criteria and to develop a complete management plan for the association's property.

As can be seen from the many illustrations set forth in this chapter, property management counseling is a diverse and challenging segment of the real estate counseling profession. The broadening of the counselor's knowledge at every opportunity is a vital ingredient of the counselor's ability to render professional services to the client.

SELECTED REFERENCES

BEAUMONT, HENRY G.   "Counseling and the Property Manager." *Journal of Property Management,* May–June 1971, pp. 127–28.

CAMPBELL, ROBERT E.   "Consultant's Role in Management of Corporate Real Estate." *Journal of Property Management,* July–August 1974, pp. 171–75.

DOWNS, JAMES C., JR.   *Principles of Real Estate Management.* Chicago: Institute of Real Estate Management, 1980.

GLASSMAN, SIDNEY.   *A Guide to Commercial Management.* Washington, D.C.: Building Owners and Managers Association International, 1981.

INSTITUTE OF REAL ESTATE MANAGEMENT.   *Managing the Office Building.* Chicago: Institute of Real Estate Management, 1981.

KELLEY, EDWARD N.   *Practical Apartment Management*. Chicago: Institute of Real
Estate Management, 1976.

KYLE, ROBERT C., and ANN M. KENNEHAN.   *Property Management*. Chicago: Real
Estate Education Company, 1979.

PETERSON, DON G.   "Industrial Tenant Check List." *Realty & Building*, June 26, 1982,
pp. 34, 36.

SHENKEL, WILLIAM M.   *Modern Real Estate Management*. New York: McGraw-Hill
Book Company, 1980.

TARR, R. GORDON.   "Management Surveys and Consultant Management." *Journal of
Property Management*, May–June 1967, pp. 111–13.

WALTERS, WILLIAM, JR.   *The Practice of Real Estate Management for the Experienced
Property Manager*. Chicago: Institute of Real Estate Management, 1979.

CHAPTER NINE
COUNSELING IN LEASE OR BUY DECISIONS

"To lease or to buy—that is the question" may be a takeoff on a famous quotation, but few more difficult decisions will confront decision makers involved in real estate in the coming decade. This chapter is intended to outline the basic requirements found in any lease or buy decision-making model and to intertwine these requirements with actual cases that have occurred.

The following items have an important impact on the requirements for any lease or buy decision:

Company ownership
The financial strength of the company
The basic objectives of ownership

As will be explained, there are different requirements for different types of property—industrial, research, or office. There are also different requirements for different types of structures—corporate, partnership, or condominium.

COMPANY OWNERSHIP

Whether their operations were conducted in a heavy manufacturing plant or a typical New England loft building, in the past companies typically owned rather than leased their real estate facilities. This was true from the industrial revolution through the 1940s, when sale-leaseback transactions evolved due to changes in tax laws and financing possibilities that emerged from the recessionary years of the 1930s.

The typical cycle of ownership was for an "incubator" corporation to start in leased space, grow, acquire its own facilities, and expand further. In a number of instances, such entities became large corporations whose major facilities were corporately owned. Expansion facilities or regional facilities that were not part of long-term planning were often temporarily leased to meet corporate goals. Today the real estate strategies of companies depend on a number of factors.

Type of Ownership

Real estate today is no longer viewed primarily as "housing" corporate operations. The issues of real estate economics have become prevalent in recent years due to the realization that real estate tends to serve as an excellent hedge against inflation and, in time, to become a major asset.

Large corporations have been known to set up real estate departments to handle real estate matters. They have been known to buy real estate on a speculative basis and then to develop and sell it, thus using their financial credit as a vehicle for profit. Sears and Prudential are prime examples of this type of thinking.

Most companies, however, view real estate as a vehicle for their own operations, and although profits from such real estate sometimes occur, they do not wish to be in the real estate business. They typically own or control long term their main facilities and lease their regional facilities. This holds true for both private and public corporations. For example, Steelcase, Inc., a major privately held manufacturer of office furnishings, owns or controls its corporate facilities and leases its regional offices throughout the country.

Distribution of Ownership

In certain instances, the distribution of corporate ownership dictates how real estate is owned. In a large corporation with many shareholders, the typical real estate ownership is by the parent company or its real estate subsidiary. An individual within the corporate structure is generally placed in charge of real estate matters and makes recommendations regarding the housing of the corporate enterprise.

In corporations held by relatively few individuals, partnerships in real estate often exist. In certain instances, individual shareholders own the real estate and lease it to the parent company. This has been especially true for retail establishments. Supermarkets, for example, are often owned by the original founders, who lease them to the company. Supermarkets typically can turn over capital three or four times a year and are not interested in nonliquid bricks and mortar. Similarly, individual owners can have the advantage of equity buildup in mortgages backed by the financial credit of the company and the direct tax benefits of depreciation that can be passed through to their own tax returns. With the fifteen-year life allowed by the new tax laws, this is going to become an ever-increasing trend.

The number of stockholders plays an important part in ownership policies. For example, with 100 or more shareholders, accounting and logistic problems make it difficult to transfer real estate ownerships to a partnership. Although this has been done in the past, it has proved to be a comparatively inflexible approach. Where corporate ownership has consisted of relatively few people, the partnership route works well. As a small group of owners age, they usually place the real estate in the names of children or other family members, which allows for continuity of control.

In service-oriented corporations, such as law firms and accounting firms, real estate is typically leased. At the same time, however, with the tax laws now allowing fifteen-year write-offs, major service firms that are the first tenant in a property are obtaining ownership. The typical vehicle is the creation of a subsidiary partnership to hold the firm's percentage ownership in the real estate.

In summary, in tightly held corporations real estate ownership rather than leasing provides an additional economic advantage. Real estate has been used as a vehicle for the transfer of both property and income to succeeding generations. Overall, the preferred type of occupancy evolves as follows:

CHARACTERISTICS	LEASE OR OWN
Large national corporations with many shareholders	Ownership or long-term control of major facilities, lease of regional facilities
Large privately held corporations	Ownership or long-term control of major facilities, lease of regional facilities
Retail corporations	Lease
Incubator or small corporations	Lease

Family-controlled entities	Ownership
	  a. By separately held realty arm
	  b. By individuals
	  c. By children
	  d. Typical format—partnership

Special corporate situations—for example, situations where there is an advantage to off–balance sheet items	Sale-leaseback

FINANCIAL POSITION OF COMPANY

Asset Position

The decision to lease or buy is usually dictated by the financial position of the company. Sometimes the extensive real estate holdings of major corporations can create an imbalance and induce financial trouble when management dreams beyond the organization's financial resources. Whims of management have been known to override sound corporate planning.

Market conditions very often govern lease or buy decisions as they impact a company's asset position. In 1978, for example, the demand for space exceeded the supply and a strong seller's market existed. To a great degree the landlord had the upper hand, which resulted in major rent increases nationwide. The company that could build its own real estate to house its facilities found itself in a lower cost position and a stronger asset position than the company that had to lease.

By 1982 the market had turned around and had become the strongest buyer's market since the depression. Tenants were scarce. Free rent and free tenant improvements were offered as inducements. Cash spoke "louder than words." The tenant controlled the market. In this case, the counselor's primary role was to supply market information on the changes that were most likely to occur, so that a corporate real estate strategy could be developed on that basis.

The asset position of a company owning real estate is weakened if that real estate is a special purpose building. From a corporate point of view, special purpose properties should be leased rather than owned due to the limited market for resale. This provides greater flexibility than ownership because a lease runs for a specified period of time and may be canceled. Although special purpose, nonmarketable real estate is shown as an asset, its ownership may really be a liability.

Liability Position

Where real estate is corporately held, the acquisition of land, buildings, fixtures, and equipment can be funded out of cash flow, paid for from depreciation, or purchased using the credit of the firm with gradual payoff from corporate earnings. Thus, real estate is simply a means for housing an enterprise tied to the manufacture or turnover of products and the profits that flow therefrom.

Where mortgage financing has been used to acquire corporate real estate, the real estate has been typically held by a subsidiary entity with the financing secured only by the property itself. In certain cases where the equity has been insufficient, corporate guarantees have been required by mortgage lenders.

Net Worth Position

Corporate decision making in a lease or buy situation is strongly influenced by the return on capital. This issue is less important for a major corporation than for a smaller company with considerable working capital requirements. Smaller companies usually wish to lease real estate, particularly under sale-leaseback arrangements, since this reduces their working capital and cash requirements. Sale-leaseback transactions have generally been made through major insurance companies or pension funds with cash to invest. Yield is tied to the prevailing market returns. In the past, after a typical twenty-five-year amortization of the real estate, the tenant's rent would drop substantially over the remaining term of the lease. This arrangement may have been acceptable under stable economic conditions, but as the rate of inflation increased, the owner found that the rent was substantially below market. In certain instances, the fair rental value of the property was three or four times the present rental levels, with the tenant having a below-market contract for twenty, twenty-five, or more years.

The Value of Space

In situations where long-term leases at fixed market rents existed, corporations discovered that they held a very valuable leasehold interest. They, in turn, could sublease for profit or sell their position in the marketplace.

Thus, real estate became a hidden asset in the net worth position of such corporations. A sale and the creation of a capital gain could result in a major payment toward new quarters on either a lease or ownership format, thus reducing their effective rental costs. In corporate structures, capital gains, capital losses, and sales of real estate assets for alternative space needs are a critical part of the decision-making process.

Return on Capital

Overall, a lease or buy decision is dictated primarily by the issue of return on capital. Major growth companies often prefer to lease rather than own certain facilities as the return on their own capital against their net worth position substantially exceeds the effective rental cost of these facilities. In addition, this alternative provides considerable flexibility for corporate planning by allowing movement or changes of offices. IBM is noted for its use of a leasing strategy that allows for changes in location and structure with the movement of its markets. Ownership of real estate is ordinarily a long-term decision. Long-term financing that corresponds to the period of ownership is a basic corporate objective. Fundamentally, a lease or buy decision rests on the cost of money and the credit strength of the corporation. One of the best sources for long-term corporate financing has been industrial bonds.

Certain ratios exist as to the typical percentage of total sales that a firm can afford to pay for rent. Rent may be measured in the form of either lease payments or debt service. As a general rule of thumb, the maximum rental that can be effectively carried is between 2 percent and 5 percent of the revenues generated, and when ratios exceed this level, the issue of overleverage and risk enters the scene.

The advantages and disadvantages of leasing may be summarized as follows:

Advantages and Disadvantages of Leasing

Advantages of Leasing

Flexibility	The lessee can move out at the end of the lease; the landlord has the vacancy problem
Capital	Leasing does not require long-term capital investment beyond the tenant's improvements
Credit	Major credit strength and being the first tenant in a new property can result in a below-market rent
Freedom of choice	A policy of short or intermediate lease terms can allow movement from location to location and the consolidation of operations

Disadvantages of Leasing

Control of decisions	Leasing results in a landlord-tenant relationship that can sometimes be divisive; this can limit internal space alterations or renovations
Loss of advantages of ownership	These advantages can include equity buildup through mortgage financing, depreciation, and the tax benefits of owning real estate
Loss of expansion option	Owned facilities can easily be expanded, particularly if excess land is involved
Cost	On an aftertax net present value basis, ownership is less expensive than leasing

CLIENT OBJECTIVES

The objectives of clients vary, depending on whether they are in an expansion mode or a contraction mode.

Expansion Mode

In the expansion mode, the first step in judging space needs is to project growth in sales and space requirements over a forecast time period. For some corporations, this period can be as much as ten years. Management's sales projections are converted to numbers of people required. This, in turn, is measured on a per employee space need basis.

There are standard ratios of space requirements for employees. Office employees usually require between 150 and 250 square feet per person. A density of 150 square feet per person is extremely tight and is generally characterized by the use of office landscaping. A density of 220 to 250 square feet per person is fairly common in service firms. Industrial employees need between 300 and 500 square feet per person. When sales projections and the number of employees estimated to create sales are known, space needs evolve:

TYPE OF USE	TYPICAL SQUARE FOOT SPACE NEEDS PER EMPLOYEE
High-density back-office use	150 to 175
Standard service-oriented use	220 to 250
Light industrial or manufacturing use	300 to 400
Industrial office or distribution facility	500 to 700

The skills of employees are important in scheduling space needs. For example, Digital Equipment Corporation created new facilities outside Massachusetts when it felt that it had fully tapped that state's reservoir of skilled employees. In addition, it located in other states, generally on a leased basis, in order to move into new markets.

Timing is an important consideration to a client who is trying to select business quarters. If the client requires immediate occupancy or space for a short period, this most often requires leased space rather than property acquisition, though purchase options can be built into lease contracts. If the client is planning for the long term, then ownership and new construction are a logical option to consider.

Basic employee costs are another consideration. Some corporations operate in several states. Their expansion is often targeted toward states that have a pool of workers capable of satisfying company production needs while meeting programmed employee costs as well as the employees' own costs for living within the area. When dealing with skilled employees, companies tend to avoid states with a high cost of living and high taxes. One of the idiosyncrasies of corporate location decisions, however, is that "the company goes where the boss wants to live." An owner's preference has been known to override corporate planning. There are known cases where the property closest to the owner's home has been acquired in preference to the logical and best site from a real estate point of view.

In contrast, corporate policy can override everything else in the choice of a company's plan and program. For example, in at least one case a major corporation studied its market, "put a dot" in the center of the market, and ordered its real estate people to choose a site or an existing property as close to the center of that "dot" as possible. The decision, though fine from a corporate point of view, was ridiculous from a real estate point of view, as the site ended up adjacent to a falling down single-family house on a side street, off a secondary road, with premium site preparation costs for construction of a building on the side of a hill. Had flexibility been allowed and site premiums considered, a number of options would have been available within several miles in existing or planned industrial parks at major highway interchanges.

With the growth of the high-technology field in the United States, building uses have changed. What used to be thought of as one-story industrial structures have become research and development buildings largely improved with air-conditioned open areas. Where an office use evolved, corporations would typically look at total building widths of between 90 and 120 feet as practical. To try to develop an office use in wider space has proved to be unfeasible from an employee morale and a planning point of view.

As space needs for the high-technology field shift toward assembly, the building width module widens, the ideal width for this purpose being between 150 and 200 feet. For almost all business activities but heavy manufacturing, a building width of 200 feet is generally considered a maximum measurement in terms of multiple options for space layout.

Another trend that has been taking place is the conversion of buildings to alternative uses as a firm's objectives change. Many industrial buildings whose building module fits certain minimums have been converted to office-type structures. In the case of "smokestack" real estate, found largely in major industrial areas of the United States, the potential of conversion just does not exist.

In summary, all of the above factors intertwine and become a study of options and alternatives that relate to the cost of moving, the cost of renovating, and other costs of overall corporate objectives. From these costs flows a real estate strategy that can be adapted to short-term and long-term purposes. In general, short-term objectives are handled by leasing. As objectives become longer term, and with costs being equal, the preference is to own real property.

Contraction Mode

The word *contraction* does not necessarily mean a decline in business or profits. A contraction mode can be reached when space becomes obsolete. For example, in the mid-1950s, the typical research space requirements produced buildings with widths of from thirty-five feet to fifty-five feet. There would be a center corridor with cubicles off the corridor in which individuals could work. As research teams evolved, this space became obsolete. If the space was leased, it became a simple matter of moving to new space when the lease expired.

In contrast, if the space was owned, two courses were often adopted. The first was simply to live within the inefficiencies of the operation. The second involved an aggressive real estate strategy in which walls were demolished to create large open areas. If this was not practical, the unsuitable buildings were generally sold, with a move to another location following.

A problem has arisen in this connection because the acquisition of space in the 1950s took place at building costs of as low as $5.00 or $6.00 per square foot and generally not above $15.00 or $20.00 per square foot, whereas the moves to new quarters would have to be made at costs of $30.00, $50.00, or more per square foot. In some instances, these costs frustrated corporate real estate strategy.

In summary, timing and cost are the two key elements in the contraction mode. If a corporation takes a long-term view of planning, it can make a considerable profit on real estate and favorably time its moves on the disposition, leasing, or subleasing of space. It is important to bear in mind that real estate markets are cyclical. RCA decided to move out of the computer business just when the real estate markets were at their bottom in the mid-1970s. The overall result was that it sold its properties and leases at less than book value. Generally, overall corporate strategy governs real estate decisions.

COMPARATIVE ANALYSIS OF FACILITIES

Although corporate planning may dictate future space needs, a set process for the study of existing occupancy in owned or leased facilities is important. An inventory of existing space by its type of use, its cost in terms of book value, and its cost of operation should be put together. This is generally in spread sheet form.

Similarly, a summary of existing leases is important from a planning stand-point. A knowledge of rental rates, lease terms, termination dates, and any special provisions is important in the timing of moves. This type of inventory can be useful in either an expansion mode or a contraction mode.

In addition, future space needs should be categorized as to type of use. Ceiling height requirements, loading requirements, shipping, and receiving are important for a company's warehouse operations. Bay sizes, building modules, and building dimensions become important when a shift is made into manufacturing or office use. What happens, in effect, is that in the abstract a plan is formulated to obtain the ideal type of facility that is needed.

Market Requirements

Market requirements dictate space needs. For example, bottle recycling plants function most efficiently where railroad access is available. At the same time, many of the new industrial parks in this country lack rail availability, which means that distribution considerations are part of the analysis that takes place in the choice of facilities.

With types of space needs and market requirements clearly understood, it is possible to study all the available space options in the real estate marketplace. Existing space that "fits" the company's needs can be analyzed, and prices of suitable space that is available for lease and for purchase can be compared.

Space Availability

Not all of the available space necessarily fits a company's needs. A typical developer option is to acquire or lease a building "shell," which provides the most flexible type of space. In this manner, a company can create its own interior. An existing building with preestablished partitions can add extra costs that will affect a lease or purchase decision.

Parking is an often overlooked issue in the decision-making process. High-density employee use in the range of 150 to 175 square feet per employee can require a parking ratio of as many as six cars for each 1,000 square feet of space. The typical site development, with a land coverage ratio in the 30 percent to 40 percent range, cannot accommodate this density of parking. Therefore, space availability must be tied to employee parking needs in both the present and the future.

Site Availability

In the past, corporations usually held an inventory of land for future use. As the cost of money has risen, corporations have been tending to place less emphasis on the acquisition of future sites. They are acquiring enough land to expand an existing facility over a period of from ten to twenty years. Corporations tend to acquire major tracts for their future needs beyond that time only when land is relatively inexpensive.

It has frequently been a mistake to acquire property in smaller cities, although the cost may be low by normal real estate standards. Markets may be thin in these cities, and it may be difficult to sell such property if changes in an operation make this necessary. Therefore, corporate real estate executives and real estate counselors are now spending considerable time studying the issue of flexibility as it relates to a company's needs.

With space, market site, and physical characteristics known the next step in the lease or buy decision process involves the study of the available alternatives.

The Condominium Alternative

With rental levels in some instances tripling or quadrupling since the mid-1970s, the option of buying office or industrial condominiums has become an important alternative. The objective of ownership is to control cost, have the benefit of equity build up and have a hedge against inflation if inflationary cycles reappear.

The typical buyer of condominiums is the small user requiring 5,000-10,000 sq. ft. of space with two to three partners plus other employees. Purchases of large blocks of space as a condominium are the exception. Previously, purchases have been primarily tax and control driven involving large national firms which typically require options on unpurchased space. They effectively control a building by taking rights of refusal.

In the decision making process, there are a series of questions that must be addressed.

Does the Company Wish to be in the Real Estate Business?

This is one of the key issues in the "to lease or to buy" decision process. For the user requiring a small amount of space, there is a strong trend toward office condominiums. Memories of inflation and increasing rental rates cause these tenants to consider real estate as a hedge against inflation. It is a way for the corporation to reduce expenses in comparison to the expense of leasing.

Over time, the history and experience of office condominiums have proven successful. However, even with the benefits derived, certain disadvantages also have occurred. Since the original developer typically does not manage the property, owners have had to assume this responsibility plus they have to set up their own property operations. In small partnerships, a problem often occurs on how to handle the property when the partnership dissolves. Typically, if a buy out between partners can not be arranged, the property is put back on the market and sold. Condominiums are not special purpose properties and they can be readily marketed to others.

Financing Issues

Small condominium properties typically have been able to be 100% financed by their owners. Financing usually is bank-related with the condominium as an additional security. Banks typically require personal liability on the part of owners, for a condominium often is regarded in the same manner as a corporate loan.

The large size condominium market is thinner in terms of financing. As a result, interest rates are 25-50 basis points above the market and more conservative underwriting procedures are required. Without corporate liability, 100 percent financing typically is not possible due to the prima facie evidence of the actual sale price of the condominium. A lender would have a hard time justifying above a 75-80 percent loan to value ratio based on known documentation. In certain instances, immediate funding can be a problem. Lenders often are reluctant to issue future commitments without substantial points up front to absorb negative arbitrage. In addition, interest rate exposure does exist as long-term fixed rate commitments become history. (See Figure 9-1 on page 126.)

Advantages/Disadvantages of Condominium/Lease Options

In summary, the following advantages or disadvantages exist in relation to the lease or buy decision process.

Advantages of a Condominium (Disadvantages of Leasing)

Control of the Future	With ownership, rent is controlled in terms of future rent increases.
Cost	Condominium ownership is historically less expensive then leasing in terms of cost. Condominiums typically produce a cost 20 percent below the cost of leasing.
Tax Benefits	In the past, there have been tax benefits from ownership of real estate. Certain benefits do exist but not at the same level as before.
Control of Decisions	100 percent control of the decision making process, separate of typical landlord-tenant relations.
Resale	The potential of profit on resale if market conditions are sound. This usually requires a long–term view.

Advantages of Leasing (Disadvantages of Condominiums)

Flexibility	The lessee can move out at the end of the lease. Rights for expansion are possible.
Capital	Leasing does not require long–term capital investment beyond tenant improvements.
Credit	Use of the firm's credit is not required in terms of obtaining a loan for a condominium.
Personal Risk of Each Partner	Beyond 75-80 percent financing, personal risk along with firm risk is realistic to assume.
Obsolescence Factors	Major firms with a life cycle of 100 or more years usually occupy a number of different locations. Over time, however, buildings do become obsolete.
	Although not readily foreseeable, there could be changes in the future which would make the ownership of a portion of a major structure obsolete. This has caused an emerging trend where a tenant obtains a limited partnership interest, rather than following the condominium approach.
Special Purpose Property Aspects	Large condominiums, as well as small condominiums, can have the problem of insufficient liquidity when prompt sale is required.
Management Policies	The management's objective is to run their business and to maintain maximum flexibility. This is why, historically, leasing has been more prevalent than the condominium mode when dealing with large space users.

A CASE STUDY

The following example describes an actual situation involving a first floor bank space containing, in total, 4,250 sq. ft. (See Figure 9-2 on p. 284). The basic assumption includes a purchase price of $650,000 with 20 percent down and a mortgage of $520,000. The mortgage interest rate is 9.5 percent with a 25 year amortization. The inflation over the period studied is expected to be 5 percent per annum. A blended income tax rate is projected at 34 percent as a maximum. The property appreciation has been conservatively estimated at 4 percent per year, or less than the rate of inflation.

The analysis is on a monthly basis. Three "snapshots" in time have been studied - Year 1, Year 5, and Year 11. The purpose of this analysis is to assess the cost of ownership versus the cost of renting property. The Year 1 and Year 5 analysis provides a ratio of cost to rent compared with the cost to own. In this case, the ownership and rental cost are approximately equal during the first five years. This is on a before depreciation basis. When depreciation is factored into the equation, the cost of ownership is less than the cost of leasing. The ratios are respectively 88-90 percent of the cost of leasing.

FIGURE 9–1 SUMMARY OF FINANCIAL SURVEY

	JOHN HANCOCK MUTUAL LIFE	EQUITABLE LIFE	CHASE MANHATTAN	BANK OF BOSTON	NEW ENGLAND MUTUAL LIFE	FOWLER, GOEDECKE, ELLIS & O'CONNOR, MORTGAGE BANKERS
Market Acceptance	Would not do as not in market	Would do only if could fund in 90 days	Would do as a corporate loan	Will finance	Could not do today as only have GIC contract funds	Financing can be arranged
Interest Rate Premium [1]	1/4%–1/2%	No premium	Tied to prime rate	1 1/4%–1 1/2% premium	1/4%	1/4% to 1/2%
Loan Term	5–7 years	Up to 10 years	—	5–7 years	Up to 10 years	Up to 10 years
Amortization	30 years	30 years	—	—	30 years	30 years
Loan to Value Ratio	75%–80% with cash equity required	70%–80% with cash equity required	—	Based on cash flow of firm. Might go over 80% of rental value if strong banking relationship	80% with cash equity required	Requires cash equity—100% loan not possible.
Liability	Either lease of firm to guarantee or personal liability	Not commented upon	Done as a corporate loan with firm/personal liability	Expect top 25–30% guaranteed	Firm must sign a long-term lease	Financial strength of borrower "expected to be on the line"

[1]Typical rates today are 8 1/2 percent–10 1/4 percent depending on loan term.

The "hidden" benefit that accrues to ownership is in the area of appreciation. This is not a cash item but, nevertheless, is considered part of the economic package associated with the purchase or lease scenario. At a conservative 4 percent annual resale appreciation for the property, this further reduces the cost of ownership as compared to leasing clearly favoring the buy option. On a before tax basis, in the long–term, ownership proves superior to leasing. The cost of owning in the 11th year is 61 percent of the cost of leasing at that same point in time.

RECOMMENDATIONS

The real estate counselor's role is to present the client with a carefully thought-out, well conceived recommendation that takes into account all the factors that may affect a decision. In many business situations, economic and financial factors can govern. Previously, the availability of financing has been know to shift the decision to ownership rather than leasing. In contrast, the requirements of corporate flexibility have turned other companies toward leasing rather than ownership.

Overall, the lease or buy decision is based on a number of factors. These include the structure of ownership, the corporate financial position, the objectives of management and the facilities requirements. The real estate counselor is paid for analysis and judgment of these items based on an accumulation of experience gained from the completion of numerous assignments in a wide variety of situations. Lease or buy decisions can be among the most difficult to make since they entail a combination of objective analysis and subjective judgment requiring the very best efforts on the part of the client and the counselor.

SELECTED REFERENCES

DeBUSK, MANUEL. "Lease Analysis—Some Practical Applications and Techniques," pp. 89–100. In *Financing Income-Producing Real Estate*, ed. J. A. Britton and L. D. Kerwood. New York: McGraw-Hill Book Company, 1977.

DOHERTY, JAMES L., and WILLIS N. COBB. "A Small Firm Makes a Buy/Lease Decision." *Real Estate Review*, Spring 1980, pp. 105–10.

DOWDEN, C. JAMES. "Commercial Condos Gain Momentum." *Real Estate Today*, May 1982, pp. 21–24.

EIMER, JACK, and TANDY O. LOFLAND. "Real Estate Development: A Commercial Tenant's Option." *Journal of Property Management*, January–February 1982, pp. 45–47.

LAUB, KENNETH D. "Evaluating the Office Condominium." *Real Estate Review*, Spring 1983, pp. 53–58.

LEVY, JOHN F. "Real Estate Lease Accounting Cookbook." *Real Estate Review*, Spring 1983, pp. 107–17.

SCHACHNER, L. "The New Accounting for Leases." *Financial Executive*, February 1978, pp. 40–47.

SCHALL, LAWRENCE D., and CHARLES W. HALEY. "Lease or Buy Analysis," pp. 601–10. In *Introduction to Financial Management*. New York: McGraw-Hill Book Company, 1980.

TRACY, BRIAN M. "Owning vs. Renting Office Space: A Financial Comparison." *Real Estate Review*, Winter 1982, pp. 86–89.

CHAPTER TEN
DISTRESSED PROPERTY ANALYSIS

One of the most challenging and difficult assignments that real estate counselors can undertake is the "work-out" of distressed properties. Some of the skills required for such assignments have been discussed in the preceding chapters, but creative, workable solutions for distressed properties—often multifaceted solutions—are more elusive than solutions to problems encountered in most other areas of real estate counseling. In addition, different types of clients will require a counselor's service and many varieties of properties can become distressed. This chapter will concentrate on an analysis procedure for distressed properties.

A counselor or other real estate professional who specializes in giving advice and assistance must be able to put a distressed property matter in perspective quickly. There are no "standard solutions" for distressed properties, given the variety of the clients and the types of property. Yet similar methods of analysis can apply to distressed situations regardless of the client and the property. It takes considerable analysis, experience, and professional ability to understand the subtle differences and create optimal solutions for the problems of distressed properties. But beware! There is not always a completely—or even a partially—successful solution. In the end, the only solution may be to abandon the property or leave the situation unchanged.

Rasmussen defines distressed property as "any property that does not generate enough income to substantiate the funds lent to develop it."[1] Rasmussen's definition clearly illustrates the financial common denominator in distressed real estate. However, properties may be in various stages of development or distress. Existing fully tenanted, income-producing real estate may become distressed; vacant land that is under development and not producing sales income may be distressed; older buildings without financing may be distressed. Quick or easy solutions should not be expected. However, there are procedures that can be followed and sources of help that are available for most distressed situations.

When a property is not producing sufficient income to maintain the debt service, the lender will take action to protect his position. Often the lender will not have the "in-house" capability to perform a work-out for the property. Even if he has that capability, outside help is often sought for troublesome loans, especially if they were originated outside the lender's immediate locale. Loan officers, though generally anxious to create loans, are in a very different mood (or have disappeared) when a loan goes bad. Many banks and financial institutions fail to recognize when a loan is going bad until it is too late. Then, because of an owner-developer's indifference or desperation, the property is likely to be in poor physical condition and the financial circumstances are likely to be comparably poor. This is where help is required, and an ideally suited assistant for the lender with a distressed property is the counselor who has extensive knowledge about local real estate, a wide range of business experience, and the good judgment to call in other qualified professionals for assistance as needed.

The counselor's first task is to evaluate the extent and scope of a property's distress. Property records from as far back as possible should be obtained and analyzed. The counselor should locate correspondence, leases, contracts, and financial data as well as all documents relevant to the loan and its default, foreclosure, or involuntary acquisition. Any advertising, public relations, or marketing information originally or currently being used should be studied for clues of the markets being pursued.

A basic checklist useful in analyzing distressed property is provided in Figure 10–1. Many of the checklist items are studied simultaneously during the initial phase. Also, the interaction between many of the items on the checklist must be considered. A word of caution is appropriate here: no single part of the analysis should become so important (or negative) that an objective perspective cannot be maintained. Almost every property can eventually be brought back to useful service. In the development of any property, sensible reasons were used to bring the property to market. Often it takes only careful and thoughtful analysis to find a particular use that will make the property a productive resource again.

---

[1]Vaughn B. Rasmussen II, "Dealing with the Buyer of Property in Trouble," *Real Estate Review,* Winter 1976, p. 39.

FIGURE 10–1　Distressed Property Checklist.

I.　On-site inspection
　　A.　Structure
　　　　1.　Exterior wall
　　　　　　Condition of masonry
　　　　　　Expansion joints
　　　　　　Mortar joints
　　　　　　Cracks
　　　　2.　Roof
　　　　　　Condition
　　　　　　Expansion joints
　　　　　　Flashing
　　　　　　Scuppers
　　　　　　Downspouts and gutters
　　　　　　Deck condition
　　B.　Portals
　　　　1.　Dock doors
　　　　2.　Seals, levelers, heights, and drive-in doors
　　　　3.　Pass doors
　　　　4.　Storefronts
　　　　5.　Windows
　　C.　Parking and driveways and grounds
　　　　1.　Surface (number of spaces in conjunction with site and use)
　　　　　　Potholes
　　　　　　Striping
　　　　　　Condition
　　　　2.　Drainage
　　　　3.　Landscaping
　　D.　Interior
　　　　1.　HVAC and other mechanicals
　　　　　　Condition
　　　　　　Capacity
　　　　　　Warranties
　　　　　　Sprinklers
　　　　　　Code violations
　　　　　　Restrooms—male, female
　　　　2.　Partitions
　　　　　　Removable
　　　　　　Movable
　　　　　　Condition
　　　　3.　Tenant improvements
　　　　　　Major per lease
　　　　　　Minor for tenancy
　　E.　Neighborhood and surroundings
　　　　1.　Highest and best use
　　　　2.　Changing neighborhood
　　　　　　Up
　　　　　　Down
　　　　　　None
　　　　3.　Security problems
　　　　4.　Traffic and street problems

Figure 10–1   Continued.

II. Off-site checks
   A. Zoning inspector
   B. Building inspector
   C. Courthouse records
      1. Site
      2. Legal
      3. Tax information
   D. Owner and bank records
      1. Leases
      2. Contracts, including maintenance
      3. Tenant agreements
      4. Financial information
         Rent roll
         Monthly and annual reports
      5. Note, mortgage, and payment records
   E. Construction information
      1. Construction contracts
      2. Plans and specifications
      3. Warranties
      4. Any data concerning construction problems

PROJECT ANALYSIS

The key ingredients of project analysis are the counselor's insight, judgment, and experience. However, the counselor must decide at the outset how the project will be analyzed. Quick decisions are sometimes very good decisions, but careful and dogged analysis will be necessary in almost every case. A careful gathering of all the facts, combined with the experience and knowledge of the analyst, is the first and most important phase of distressed property analysis.

Physical Inspection

The eye of the trained real estate counselor is essential in determining what is "right" and "wrong" about the physical quality of a property. The physical construction characteristics of the property and its basic engineering, structural, and architectural countenance must be considered. Often, while a property is falling into a distressed state, the owner-developer will defer maintenance to pay other bills. The degree to which maintenance on a property has been deferred will eventually determine a major portion of the work-out cost. Defects caused by lack of care can sometimes be corrected by a quick and direct program of immediate inspection and repair.

An inspection of the roof usually comes first. Items to be considered are its condition and construction; whether the expansion joints were properly installed and the flashing is properly attached; whether the ballast, if any, is still intact; and whether all ventilators, skylights, and mechanical equipment have been properly installed. Exterior walls may show some telltale signs as to the condition of the roof depending on downspouts, flashing, scuppers, firewalls, and parapets. A quick look at the roof can reveal any cracking and whether there are any wind-related lift-off problems. Exterior and interior roof conditions can help to determine whether maintenance has been deferred or tenants have misused the facility. After the roof has been inspected, the parking lot, driveways, and service areas become the next most serious areas of exterior investigation.

An interior inspection of the mechanical and structural components of the building is necessary. The heating, ventilation, and air conditioning (HVAC) must be looked at for condition, adequacy, and fuel conservation. Piping, wiring, and ducting are the most obvious indicators of problems. An indication of rust on water or steam lines, fraying or improper circuitry on the wiring, and blocked or misdirected ducting can be primary causes of problems. Look at furnaces or air conditioning units for maintenance and operational defects. These are not always apparent; it might be wise to bring in a trained professional for assistance.

A good look at the condition and load-bearing capacities of the floors is also necessary. The condition can be determined by wear patterns, cracking, lifting, and deterioration of the concrete or whatever material has been used. Column spacing must be determined to be adequate for the use. Older buildings often have too narrow a column spacing for proper division or operation (for example, the use of tow motors and other material handling equipment). Ceiling heights must also be considered: low ceilings for warehousing make full use of the property difficult.

The general appearance of the facility helps determine the extent to which an owner-developer has taken care of the property. Sometimes tenants will step into the owner's position and take care of their areas as if they were their own. This situation helps the basic underlying appearance and may make the job of turning the property around somewhat easier. The initial design and layout of the property are very important. To a great extent, whether or not the property was originally well planned will determine what solutions are necessary and can be taken to change traffic patterns, parking layouts, entries, and exits.

A trained real estate counselor will know when to call on other disciplines to help in making the analysis of a property in trouble. Professional engineers, architects, registered land surveyors, and vendors of various materials (roofing, asphalt, sheet metal, etc.) can be brought in to help complete the analysis. They usually know what the cost will be to restore each of their specialized areas to proper condition. A counselor should never hesitate to use outside help to aid in the complete analysis of any property.

Record Check

An important part of the analysis is looking at the financial data available. The counselor should determine what leases are in place and whether the owner has been using a standard form or has allowed the tenants to use their own lease forms. If the owner has used a standard form, the circumstances are bound to be better and the job of lease analysis has, at least, a common denominator. However, if the builder-developer-owner has allowed tenants' forms to be used, he has probably been whipsawed from the very beginning by the tenants and made concessions to one or more tenants that were not made to others. This, of course, brings additional problems because a tenant who learns that another tenant has favorable lease terms is going to want them too. So the existence of lease variations among tenants is a problem needing curative action that is prompt and firm, yet diplomatic.

How rent collection has been maintained is also very important. The items to be considered include the following: (1) Were late notices sent on time? (2) Were renewals and options exercised at the right time? (3) Was rent collection an important part of the developer's operation, or did tenants take unfair advantage? The longer collection problems existed, the more difficult it was for the owner to bring tenants' accounts current, probably exacerbating other financial problems as well.

Both the level of maintenance that the owner instituted and the owner's written statements regarding tenant policy will provide indications of the caliber of management that the property has experienced. If the tenant policies were slipshod or sporadic, tenant dissatisfaction was likely. On the other hand, a professionally managed property will generally have well-directed procedures and policies in operation.

If the owner-developer had other problems and was managing the property improperly, it will often be found that it was very easy to defer maintenance to pay Peter from Paul's proceeds. Here the counselor should look to a certified property manager (CPM) for assistance with regard to proper management policies and procedures. Then it will be fairly certain that a good maintenance policy can be put in place and will continue during the work-out period and beyond.

A detailed analysis of the initial budget projections versus the operating experience, the amounts of mortgage money and initial equity available, and the cost overruns that occurred early in the project may indicate signs of project weakness that multiplied over time. If the project equity was "thin" and the cost overruns occurred toward the end, then the builder-developer-owner probably had the operation under control until uncontrollable strikes, economic downturns, or other setbacks occurred. A property that was kept under continual control has a greater chance of success than one in which the developer allowed matters to go awry by not taking the proper steps to solve problems as quickly as they occurred during the development stage.

A close look at the mortgage debt repayment history is very important in determining the scope of the analysis. This is an area where a real estate professional can discover problems early. If delinquencies occurred at the outset, there should be indicators of problems, but if delinquencies occurred late in the project, perhaps the developer tried to work with a financial institution as long as possible to keep the project out of trouble and productive. Once the status of the mortgage has been determined, attention is directed to the lender. What is the lender's attitude toward delinquencies? Will the lender under proper circumstances (good management, third party work-out or supervised owner in possession of the property) give some positive indication that analysis of the physical and financial aspects of the work-out can be accomplished satisfactorily?

Location Analysis

Determination of the precise uses of the project (office building, housing, industrial, shopping, or mixed use) and an analysis of the project's location are next. Here the experience and instinct of the seasoned professional can often tell at an early stage whether the scope and type of project were right for the location. Many factors, supported by demographic studies, zoning requirements, neighborhood attitudes, and adaptability, must be considered at this point. If the property requires a reuse, what neighborhood qualities are important? The surrounding area must be in keeping with the building's present use in order to successfully continue that use. If a shopping center was developed twenty years ago in a well-kept residential neighborhood that is now either run-down or changing into an industrial or warehousing district, then the shopping center may have to be converted to a use in keeping with the surrounding area. The highest and best use, or reuse, of the property being analyzed must be determined. Obviously, there must be a determination of the number of square feet or units on the market and the absorption rate of net square footage or units for sale or rent in competitive properties. The present stability and the future of the area in which the property is located come into play when analyzing the location of a property in difficulty. Total reuse may be indicated by user demand, but it may be barred by leases in place, zoning complications, or a myriad of other problems.

Tenant Interviews

Interviewing tenants to discover their property-related problems and what they perceive to be solutions to these problems can be very useful. The counselor should always be attuned to the tenants' needs but should make no commitments while talking to them. Many times a disgruntled tenant will complain unduly about items that cannot be taken care of economically or will be unable to maintain an objective view of the landowner or developer. However, the legality of a lease document in place and tenancy has to be given primary consideration. Often a tenant will be satisfied with small changes. When such changes can be determined, the counselor should be sure to specify them and to structure them into the financial requirements of the property if possible. Then, in the final recommendation of the analysis, the counselor will find it easier to identify in just what direction the owner or lender may want to go to protect the investment. It is important to determine who the satisfied tenants are and who the disgruntled tenants are in order to treat each category appropriately. In the initial research, however, as much information as possible should be obtained from the points of view of *all* the tenants.

Squabbles among tenants sometimes happen, and they can be disconcerting, but they must be attended to judiciously. In most cases, professional management will exercise the proper care and treatment of tenants and keep them satisfied in their space. Usually small offers of help rather than threatening the tenants provide a basis to build on during the recovery period. There are exceptions to this rule, particularly when a major tenant of the building has become dissatisfied and his departure appears certain. Then a large vacancy and rent-loss factor have to be structured into the financial side of the analysis.

Highest and Best Use Analysis

This is the most sensitive part of a counselor's determination of why a property is currently distressed. Were the site and location properly selected by the developer-owner in the first place? Will today's use be appropriate for the property in the future? Various factors, including why the developer-owner determined that the present use was appropriate when he began the project, should be taken into consideration. Trying to analyze what is wrong today may require a complete and total rethinking of the best use factors. Overbuilding for the market, under- or over-utilization of the site, and imitation of a successful project where absorption has not kept pace with the market are some major considerations.

Many properties, especially mature, older, historic, or industrial buildings, require a complete change of use. A reuse analysis should be employed in such situations. Many of the factors used for analyzing the property as it is are also useful in a reuse analysis. Imagination, practicality, and structural condition are the major concerns in a reuse change. Zoning and local land use plans are also an important concern in the decision regarding an alternative use. In many cases, especially with older industrial and office facilities in less desirable areas, governmental authorities can be very cooperative in creating any kind of reasonable change. With the help of local Economic Development Authority (EDA) and Urban Development Action Grants (UDAG) from federal or state sources, financial and other kinds of support can be made available.

Effect of Tax Structure on the Project

In most instances, newer properties in distressed situations have to be kept within the bounds of existing financing and local tax structure. However, there are a number of advantageous local and federal tax programs that might be considered when making a decision about whether a distressed property can be revamped into a profitable venture. From 1976 to the present, there have been numerous federal income tax regulations that have allowed more attractive tax treatment, especially for older properties. With the new depreciation rules that are currently in effect, equations both mathematical and problematic can be altered on a sensitivity basis to allow successful uses and reuses of today's problem real estate. The counselor should not hesitate to contact local and state historic preservation and planning commission staffs to determine what programs are available and how they can be used. There are also some well-known nationwide consultants who are available for assistance with properties that may enjoy very specialized circumstances.

FIGURE 10-2   The former Carling Brewery in Natick, Massachusetts. The brewery was built in 1954 and had a gross area of 307,565 square feet. Courtesy Leggat, McCall & Werner, Inc., Boston, Massachusetts.

Value "As Is" versus Completed Value

This part of the overall analysis is important for a project that is in an early stage of development but has not been substantially completed. As a project draws closer to completion, the use and reuse become much more limited due to the structural and physical improvements that have been made. However, there are times early in the development phase when, if a project is in trouble and is proving to be financially infeasible, thought should be given to what can be done to change its use entirely in order to make it a viable enterprise. This opportunity does not always call for a major design, finance, or marketing change, but any chance to achieve success by converting to an alternative use should be investigated. Pro forma investigation using all the "what if's" of income, expense, cost, available financing, and rent-up term can help in determining the highest value if the project goes ahead "as is," is completed as created, is partially modified, or is just stopped altogether.

Recommendations

Once the analysis has been completed, the most important alternative considerations to be included in a recommendation are:

Retain "as is."   If the project has been properly conceived and is continuing along a proper and orderly process of development, it may be recommended, after the analysis has been completed, that the project go ahead on its present course. Obviously, a distressed property has problems that require solutions. If the solutions are somewhat easy to effect, a recommendation to continue as is can be made. In most cases, the owner-developer had a good idea in the beginning and all he needs to do is to complete the project as conceived while making a few of the important changes that the counselor might suggest. The owner-developer or the mortgage

FIGURE 10–3   Postrenovation view of the former Carling Brewery, which was renamed Prime Park and leased entirely to a minicomputer firm. Courtesy Leggat, McCall & Werner, Inc., Boston, Massachusetts.

lender may have to make and implement some difficult decisions, but the superior course of action is to continue as is.

Retain after redesigning or renovating.   In this case, with architectural and engineering help, simple or complex solutions can improve the basic design of the project. Encompassed in A of the checklist in Figure 10–1 (on-site inspection) can be recommendations to modify the design of the facility to such a degree that spending some additional money will help ensure the complete and successful workout. The older a facility is, the greater the chances are that it will need to be redesigned or renovated. In some cases, however, a new facility will require structural alterations to improve its appeal.

Modify marketing program.   This is a very important part of the general view of a project because usually problems have occurred because of the lack of tenants or insufficient sales. After the location and highest and best use analysis, identification of the probable tenant mix or purchaser's market is most important. For example, a large industrial building being offered in increments of 20,000 square feet might be made more attractive in the appropriate marketplace and better rented if those 20,000 square feet were broken down into 5,000-square-foot units.

A frequent problem is the sale of residential condominium units priced higher than the local market can absorb. The best recommendation might be to market a less expensive unit that could be sold more quickly, thereby reducing the carrying costs. This method, of course, takes some "bullet biting." Generally speaking, more out-of-pocket expenses will have to be incurred or profitability will have to be lessened to create a successful project. Drastic changes in financial projections, including profit potential, may become necessary. But success in one recommendation often breeds additional successes, and though there may be a temporary dip in the profit curve, the overall performance of the project must be considered.

Sell partial or full interest.   It may be necessary to get the present owner-developer out of the project and to bring in investors with new concepts and additional money. Again, the financial determination from the pro forma analysis will help show what needs to be done to rescue the project (and perhaps the developer's financial health). Pride always has its place in these matters, and at times an owner-developer is reluctant to sell something that has been his "baby." The financial institution behind the project may have more to say about a sell decision than anyone else. Sometimes these changes are difficult medicine for a lender to "swallow," but they may be required for a successful work-out of the distressed property.

Time for recovery estimate.   In any consultation the owner-developer is going to want to know how long the counselor thinks it will take to bring the project back in line. The lender will be even more anxious to have this estimate. Because of the difficulty of a distressed property situation, all concerned will want a "quick fix"—a simple solution that may not be possible. It is nevertheless necessary to estimate the time for recovery in realistic terms. Unless there are some absolutely apparent and indisputable reasons, the recovery time should never be estimated at less than the time the project has absorbed to date, plus a 10–20 percent margin of safety factor.

Computer analysis.   In today's sophisticated market there are many computer programs with which the real estate professional can create "what if" models for a project. If computer analysis was not done previously, it should be done now. The counselor should create a desired return on investment model employing realistic time spans, properly estimated rent-up periods, and income and expenses that can go from the low end to the high end of the spectrum. This approach will determine the best approach through an analysis sensitive to all the variables relevant for the owner-developer and the lender. The "best" and "worst" solutions should be sought, as well as the solution that would be, under reasonable circumstances, the "most probable." Computer-assisted analysis is the "state of the art" for asset management and is fast becoming a necessity in real estate consulting work.

RECOVERY PLAN

A recovery plan is the next product that the counselor must present to the owner-developer or lender of a distressed property. Assuming that all determinations have been made and that a successful recovery is deemed possible by the counselor and any necessary outside experts, a plan for recovery can now be drafted. The certified property manager, architect, engineer, SIR, or other marketing expert and contractor who have assisted previously can be brought into the recovery plan.

Retain or Change Management

This decision is made based on thorough knowledge of the condition of the property and the current management's track record and degree of control over the property. A lender may demand a clean sweep, ousting current management in favor of new management. Factors such as maintenance, rent collection, and tenant relations will be studied in determining whether the present management has been doing everything possible to make the property successful. The present management's intentions and commitment to the property must be determined. The owner-developer's desires must also be probed since he is often the individual who is best equipped to manage the work-out. If there has been a great deal of difficulty in maintaining a good level of management for the property, then a change in management is indicated. The new manager should always be a person or firm that is willing to spend the time, energy, and money necessary to get the job done well. There are a number of national management firms that are experts in work-out management situations, particularly for large projects.

Introduce Management Controls

Obviously, if new management is going to be employed, more direct controls will have to be initiated. If the present manager is retained, those controls can be imposed on the present manager for his own good and the benefit of the owner as well as the lender. It is usually necessary to reduce operating costs, to get tax reductions, and to control the operating losses by prompt and proper rent collection. It is also necessary to reduce vacancies and turnovers. This improvement is sometimes accomplished by moving some of the present tenants to smaller space and others to larger space. Concessions can be made, if necessary, to create a higher cash flow. As discussed previously, undesirable tenants should be dealt with promptly and effectively. Relations with the remaining tenants can often be improved through better communciation. The rent schedule should be examined to see whether income is at an appropriate competitive level and if not, what can be done to improve it.

Restructure Mortgage Financing

If a lender desires a work-out (and lenders usually do), the counselor should be prepared to ask for adjustments in the present debt service, or perhaps for a larger loan. Determining whether new capital in the project is going to be "good money thrown after bad" must be carefully judged, but it is often preferable for a lender to put more money into the project than to have it foreclosed. A good working relationship between the financial institution and the work-out manager can dramatically aid the work-out situation. Given such a relationship, positive cash flows can be achieved more quickly and success is better assured.

Improve the Maintenance Program

Improving the physical condition of the property is not always required, but in some cases it is necessary due to the maintenance deferral problems discussed earlier. Much can be done to accelerate a turnaround by cleaning up small items and upgrading amenities. Spending a few dollars initially rather than just talking about future changes can improve tenant morale and help to retain tenants. Generally speaking, much of this improvement can be done from current cash flow and does not require new funds from the lender. It should be remembered, however, that the restructuring of the financing has to be skillfully coordinated with the anticipated maintenance programs to help get a distressed property out of trouble.

Initiate a Training Program

If the present management stays with the project, some changes will be required. With the help of a consulting certified property manager (CPM) or through the exercise of common sense and good business practices, the present management can often be retained in order to manage the property more effectively. All books and records must be brought up-to-date. Rent collections must be made current, and maintenance policies must be established. If a new manager is employed who is not familiar with work-out problems, a training program will be necessary to ensure success. The retraining of a distressed property's tenants is also important. The tenants will have to understand that rents must be made current and paid when due (without deductions) and that their own housekeeping responsibilities must be performed on time and efficiently. Once management demonstrates what can be done with the property, the tenants must be willing to comply with the changes. Housekeeping, rent-paying habits, and compliance with new rules and regulations may be unpleasant for the tenant, but once good operating standards have been established, tenant compliance will have to be maintained. In almost every case where a work-out is required, attitude adjustments must be made by all concerned: the manager, the owner, the tenants, and the lenders.

Redirect the Marketing Efforts

When a project is determined to be ready for renewal and the physical and economic matters have been addressed, the marketing program for the project may require some changes before recovery is initiated. Often new signs or a new name for the project can indicate to the public that something positive is happening. In one example, a retail project in a midwestern city had gone into default and a work-out analysis determined that the project should have been office space from the outset rather than retail space. Even the name of the project had a negative local connotation. By changing the name into a more suitable, positive one and changing the use to office space, the work-out became successful. A new, professional marketing approach, oriented toward office space users that could not afford "uptown" rates helped lease up the project and keep it full.

When the work-out program has been completed and the project is placed back in service, it is up to the counselor to monitor the operation periodically. The postanalysis monitoring should be a very important part of the original proposal when the decision to pursue the work-out is made. Once work-out recommendations have been made, it is imperative that they be put into effect as soon as possible. Tenant turnover and the total occupancy level must be monitored. Projections must be made as to the timing of new tenants as well as the retention of old ones. Operating budgets, when established, must be adhered to, and that is a direct responsibility of management and therefore part of the manager's performance criteria. Ongoing supervision by someone other than the owner-developer-lender and the manager can keep a project from falling into the same circumstances that caused it to become distressed in the first place.

SELECTED REFERENCES

ARNOLD, ALVIN L., and DEBORAH J. LAWNER. *How to Handle Real Estate in Distress: Cure and Prevention*. Boston: Warren, Gorham & Lamont, 1975.

BRADY, PAUL M. "Determining Loss Reserves on Distressed Property." *Real Estate Review*, Summer 1978, pp. 77–82.

BUCKWALTER, NANCY. "New York State MLC: Private-Sector Professionals Join Public Sector to Solve Distressed Property Problems." *United States Banker*, November 1981, pp. 54–56.

CAMPBELL, KENNETH D. "Doctoring Sick Properties." *Professional Builder*, January 1975, p. 38.

Case Studies: A Review of Problem Income Property Loans. Chicago: United States League of Savings Associations, 1977.

GRUBB, ROBERT C. "Making the Hold/Sell Decision for Distressed Property." *Real Estate Review*, Fall 1977, pp. 45–53.

HAYMES, ALLAN. "Bank Ineptness as a Cause of Real Estate Distress." *Real Estate Review*, Fall 1977, pp. 17–18.

HOPFL, CHARLES E. "Aid for Apartment Owners under Section 223(F)." *Real Estate Review*, Fall 1976, pp. 67–71.

KELLEY, EDWARD N. "Lenders Must Recognize Own Limitations, Seek Outside Management for Distressed Properties." *The National Real Estate Investor*, August 1976, pp. 29–30.

LEFRAK, SAM. "Real Estate Bargain Hunter." *Business Week*, May 31, 1976, pp. 50–54.

LIVINGSTON, FRANK H. "Community, Residents, Owners Benefit from Turnaround of Distressed Apartment Complex." *The Mortgage Banker*, February 1978, pp. 79–81.

NICHOLSON, SY. "Workout Query: Are the Lenders Being Realistic?" *The National Real Estate Investor*, June 1976, pp. 34–35.

O'NEILL, RICHARD W. "Sloppy Lending Was the Real Reason Real Estate Projects Went Bad; Now Here's What to Do about Them." *Banking*, September 1976, pp. 106, 108, 110.

"Problem Properties: Builders, Lenders Seek Aid from Restructured Financing, New Management." *The National Real Estate Investor*, August 1975, pp. 20–24, 35, 36.

RASMUSSEN, VAUGHN B., II.   "Dealing with the Buyer of Property in Trouble." *Real Estate Review,* Winter 1976, pp. 39–44.

SIEGELAUB, HAROLD, and HERBERT A. MEISTRICH.   "Specialists Should Receive Incentives, Full Cooperation When Working Out Problem Loans." *The Mortgage Banker,* October 1977, pp. 113–14, 116, 118.

ZELL, SAMUEL.   "The Grave Dancer." *Real Estate Review,* Winter 1974, pp. 31–38.

CHAPTER ELEVEN
COUNSELING THE RESIDENTIAL CLIENT

The types of residential clients are varied; the residential client may be either a buyer or a seller, a renter or a landlord. The interests of residential clients are diverse; they may want to buy, sell, or rent a single-family detached residence, a condominium, a multifamily property (two or more units), or even a multi-unit building. Their needs are diverse; these may vary from a pressing need to promptly obtain shelter to the more postponable need to find a future retirement home. The residential client may be a corporate transferee or a local investor. His community needs may vary from a need to be active in local government to a need to be close to a transit system. He may be motivated by avoidable tax considerations or by a need to satisfy local zoning requirements prior to a sale or purchase. He may be responsible for the disposition of an estate or desirous of creating one. Separation of the marital partners may require that the property be sold outright or that one of the parties be capable of buying out the other. The family unit may have increased or decreased, necessitating a change in housing accommodations, or perhaps job status and incomes have shifted, so that a more or less expensive home is desired.

Regardless of the problem to be solved, the motivation of the buyer or seller, or the immediate need to be satisfied, objective advice, unencumbered by a prospective sales commission, is generally in the best interest of the residential client. The service of the real estate counselor, therefore, is an independent advisory service, and the advice of the real estate counselor is similar to the advice that one would expect from a personal investment counselor or a family physician.

A large number of clients in this area of counseling are people who want to buy or sell a residential-type property. Counseling for single-family homes and condominiums has not been common because people tend to avoid as many costs as they can. This is particularly true in the case of first-time home buyers, who often operate with limited funds. But as prices continue to climb, as regulations multiply, and as financing becomes more complex, the need for counseling becomes more apparent. Therefore, this chapter focuses primarily on the residential client.

COUNSELING RESIDENTIAL BUYERS AND SELLERS

The counselor who works with single-family clients must first recognize his client's self-interest. Seldom are the needs of buyers and sellers compatible. The seller wants to realize as much as possible from his property in the shortest possible time and with the least possible inconvenience. For him, the ideal situation would be an all-cash sale, in which he does not become personally involved in the financing arrangements by taking back a note or mortgage. The buyer, conversely, wants to secure a "good deal" that will meet his family's location and space requirements and be within the framework of his budget and income. He is also concerned about the many pitfalls of purchasing property—the structure itself (is it sound?), the mechanical systems (are they in good working order?), the title (is it free and clear?), and the survey (is he getting what has been represented as the land area?). The proper research of these matters is time consuming. The counselor must make the client realize that for a transaction to occur, it must be equitable to both the buyer and the seller.

BUYERS

The qualification process that a broker goes through can be a guideline for the counselor. Both counselors and brokers need to understand the buyer's *needs* and *motives*. Therefore, it is necessary to determine the buyer's needs and to ascertain why the buyer wishes to purchase or why the buyer is considering a move to a different location.

The counselor may begin his questioning by inquiring about the buyer's lifestyle and interests. Is the buyer a gardener, joiner, doer, golfer, birder, and so on? Usually, by ascertaining the buyer's lifestyle and monetary position, the counselor can tell which towns or cities the buyer ought to consider. After having narrowed the choice down to this point, the counselor can suggest several brokers in the specific area who would be helpful. With the aid of a checklist (such as the

FIGURE 11–1   Buyer's Search Checklist.

Municipality
Assessor's office
  Tax rate over past five years? _____
  Date of last reassessment, if recent? _____

Chamber of commerce (board of trade)
  Principal employer?_____   Secondary employer? _____
  Population growth rate over past five years? _____
  Predominant growth sectors in community? _____

School department
  School building program? _____
  Tax impact? _____
  Pupil-teacher ratio at each school level? _____
  Cost per pupil? _____
  Teachers' pay scale? _____

Building department
  New construction permits: Number residential?____
  Number commercial or industrial? _____
  Building program for other municipal buildings? _____
  Tax impact? _____

Planning office
  New highway proposed? _____
  Median income in subject census tract for latest census? _____
  Master plan for community—zoning plan and map? _____

Full-time fire department? _____
  Distance of fire department from dwelling and distance of dwelling from nearest fire
hydrant (re fire insurance coverage and rate)? _____

Full-time police department? _____

Public library? _____

Medical services available?_____   Where? _____
  Hospitals? _____

Municipal services: Sewer?_____   Water?_____   Gas? _____
  Electricity?_____   Rubbish removal? _____

one shown in Figure 11–1) and the assistance of a capable broker, the buyer can consider the purchase of a home in an informed manner.

Establishing Criteria

Many times, buyers get caught up in the emotionalism of their potential purchase and overlook important factors such as the ease and cost of getting to work, real estate tax burdens, and the quality of schools. A checklist can alert buyers to factors of which they may be unaware. It can help them to focus on the criteria that are most important to them, so that they will be able to arrive at a sound decision based on facts, with the guidance of a counselor. For instance, in surveying a region, buyers will narrow their search down to a few areas—municipalities that meet their social, economic, and aesthetic preferences. The buyers' priorities will then function to eliminate some of these areas. For example, a doctor who wants to live in the country would be restricted to areas whose roads he or she could use if called to the hospital in the middle of the night. Parents of a child with special needs may settle on a city with access to programs that address the problem. The checklist prompts the buyer to ask many of the questions that must be answered in order to make an informed decision.

Assessing Housing Requirements

The counselor can provide two other forms of assistance to the buyer at an early stage. First, the buyer can be asked to complete an inventory of housing essentials (Figure 11–2) that will reveal the basic features strongly desired. This inventory requires the buyer to fully assess his housing requirements. It also forces him to determine, in order, which features are most important to him. By comparing the information on municipalities with the inventory of housing essentials, the client is directed toward those areas that are most likely to fulfill his needs. Suppose the

FIGURE 11–2 **Inventory of Housing Essentials.**

Nongovernmental services: Telephone? _____ Water?_____ Gas? _____
                          Electricity? _____ Rubbish removal? _____
Any proposed municipal service installations for the total municipality, such as sewerage treatment plant?
    If so, how is the debt to be repaid? _____
    How will this affect the tax rate? _____
    _____

Neighborhood
    Composition of neighborhood (old, young families, etc.)? _____
    Appearance and maintenance of properties? _____
    Uses other than single-family residential? _____ Effect? _____
    Distance from shopping, schools, and churches? _____
    Distance to transportation? Public? _____ Highway? _____
    Range of sale prices? _____
    _____

    Any negative factors? _____
Property
    Does it fulfill your family needs? _____
    Can the home that you propose to buy be financed? _____
        By whom? _____ Terms? _____
    How does it compare in value with other homes that you have inspected in the same town?
    _____

Same neighborhood? _____
What homes have you inspected that sold recently and are like the home that you propose to buy?
    (1) How many rooms? _____ Baths? _____ Garage? _____ Other? _____
    (2) When did it sell and for how much? _____
    (3) To whom? _____
    Termite inspection results? _____
    Structural and mechanical equipment inspection results? _____
    _____
    _____

client wishes to raise horses and his work requires that he live within a half-hour drive of his employment. After surveying the towns that are within the circumference of a half-hour drive, he focuses on two that would be ideal communities for operating a stable. He learns from his research that one of these towns is undergoing a school building program (which would raise the real estate tax bill) and that the other has taken steps to broaden its tax base by encouraging light industry in a well-controlled industrial park (which would lower the real estate tax bill).

Determining Home Affordability

Next the prospective buyer can provide a realistic idea of how much home he can afford by computing the amount of cash available for a down payment and the amount of housing expenses he can carry (see Figures 11–3 and 11–3A).

The typical first-time home buyer might be a couple who have been married three or four years and are in their mid-twenties. They are both employed full time,

FIGURE 11–3   Affordable Price and Monthly Payments.

Cash available for down payment		
Cash in checking account	$ _____	
Cash in savings account	$ _____	
Expected net sale proceeds from sale of present house	$ _____	
Other (savings bonds, parental gift, etc.)	$ _____	
Total		$ _____
Average monthly expenses		
Food	$ _____	
Medical and dental	$ _____	
Car expenses	$ _____	
Installment or recurring debt (appliances, credit cards, etc.)	$ _____	
Insurance (life, auto, major medical, etc.)	$ _____	
Telephone	$ _____	
Laundry and cleaning	$ _____	
Charitable and church contributions	$ _____	
Educational expenses	$ _____	
Entertainment and recreation	$ _____	
Clothing	$ _____	
Utilities	$ _____	
Savings	$ _____	
Total monthly expenses		$ _____

Summary

Total monthly income (after income taxes and payroll deductions)	$ _____
Less monthly expenses	$ _____
Amount available for housing expenses (including real estate taxes, mortgage payments, electricity, special assessments, and estimated repairs)	$ _____

and they have no children. Their gross income is about $40,000. They are apartment dwellers, and they enjoy a moderate social life. They own one car, and their only unusual expense is the repayment of a higher education loan. For the last two years they have been saving actively to purchase a home. As their savings appeared to increase, inflation decreased the purchasing power of the savings and property prices continued to increase. It was apparent that the only real solution for them was to get into the inflation spiral as quickly as they could qualify for a mortgage loan. With the aid of the income and expense analysis they will be able to realize the actual amount that is available for housing expenses. The most devastating expenses are often the expenses that are unexpected and not immediately apparent, such as furnace repairs, roof repairs, and sewer charges. Use of the form in Figure 11–3 will also alert the client to excesses that could be eliminated or reduced. The amount of money available for disposable income after the housing expense deduction is entirely dependent on the comforts expected by the client.

FIGURE 11–3A Affordable Price and Monthly Payments.

Cash available for down payment
Cash in checking account	$ 500	
Cash in savings account	$ 9,500	
Expected net sale proceeds from sale of present house	$ -0-	
Other (savings bonds, parental gift, etc.)	$15,000	
Total		$25,000

Average monthly expenses
Food	$ 258	
Medical and dental	$ 80	
Car expenses	$ 388	
Installment or recurring debt (appliances, credit cards, etc.)	$ 50	
Insurance (life, auto, major medical, etc.)	$ 150	
Telephone	$ 40	
Laundry and cleaning	$ 25	
Charitable and church contributions	$ 40	
Educational expenses	$ 50	
Entertainment and recreation	$ 100	
Clothing	$ 100	
Utilities	$ 60	
Savings	$ 00	
Total monthly expenses		$ 1,341

Summary
Total monthly income (after income taxes and payroll deductions)	$ 2,400
Less monthly expenses	$ 1,341
Amount available for housing expenses (including real estate taxes, mortgage payments, electricity, special assessments, and estimated repairs)	$ 1,059

In the preceding example, the clients' expenses were 55 percent of their net income. Most of the expenses would be ongoing, so there is little room for short-term decreases.

Assuming that the buyers have determined to put 20 percent equity into their purchase and that the counselor has advised them to retain a minimum of $6,000 for closing expenses, they have available $19,000 for a down payment on a purchase price not to exceed $95,000.

The counselor has determined that a mortgage interest rate of 10 percent can be obtained on a three-year review basis, payable, however, on a thirty-year term with 20 percent down. This translates into a monthly cost of $666.95. Taxes are $2,000 divided by 12 = $166.66, which brings the total to $833.62 monthly. This leaves something to cover insurance, heating costs, repairs, and other assessments. The counselor would advise the clients to make allowances for the other monthly expenses which could occur.

After a thorough search, the buyers, like most buyers, will become their own appraisers. After viewing many properties, they will develop a feel for the housing market and for values. If, for any reason, a professional appraiser is needed, the counselor will retain one. Sellers generally need an appraiser; buyers generally do not, except when they have quickly found a home that suits their needs and have not had time to thoroughly examine the market.

When buyers find a home that satisfies all of their requirements and they want to make a purchase, they check with the counselor. He will ask them about the physical condition of the property and about the forms or contracts that they have been asked to sign.

If this interview indicates that property inspections are needed, the counselor will order them. If the buyer-client comes in with a purchase and sales agreement in hand, the counselor checks the agreement and may recommend the employment of an attorney. If the purchase and sales agreement is straightforward, an experienced real estate counselor may feel that he can properly comment on it; otherwise, he will call for assistance.

The counselor hires specialists in specific fields where the needs of the client require additional expert advice. The assistance of a good accountant, real estate attorney, appraiser, property manager, broker, or other counselor can only enhance the counselor's position by producing better advice for his client. Part of anyone's practice is knowing whom to tap for assistance without unnecessarily driving up the purchase costs. Restrictive covenants recited in the agreement may need to be clarified, or a change in zoning may be necessary prior to closing. The seller may require occupancy past the closing date. If necessary, the counselor would not hesitate to call in other professionals to assist him in determining the course of action best for his client.

A physical inspection of the land and buildings is needed to assure that all items are either included in the agreement or accounted for in some manner and that all necessary inspections have been ordered. Normally, the counselor will represent the buyer at the transfer unless an attorney has been retained.

SELLERS

Sellers naturally want to receive the maximum price for their property. They also want their property sold in the minimum amount of time with the least amount of bother. To accomplish these objectives, the counselor should advise them to get an opinion of value from an appraiser or from several local brokers. The value provided by either should be substantiated by an analysis based on confirmed sales and detailed property information that is usually provided in writing.

Selecting a Broker

The next consideration is the selection of the broker. Many sellers of single-family homes have the idea that they can sell their homes themselves and save the commission. It is important that the counselor point out the advantages of listing with a successful, experienced broker. An interview session should be set up for broker selection with the seller and the counselor both being present. During the interviews questions should be raised about the brokers' marketing program, their organization, the number of sales they have made in the current year to date, their present number of active listings, and their method of showing or presenting property. One broker usually makes the most impressive presentation. When this is evident, the seller probably should be advised that the broker be employed on an "exclusive right to sell" basis, which means that the broker is entitled to a commission on the sale of the property by anyone, including the owner. The broker should be told to place the property in Multiple Listing Services (MLS) immediately in order to ensure wider marketing visibility. The counselor then instructs the broker as to the purchase and sales forms to be used, the price and terms at which the property is to be listed, the acceptable contingencies, and the time allotted for these contingencies. It may be advisable to limit the exclusive right to sell agreement to thirty days, with a renewal at the end of each thirty-day period based on the broker's performance. The counselor also suggests a method by which the broker is to report his activity to the seller.

Financing

The counselor may want to check with the local banks concerning *available* mortgage money and current interest rates and loan terms to satisfy himself that any mortgage contingenices presented can be satisfied. Creative financing has become popular and is an accepted part of transactions, particularly in times of tight money. The counselor's ability to explain the precise meaning of terms such as balloon payments, wraparound mortgage, mortgage assumptions, and nonrecourse notes helps clients to determine whether these are things they want to do. For example, a client selling her home subject to the existing mortgage must understand that her name is still on the note held by the lending institution and that she is still liable for the debt in case of default. The seller is then given advice about preparing the house for sale. The counselor may also become involved in the negotiations when a sales contract is presented, and he may attend the transfer as the seller's representative.

LETTER OF UNDERSTANDING

Prior to working with a client, the counselor should have the client sign a letter of understanding so that the fee and all other services are clearly understood. An example of such a letter is contained in Figure 11–4. It may help to give the client a general estimate of the amount of the fee, such as a not-to-exceed amount, while explaining that the fee is ultimately based on the amount of time involved in a particular assignment. Submission of a time sheet, such as that shown in Figure 11–5, with the bill is an accepted practice.

COUNSELOR'S BILLING FOR WORK

Each counselor's billing will vary, depending on how he or she sees the assignment. People work at various rates, depending on their perception of the job. Therefore, it is suggested that the fee be spelled out in the letter of understanding. Some firms and individuals add a percentage to the fee to cover overhead, and this can be explained in the letter.

If research people are used for fieldwork, their time is billed at a much lower rate, generally, than the senior counselor. The use of such people can reduce the charges to the client while expediting completion of the assignment. For this reason, the counselor may detail some of the services to be supplied, such as property inspection, commentary on the purchase and sales agreement, and marketing advice.

Recognition of the advantages of employing a real estate professional to represent one's best interests is becoming more common in residential transactions. Novice buyers want to avoid making costly mistakes; homeowners reaching retirement need to plan carefully; owners of excess land may have a potential added asset—all of these people need impartial answers. Evaluating the merits of a real estate transaction is not for amateurs—the counselor's role is to make sure the client does not step on any broken glass along the way.

In guiding the client around the scattered and often hidden difficulties of a real estate transaction, the residential counselor is forced to be a generalist. Inner-city counselors normally deal with commercial-type real estate and the problems attendant thereto. If such counselors come to the suburbs or to a rural area, it is usually to solve an industrial or commercial problem for a client contact that originated in the city.

FIGURE 11-4 Sample Letter of Understanding.

November 3, 19—

Mr. and Mrs. Lovely People
1000 Peachtree Lane
Anytown, U.S.A. 00001

Dear Mr. and Mrs. People:

To clarify our working relationship during the time that I will be counseling you on the [purchase or disposition] of real estate, I herewith submit an outline of our services and the corresponding fees.

A counselor is employed to provide advice in the field in which he has expertise. His advice will be objective and impartial. The counselor will attempt to solve any real estate problems that occur and will try to solve them for the benefit of his client.

Counseling is the sale of time based on the background and experience of the counselor. My time will be billed at [$xx per hour, $xx per day, or $xx per assignment] plus out-of-pocket expenses.

My billing will be on a [monthly, weekly, or when the assignment is completed] basis.

All reporting will be verbal unless otherwise called for.

If all that has been stated in this letter agrees with your understanding of my employment, please sign and date the enclosed copy where it says "accepted" and return it in the enclosed envelope.

I look forward with pleasure toward working to assist you on this assignment.

Sincerely,

Mark M. Y. Words

Accepted

_____

PROBLEM-SOLVING SKILLS NEEDED

The residential counselor, one who solves problems for individual home buyers or sellers, must be prepared to solve all types of problems attendant to the area in which he or she serves. Usually residential counselors are located where there are

FIGURE 11–5 Log and time sheet.

Client: _____

Address: _____

Property address: _____

Purpose of assignment: _____

Date started: _____ Date promised: _____

Assignment performed by: _____

LOG DETAILS OF WORK PERFORMED	EXPENSES, IF ANY	DATE	TIME EXPENDED	$ COMPUTED

many single-family units. This could be in an urban, suburban, or exurban location. Therefore, in addition to counseling clients on buy and sell situations, the counselor will be involved in questions of zoning, appeal board hearings, planning of residential subdivisions, ad valorem taxation, and sometimes the improvement of communication between a citizen and the municipal government.

For example, a citizen owned a property adjacent to a group of municipal buildings. The town wanted the property for parking and future building expansion.

The town approached the owner, and both agreed on an appraisal, which was subsequently ordered and submitted. Nothing else happened. Rumor had it that the owner was stubborn; rumor also had it that the selectmen were going to proceed to take the property by eminent domain. Everyone, including the selectmen and the owner, was feeding off *rumors*. The owner came to a counselor seeking an appraisal. The counselor asked him why he wanted one. He replied, "To prepare for court action." He was asked whether he was satisfied with the value estimated by the town's appraiser. He said he was. It was an acceptable value. He was then asked why he and the selectmen had not gotten together and completed a transaction. He said the selectmen would not talk to him. It was suggested that the counselor talk to the selectmen on his behalf. He agreed. As a result, a motion was made at a town meeting for an appropriation of money to purchase the land based on the appraised value. The motion passed, the land was purchased, the owner retired to another state, and the town has a parking lot.

As to appeal board hearings: A counselor once advised the owner of a single-family home to retain a parcel of land contiguous to his residence of about 1.5 acres after he sold off a parcel of land and the dwelling. There was a problem with the back land in that it had 50 feet on an accepted street. The zoning required 110 feet. The minimum lot size in the area was 15,000 square feet, based on the current zoning bylaws. The counselor reasoned that the town would accept the larger lot (4.36 times over the present requirements) even though the frontage was less than 50 percent of the minimum requirement, from the owner's standpoint. The counselor also thought that time would contribute to an increase in value. The client concurred with this reasoning and four years later told the counselor to do whatever was necessary to prepare the lot for sale. This required a hearing, which the counselor scheduled. The hearing went as it was expected to go—the land received a variance; the counselor advised the town that his client would not subdivide if a variance was granted; and the lot was subsequently sold as a building lot, with a value that was much more than back land value.

An article on the counselor's practice—"Now, a Guide for Tenderfeet on a Realty Safari"—appeared in a metropolitan newspaper. As a result of this article the firm received a call from a woman who owned property in another state. At the time of the call there were no CREs in that state. The woman was a joint owner of a cottage in a coastal town. She received her interest by inheritance. Her brother was the other owner. The brother wanted to sell the cottage; the client wanted to retain it, rent it out temporarily, and eventually retire and live in it.

The counselor determined from the woman that she needed to know whether the cottage was rentable and for how much, the probable lease term, and its salability and market value.

The procedure was to retain a local appraiser (who was recommended by a Realtor known to the counselor) to do an appraisal and a rental study. As a result of his work the counselor was able to give the client the pros and cons of renting, the fair market value, and some advice as to how she might utilize the proceeds from a sale to meet her future needs. Her brother challenged the appraised value. He said it was much too low and that he had a buyer in hand that would pay much more than the appraised value. The counselor gave him the opportunity to bring in his high-priced buyer, which he could not do. The ultimate disposition of the property is unknown in this case. What is important, however, is that the counselor saved the client some money by using local talent and giving her his best advice. Of course, when such advice is given, it is not always followed.

Because small-town counselors are not involved in inner-city transactions and, therefore, in the politics of the inner city, they sometimes become attractive to institutions that want a type of objectivity that is not available from a counselor who may be directly or indirectly involved in business that bears on their problem. Such was the case of an institution that hired one small-town counseling firm to check the activities of a consultant whom it had hired to advise it regarding the economic viability of a large housing project. The counseling firm was able to render a totally unbiased opinion, a fresh approach to a messy situation, and some positive suggestions as to how to remedy it.

POTENTIAL OF RESIDENTIAL COUNSELING

The counseling of residential clients is a large untapped market that cries for attention. The single-family residential broker who can take off the broker's hat and put on the counselor's has an additional asset. There are diverse opportunities with people who want to sell their own property, with buyers who will not work with a broker, with industrial transferees, with legal and accounting firms that transfer people regularly, with attorneys who are not familiar with the area or with real estate transactions generally, and with brokers whose clients want unbiased real estate advice. The possibilities are endless.

The caveats are, however, that you cannot doff the counselor's hat in the middle of a given transaction and that you must recognize the limits of your experience and call for help when you do not have the answers.

SELECTED REFERENCES

BEATON, WILLIAM R. *Real Estate Financing* (2nd ed.). Englewood Cliffs, N.J.: Prentice-Hall, Inc., 1982.

BLOOM, GEORGE F., and HENRY S. HARRISON. *Appraising the Single Family Residence*. Chicago: American Institute of Real Estate Appraisers, 1978.

BOYCE, BYRL N., ed. *Real Estate Appraisal Terminology* (rev. ed.). Cambridge, Mass.: Ballinger Publishing Co., 1981.

BOYKIN, JAMES H. *Financing Real Estate*. Lexington, Mass.: Lexington Books, 1979.

HARRISON, HENRY S. *Home Buying: The Complete Illustrated Guide*. Chicago: Realtors National Marketing Institute, 1980.

———— *Houses* (8th ed.). Chicago: Realtors National Marketing Institute, 1979.

KRATOVIL, ROBERT. *Buying, Owning, and Selling a Home in the 1980's*. Englewood Cliffs, N.J.: Prentice-Hall, Inc., 1981.

Marshall Swift Residential Cost Manual (updated monthly).   Los Angeles: Marshall and
    Swift Publication Company.
REALTORS NATIONAL MARKETING INSTITUTE.   *Real Estate Sales Handbook*. Chi-
    cago: National Association of Realtors, 1975.
SUMICHRAST, MICHAEL, and RONALD G. SHAFER.   *The Complete Book of Home
    Buying*. Princeton, N.J.: Dow Jones Books, 1980.

CHAPTER TWELVE
MOTEL-HOTEL
PROPERTIES

This chapter presents a brief overview of some of the important elements involved in the evaluation of hotels. Since hotels are primarily a retail business, the chapter covers the physical real property attributes necessary for a successful operation, as well as some of the business elements (management and chain affiliation), which should be evaluated by the counselor advising clients in hotel investments.

Among the topics discussed are the following: hostelry types, ownership forms, feasibility analysis, existing facility investment analysis, evaluating a franchise, and evaluating a managing agent.

HOSTELRY TYPES

Hostelry types can be discussed from many viewpoints. However, they are generally characterized by three factors: location, market orientation, and operation.

Location

Location in relation to area amenities and generators of demand is one of the most important elements in the discussion of a hostelry because it is one of the major factors influencing a hostelry's success. Access and visibility are also vital characteristics of the analysis of any hostelry.

Airport hotels are generally located on airport property or within a five-mile radius of it. Their room demand stems substantially from direct airline crew and related business and commercial activities around the airport. Downtown properties are center-city hotels that are generally located in the commercial or financial districts of metropolitan areas and depend primarily on the traveling businessperson for their room demand. Resort properties are located in destination areas and appeal primarily to tourists and vacation-oriented conferences. Highway lodging facilities are located on interstate or major local routes and depend heavily on the in-transit businessperson and vacationer for the bulk of their room demand. Areas such as office parks and industrial developments also create demand for these facilities.

Market Orientation

Location and facilities are often indications of a hotel's market orientation. Hostelries that have limited public facilities such as meeting rooms and ballrooms accommodate mainly individuals or families. These may be businesspersons or tourists who are either in transit or have arrived at their final destination.

The group-type hostelry generally has more extensive meeting and banquet facilities and a larger number of guest room units. The corporate-oriented facility is found in cities or near office parks; it usually features small meeting rooms and excellent food and beverage facilities. The hostelry oriented to conferences or conventions can be in a resort area, a city, or near a major airport; it is characterized by large meeting and banquet facilities. Group tours represent a substantial market segment for a few hotels, though this is generally filler-type business for most properties.

Operation

Hotels have various methods of operation. First, there are franchised properties that obtain a license to operate under a given name (for example, Best Western, Days Inn, Howard Johnson's, Holiday Inn, Hilton, Quality, Ramada, and Sheraton). Second, there are hotels that are owned, operated under management contract or leased by a hotel chain (for example, Aircoa, Amfac, Canadian Pacific, Doubletree, Dunfey, Embassy Suite, Four Seasons, Hyatt, Marriott, Meridien, Hilton, Radisson, Sheraton, Sofitel, Stouffer, Trust House Forte, and Westin). The referral organization allows an independently owned hotel such as a Best Western or a Friendship Inn to be associated in a national network primarily for reservations benefits. It should be noted that both of these methods of operations are used by such hotel companies as Hilton and Sheraton.

Finally, there are independently owned and operated properties that have no chain (brand name) affiliation.

FIGURE 12–1   The Hyatt Regency Maui on Kaanapali Beach in Lahaina, Hawaii, is a resort hotel. Courtesy of Hyatt Hotels Corporation.

OWNERSHIP FORMS

Hotel ownership takes many forms. Hotels may be owned in fee, or the ground, building, and chattels may be leased. The day-to-day operation of a hotel is often entrusted to a third-party professional agent, though the owner may take the responsibility. Owners sometimes lease their hotel properties to third-party hotel operators, but this form of transaction is most unusual in today's market. Twenty years ago, hotel companies were willing to accept the risks and obligations associated with long-term leases. However, this is not the case now due to the high fixed costs of debt service normally associated with newer hotels, which until recent 1986 tax legislation, were typically highly leveraged. With the 1986 changes in the tax laws we should see greater equity and less fixed debt in order to assure the viability of the equity investment. The most commonly used type of deal structure is when a developer/investor employs a management agent—the owner enters into a management contract with a hotel operator for the operation of the hotel. Management contracts may require a capital investment in the property by the operator-via loan for shortfall, etc.. Such contracts usually stipulate the operator is to receive a base minimum fee (generally a percentage of gross sales) plus an incentive fee based on defined profits. (A complete analysis of hotel management contracts is found in James Eyster's book, *The Negotiation and Administration of Hotel Management Contracts.*)

FEASIBILITY ANALYSIS OF PROPOSED HOSTELRIES

The feasibility of a hotel is ultimately determined by its cost versus its profit and tax benefits. This information is generally obtained in the concluding step of the feasibility analysis. The initial step of the hotel feasibility study is an analysis of the site, which is followed by a thorough evaluation of competition and market demand. Once the existing supply and demand characteristics of the market have been analyzed, projections of future supply and demand and estimates of market penetration by the subject property must be made. From these analyses, realistic projections of income and expense and, ultimately, return on investment can be completed.

Location

The old adage of E. M. Statler that the three most important elements in a hotel's success were "location, location, and location" is still very true today. As a public facility, a hotel should be conveniently accessible and highly visible. Ideal neighborhoods have nighttime activities and residential or commercial complexes located nearby. Obviously, the neighborhoods should be free of deterioration and crime. Hotel developers prefer locations in growing areas or areas that demonstrate strong and stable characteristics. Proximity to generators of transient lodging demand is also important. These generators may be airports, office buildings, convention centers, or, in the case of resorts, natural amenities such as ski slopes, beaches, and marinas. The counselor performing the feasibility analysis should be most careful to analyze all of the factors that concern location (access, visibility, area activities, residential or commercial backup, neighborhood characteristics, and growth patterns), as well as the overall economic climate and growth within a given metropolitan area or development.

Demand

The second step in any hotel feasibility or market analysis should be a thorough review of the past, present, and future demand generators of transient visitation. Broadly, these generators fall into two categories, individuals and groups. As discussed in the "Hostelry Types" section, there are various subcategories in each of these demand segments. Each hotel operator may categorize individual or group business differently; however, properties in a particular area generally cater to similar markets. Identifying and quantifying specific segments of demand is an interview process with hotel operators, chambers of commerce, major employers, convention and visitor center personnel, airport officials, and so forth. The key to any feasibility analysis is an estimate not only of existing demand but of potential future demand that may be affected by various new developments such as a proposed shopping mall, sports arena, office or industrial park, or amusement or entertainment complex.

Supply

The supply analysis involves a detailed review of the existing and proposed hostelries within a given market area. These should be compared with the subject property on the basis of location, price, facilities, chain affiliation, management, and other factors. Also necessary is an assessment of the likelihood that proposed hostelries will actually be developed and of the time when they will be opened to the marketplace. Obtaining this information may require interviews with developers and with building department and financial institution personnel. The information is extremely important because the amount of proposed competition that actually materializes can significantly affect the financial success of any competitive hotel. Witness the overbuilding of hotels in many areas during the 1970s and the numerous resulting hotel bankruptcies and foreclosures. The possibility of a recurrence of this experience was evident in some cities in the early eighties and is occurring again in the mid 1980s.

Targeted Market Penetration

Based on the analyses of existing and proposed supply and demand conditions, the consultant should arrive at a market penetration potential for each of the subject property's target markets. This involves analyzing the quality and strength of demand and the projected growth of each of these market segments. Because of the subject property's location and physical facilities, its market penetration may be different in each category. For example, a proposed 100-unit economy motel may represent only 10 percent of the available rooms in a community that has 900 rooms in existing competitive hotels. Because of its reduced room rates, however, it may be able to attract 20 percent or more of the available price-sensitive markets (for example, salespersons on per diem, government employees, family tourists, and senior citizens). Similarly, because of its reduced facilities and services or because of its location in relation to generators of demand and competitive hotels, it may not be able to capture a fair market share (10 percent) of the available groups and conventions or expense account executives.

As was just indicated, the price sensitivity of each market segment must also be analyzed. A few developers have made the error of constructing a four- or five-star hotel or even a quality suite hotel in a secondary or tertiary city that does not have a strong corporate headquarters base. Such hotels are examples of over-improvements, which may or may not be permanent, and economic obsolescence, that form of depreciation most difficult to quantify.

Market penetration should also be analyzed from the point of view of how long it will take the proposed facility to reach a stabilized operating position. Stabilized position refers to the annual occupancy and the average rates that a hotel is expected to achieve. For example, a proposed hotel may be projected to obtain an average occupancy of 75 percent over its economic life. Typically, however, it requires two to four years of operation and marketing plus strong preopening sales to reach this level. Average rates are typically estimated in terms of current-value dollars by comparing the subject hotel with locally competitive hotels. These rates are then inflated forward to the year in which stabilized occupancy of the new hotel is to be reached. Assumptions as to inflation should be very clearly stated and considered because many hotel projects cannot be proved feasible in terms of current-value dollars.

Projected Feasibility

Once the market penetration and the facilities of the proposed hotel have been determined by the consultant, projections of income and expenses can be made. These projections should cover not only the stabilized year but all years prior to it, so that the developer is made aware of the potential "shortfall" in the early years of the hotel's operation. Typically, it requires three to four years for a hotel to mature and reach a relatively stable level of occupancy. An example of a three-year projection of this kind is shown in Figure 12–2.

Project Cost

Once the initial market study aspects of the feasibility analysis have been completed, a meeting is usually held between the counselor and the developer to review these preliminary findings. At this point the developer may decide to move forward with the project by retaining an architect to prepare preliminary schematic plans based on the counselor's recommendations. If an architect was retained prior to the counselor, the counselor is generally asked to comment on a set of preliminary plans and project cost estimates.

Cost versus Profit

To develop a pro forma statement of available cash flow for the owner, one analyzes projected profitability generally with some assumption as to debt service. Financial institutions such as banks, life insurance companies, credit companies, and pension funds finance hotel development, but often not as fixed-rate long-term lenders. More and more, creative financing packages are being put together in order to enable the hotel industry to continue its growth. In the early 1980s these ran the gamut from government of quasi-government participation to tax-sheltered, equity syndications. With the 1986 tax legislation, tax shelters will no longer be a viable means of project financing and governments grants and loans will be greatly reduced.

FIGURE 12-2 Proposed Hotel Projection of Income and Expense

	YEAR 1		YEAR 2		YEAR 3		YEAR 4		YEAR 5	
NUMBER OF ROOMS	374		374		374		374		374	
OCCUPANCY PERCENTAGE	63%		68%		72%		74%		75%	
AVERAGE ROOM RATE	$147.00		$169.00		$186.00		$199.00		$213.00	
REVENUES										
Rooms	12642	66.62%	15688	69.43%	18281	71.13%	20102	71.93%	21807	72.64%
Food	4040	21.29%	4323	19.13%	4582	17.83%	4811	17.21%	5004	16.67%
Beverage	1535	8.09%	1643	7.27%	1741	6.77%	1828	6.54%	1901	6.33%
Telephone	506	2.66%	628	2.78%	731	2.85%	804	2.88%	872	2.91%
Other	253	1.33%	314	1.39%	366	1.42%	402	1.44%	436	1.45%
Total Revenue	18976	100.00%	22594	100.00%	25702	100.00%	27948	100.00%	30021	100.00%
*DEPARTMENTAL COSTS**										
Rooms	3350	26.50%	3922	25.00%	4296	23.50%	4523	22.50%	4798	22.00%
Food & Beverage	4850	87.00%	5071	85.00%	5248	83.00%	5444	82.00%	5593	81.00%
Telephone	531	105.00%	628	100.00%	695	95.00%	748	93.00%	785	90.00%
Total Dept. Costs	8732	46.01%	9620	42.58%	10239	39.84%	10715	38.34%	11176	37.23%
GROSS OPERATING INCOME	10244	53.99%	12974	57.42%	15462	60.16%	17233	61.66%	18845	62.77%
UNDISTRIBUTED EXPENSES										
Administrative & General	1708	9.00%	1875	8.30%	1953	7.60%	2012	7.20%	2101	7.00%
Marketing	1233	6.50%	1356	6.00%	1491	5.80%	1593	5.70%	1681	5.60%
Repairs & Maintenance	740	3.90%	904	4.00%	1054	4.10%	1174	4.20%	1261	4.20%
Utilities	780	4.11%	826	3.66%	876	3.41%	928	3.32%	984	3.28%
Total Expenses	4461	23.51%	4961	21.96%	5374	20.91%	5708	20.42%	6028	20.08%
HOUSE PROFIT	5784	30.48%	8013	35.47%	10089	39.25%	11525	41.24%	12818	42.70%
FIXED EXPENSES										
Insurance	88	0.46%	95	0.42%	103	0.40%	111	0.40%	120	0.40%
Real Estate Taxes	1968	10.37%	3000	13.28%	3075	11.96%	3152	11.28%	3231	10.76%
Total Fixed Expenses	2056	10.83%	3095	13.70%	3178	12.36%	3263	11.67%	3350	11.16%
INCOME BEFORE MANAGEMENT FEE AND RESERVES	3728	19.64%	4918	21.77%	6911	26.89%	8263	29.56%	9467	31.54%
Reserve for Replacement	190	1.00%	226	1.00%	257	1.00%	419	1.50%	600	2.00%
INCOME BEFORE MANAGEMENT FEE	3538	18.64%	4692	20.77%	6654	25.89%	7843	28.06%	8867	29.54%
Management Fee	759	4.00%	904	4.00%	1028	4.00%	1118	4.00%	1201	4.00%
*NET INCOME AVAILABLE FOR DEBT SERVICE **	2779	14.64%	3789	16.77%	5626	21.89%	6725	24.06%	7666	25.54%

* Departmental percentages expressed in ratio to departmental revenues
**Does not include income derived from rental of approximately 6,900 square feet of retail space

As all developers realize, a project is feasible only when a financial package is in place (even for the short term), regardless of supply and demand. Many other factors also affect a project's feasibility, such as equity returns with and without tax benefits, appreciation of an area's real estate values, holding period, form of ownership, and risk of capital exposure.

INVESTMENT ANALYSIS
OF AN EXISTING FACILITY

In preparing an investment analysis of an existing facility, a review of location, demand, and supply, and projected profitability is necessary. All of these items were discussed in the preceding section. With the investment analysis an internal rate of return on the investment as well as other investment benefits can be calculated. These other benefits include tax benefits and a favorable impact on the value of adjacent land and of proposed and existing developments.

Specific Risks or Benefits
of a Particular Deal

Analyzing the specific risks or benefits of a particular deal requires an understanding of the type of property and the nature of its occupancy. This includes knowing how secure that occupancy is and what can happen to detract from or add to it. A hotel is a retail business, and its major source of "profit" comes from the sale of its rooms. A room rate that constantly increases at or above inflation rates and an occupancy that can hold at a "stabilized level" except for times of recession are indeed desirable characteristics.

Review of Existing Debt or Lease

Analyzing existing debt is of great significance, for when a purchaser can assume or take over a property subject to existing financing, he may be borrowing a portion of the purchase price at a rate of interest below the rate that is available today. Existing debt and seller financing provide the means of financing in the many hotel-motel transfers.

Lease analysis requires an understanding of the obligations of both tenant and landlord and of their potential risk-reward positions. A principal reason for analyzing a hotel lease is to learn more about what is required of the tenant (maintenance, payments, records, etc.). It is also important to examine how the landlord may benefit as the tenant's gross sales improve, even if the tenant's net profit does not. Other important lease provisions may address such matters as subordination, defaults, termination, renewals, restrictive use, and the right of first refusal—all of which can affect the current value and future profitability of the property. A typical example is the following ground lease clause pertaining to the tenant's right to mortgage its leasehold interest:

Mortgages may be taken out for a term of not less than ten years and in amounts not to exceed two-thirds of the market value of the premises, not including land. Interest is not to exceed 10 percent per annum, and amortization shall not be less than 2 percent per annum. The total debt service constant is not to exceed 12 percent in any one year except for the year the loan is due.

Physical Inspections and Review of Capital Budgets

Physical inspections and review of capital budgets are extremely important in evaluating an existing facility. It is often advisable to use consulting engineers or in-house engineers because the condition of a property's physical facilities can have a great impact on a hotel's value, can move a property from one class to another, can increase occupancy by adding facilities, can increase rates by changing room characteristics, and so forth. The facility should be viewed both from a deferred maintenance standpoint and from an upgrading-expansion standpoint.

Evaluation of Management

An evaluation of management begins with an analysis of the management contract and moves into a review of management's motivation and training procedures; supervision of on-site management from the management agent's office; and communication between the management agent, the on-premise management, the owner, and other involved parties. Management contracts range from informal agreements to voluminous formal documents specifying the rights, obligations, liabilities, and so forth of both the owner and the manager.

Asset Management

Asset management has become a frequently used service by institutional and syndicate investors. By retaining a third party hotel consulting and management firm to become the liaison between property management and ownership, the owner is provided with greater assurance of properly positioning the hotel, financial reporting and monitoring of capital improvements. The asset manager's primary responsibility is the preservation and enhancement of property value. Asset managers advise on refurbishing, marketing plans, adherence to budget, annual plans, changes in a market's supply/demand ratios, room rate and product pricing policies, etc.

Business versus Real Estate Income

It is rather difficult to distinguish between business and real estate income except in the case of a net-net lease, where the landlord is paid primarily for the use of real estate and the tenant profits primarily from his business expertise. Often, however, the landlord also shares in the business profits through a share of gross sales. Where there is no landlord-tenant relationship, the estimation of business versus real estate value becomes more difficult. A case in point would be the valuation of a casino building whose business value substantially exceeds the total of the "bricks and mortar" and land real estate values.

Tax Consequences

Tax consequences involve allowable tax write-offs because of the amount of dollars spent on furniture, fixtures, and equipment (FF&E) as well as the building. At times, the equity positions of hotels have been bought and sold primarily for their tax-sheltering capacity rather than their ability to provide cash flow. The federal tax legislation enacted in 1982 permitted greater allowable depreciation making the tax-sheltering capacity of a hotel even more than before. Hence, tax-oriented equity investors and syndicators reduced their projected "cash on cash" return requirement (at least for the initial years of their ownership). The 1986 tax legislation will reduce or remove many of these tax benefits (longer depreciation, no ITC, non-allowable passive losses against ordinary earned income, etc.) However, hotels appear to be classed as businesses not as real estate and in some cases may appear to be a window for structuring tax incentive transactions.

Valuation of the Future Income Stream

The valuation of the future income stream depends primarily on the increases in room rates and occupancy that the consultant believes are obtainable. An internal rate of return can then be applied to this income stream and the project cost. In the hospitality industry internal rates of return of 20 percent or more over a fifteen-year period now appear generally acceptable. Caution must be exercised in the projection process when using a rate of inflation on room rates. When double-digit increases in room rates are experienced, it may not be possible to forecast such rates of increase over an extended period with any reasonable degree of certainty. The hotel industry, like most others, is cyclical, and typically it lags behind the general economy during both its periods of recovery and its periods of decline.

Highest and Best Use and Alternative Use Analyses

Highest and best use analysis and alternative use analysis are concerned with the viability of a hotel for uses other than its present use. For example, the present use might change from first class to economy, from first class to luxury, or even from use as a hotel to residential use, (rental, condominium, or cooperative), time share use, or use as a condominium rental pool. Usually a hotel should be demolished or completely recycled when the land value is greater than the value of the land and building as a going hotel. Perhaps the hotel should be converted to such uses as office space, user-occupant space, or conference center space. The purpose of highest and best use analysis is to carefully consider possible uses in order to identify most profitable use or uses for a hotel property.

How and When to Sell or Buy

A hotel should be sold if it has been determined with reasonable certainty that the present operating conditions have attained maximum profitability and will fall off without major refurbishing and the present owner does not wish to become involved in a long-term capital expense program of this nature. A hotel should also be sold if the present owner is a ''hotel operator'' and believes that the hotel should be converted to another use and or if the present owner wants to move from the active to the passive investment role. The tax shelter capability of a hotel, or the lack thereof, is often an inducement to buy or sell a hotel.

EVALUATION OF A FRANCHISE OR CHAIN

The evaluation of chain affiliation via a franchise requires a cost-benefit analysis. The costs of franchise memberships vary. They involve not only the expense of physically complying with franchise standards but also the ongoing royalty fees, which are generally a percentage of gross room sales plus marketing and reservation fees. These costs typically range from 2 percent to 5 percent and more of gross room sales. The benefits derived from chain affiliation are increased sales due to brand name identification, national sales and reservation systems, and other chain services. These benefits are frequently difficult to measure because of the uncertainty of the impact of a specific brand name on a particular market. Although many franchises have national representation, the market strength of others is more regionalized. Discussing a franchise's strengths with an existing franchisee in a similar but not competitive market area can often be most helpful.

Chain Financial Strength

The financial strength of chains is usually easy to determine because many chains are public corporations. However, an understanding of a particular chain's share of the market and its national or regional strength is needed to determine its impact on a hotel's value. The strength of chains is measured not only in their ability to produce and increase sales but also in their home office services and specializations in such operating areas as front office, housekeeping, food and beverages, engineering, architecture, design, internal control, and purchasing. Also association with a particular chain may facilitate obtaining financing for a hotel based on the chain's previous track record.

Ability to Generate Sales

It must be understood that chains charge a great deal for the use of their name. Therefore, such use has to be an asset that can bring enough additional business to create higher gross sales and net profits after deducting all franchise expenses.

The reservation system of a chain has to be analyzed in terms of its sophistication, the number of reservations it processes, how these reservations are "sold" to prospective guests, and its performance for others who currently own properties associated with the chain. A chain reservation system should be evaluated by its ability to create sales over and above the sales that a comparable independent hotel could realize. Details concerning the chain's market strength on a year-round basis and in particular market segments (for example, families, corporate executives, and price-sensitive travelers) should also be considered.

The best way to learn about a chain and its franchise system is to visit both its home office and individual operations of third-party owners. The comments of owners are especially valuable when the owners' product is located in a market similar to that of the subject property and the facilities are physically comparable. Important concerns are the number of reservations that the chains generate on a monthly basis, seasonal variations, the ratio of chain-generated room nights to total room nights, and the number of room nights denied on the reservation systems because the property was at full capacity.

Obviously, if other members of the reservation group are in the market area of the subject property, one must make sure that they have overflow business available. However, overflow business is rarely the only reason to become associated with a particular brand name. A hotel should be able to attract its own market share due to its location and facilities and not just capture existing markets from those using the same brand name within the area. The franchise affiliation is sought for many reasons, including the security of "brand name" identification, the reservation system, purchasing services, management systems and training, and the facilitation of project financing or investor acquisition (and also as a method to obtain a relatively high stabilized market value for the product).

If a chain produces group sales leads (leads given to individual hotels concerning groups planning to meet in a particular city), this indicates that the chain itself has salespeople on the road and offices throughout the country selling its product. However, it is up to the management of the individual property to make the most effective use of these leads and convert them into sales. Corporate leads and sales are important, as are the local and national advertising programs executed by the national chain. If these are directed for a product similar to the property in question, they can be very helpful in creating consumer awareness and perceptions of quality.

EVALUATION OF A MANAGING AGENT

Organization

Evaluating a managing agent is fairly straightforward. The counselor should make sure that the agent has an organization that includes at least a director of operations and regional directors and that it has management systems such as those required to market, control, and train as well as a meaningful operations manual. One should be certain that the agent has sufficient strength to assemble the management team needed for a hotel and is capable of directing that team.

It may not be necessary to have an expensive management agent for a simple 150–300-room motor hotel, but a 1,000–2,000-room convention hotel would be expected to have a full-fledged management agent with a national brand name. The agent organization should be evaluated on the basis of owner needs. Some agents offer full architectural and design services in addition to operational, accounting, and financial specialists. Most agents charge for these specialized services in addition to their standard management fees.

Accounting

The accounting systems of an agent should follow the standard hotel-motel accounting system approved by the hotel community and should give the owner monthly reports by the twentieth of the following month. These reports should incorporate a comparison between actual and budget and that of the same period a year ago and should assure the owner that the "internal control system" is being properly monitored. Although most agents decentralize the accounting function at the hotel level, some agents continue to offer centralized accounting. In either event, the reporting systems should accurately reflect the operation as well as maintain a high degree of control and supervision.

Engineering

Engineering capability refers to a complete system of preventive maintenance and capital project evaluation and implementation. It includes the ability to put together an engineering section in an annual plan that fully analyzes the physical condition of a property, indicates improvements categorized as either "desirable" or "necessary," and provides a cost-benefit analysis of those improvements that have revenue or cost impact. Once the owner decides to implement various projects, the engineering personnel should be able to bid them out and monitor their implementation. Engineering costs, whether of a capital or repair nature, should relate to a flow of income, both present and future.

Marketing

Marketing, obviously, is one of the key ingredients for hotels as for retail businesses. A detailed marketing plan setting forth strategies and goals is essential to the orderly monitoring of the marketing program's cost effectiveness. Marketing strategy details should be clearly set forth and made part of the annual plan used by the agent and the owner. Marketing supervision of on-premise personnel is needed, for cost-effective marketing is the result of the combined efforts of the people at the hotel who sell the hotel and of the management agent that supervises these people and gives them the necessary tools to make their program succeed.

Systems, Procedures, Controls

Systems, procedures, and controls differ greatly among managing agents. However, management agents that handle numerous "brand name affiliations" (franchised properties) and independents usually have designed systems to include procedures and controls that are adaptable to most properties and that allow the on-premise management team to effectively run the individual property, while also allowing the agent's home office and regional directors to monitor progress.

Evaluating a hotel investment, whether it be existing or proposed, is a detailed and time-consuming process. Reliance on operating statements alone can be misleading because the hotel industry historically has been very volatile and because each facility has its particular characteristics and market mix. Knowledge of the past operating history, current and future market supply and demand conditions, physical facilities and their condition, management, franchise and chain strengths, and many other factors is necessary to a proper hospitality industry investment evaluation.

SELECTED REFERENCES

BRENER, STEPHEN W.   "Factors Involved in a Motel's Site Survey." *Valuation*, 1969 pp. 9-16.

BRENER, STEPHEN W.   "Management Contract." *Resort Management*, May 1972, p. 8.

EYSTER, JAMES,   *The Negotiation and Administration of Hotel Management Contracts.* Ithaca, N. Y. School of Hotel Administration, Cornell University 1977.

BRENER, STEPHEN W.   "Room at the Top" *Forbes Magazine*, March 1984.

BRENER, STEPHEN W.   "Repositioning and Marketing a Transient Lodging Property" *Journal of Property Management*, November/December 1984.

CHAPTER THIRTEEN
COUNSELING THE
OFFICE BUILDING CLIENT

Office building counseling has expanded to new horizons within the past decade. In the past office building clients were interested in the bottom line: Will the income generated from the project cover the expenses and debt service and give the investor the required return? Today these clients are much more sophisticated. Among the important concerns of the office building counselor are such things as supply and demand for office space, historical and current absorption levels, rental rates, expense escalation provisions, design aspects of the building, and the ability of the building to compete successfully in its market. Of equal concern is the overall project feasibility.

This chapter will consider the different types of office building counseling.

FUNCTIONAL TYPES OF
OFFICE BUILDINGS

Basically, there are four functional types of office buildings: single-tenant, multi-tenant, and special use occupancies and the condominium office building.

Single-Tenant Buildings

The single-tenant office building generally has a large floor plate (the gross square footage of the floor area) of 20,000 square feet to 60,000 square feet. Historically, these buildings have been rented on a rentable area basis. The Building Owners and Managers Association International has promulgated a uniform method of measuring areas within office buildings. This method, known as the American National Standard, defines *rentable areas* as

> the area measured to the inside finish of permanent outer building walls, or from the glass line where at least 50% of the outer building wall is glass. Rentable area shall include all areas within outside walls, less stairs, elevator shafts, flues, pipe shafts, vertical ducts, air-conditioning rooms, fan rooms, janitor closets, electrical closets, and other such rooms not actually available to the tenant for his furnishings and personnel, and their enclosing walls. Toilet rooms within and exclusively serving only that floor shall be included in rentable area. No deductions are made for columns and projections necessary to the building.[1]

The single-tenant office building has a much higher efficiency ratio (rentable area to gross building area) than do other types of office buildings. This is because they have larger floor plates, greater bay depth (the distance from the central core to the outside walls), less partitioning, and more efficient use of building cores.

The single-tenant office building has the following advantages:

More rentable area per floor (greater efficiency)
The greater creditworthiness and the greater income security offered by larger tenants
Less tenant turnover and loss of income from vacancies, leasing commissions, and remodeling expenses
Ease of management
Enhanced mortgageability

Multitenant Buildings

The multitenant office building generally has a floor plate of 10,000 square feet to 24,000 square feet. Historically, such buildings have been leased on a usable area basis. *Usable area* is defined as

> the area measured to the inside finish of permanent outer building walls, or to the glass line if at least 50% of the outer building wall is glass, to the office side of corridors and/or other permanent partitions, and to the center of partitions that separate the premises from adjoining rentable areas. No deductions are made for columns and projections necessary to the building.[2]

Increasingly, multitenant building managers have been getting away from the usable area method of space calculation in an attempt to "recapture" the rental value of certain areas in the building that are common to all tenants but are not contained

[1]Building Owners and Managers Association, American National Standard, Z65.1–1980.
[2]Ibid.

within the specific area of an individual office suite. In California, this is known as a "load factor."

This can be accomplished in a number of ways. One common method is to simply calculate both the rentable area and the usable area of the building and to divide the usable area into the rentable area to obtain a factor that can be applied to each office suite to determine its rentable area equivalent. This conversion factor can be applied either to the individual suite's area or rental rate to effect the desired adjustment.

In different parts of the country, different methods are used for measuring rentable areas. However, the definition used earlier is in most common use in New York City. For example, the main floor common areas (entrance foyer, elevator lobbies, mail rooms, etc.) are also allocated, pro rata, to the building's rentable area.

The multitenant office building has the greatest necessity, and usually the best opportunity, to capitalize on architectural design. The multitenant office building has the following advantages over the single-tenant office building:

> Higher rental rates can generally be charged.
>
> The tenants' leases do not all expire at the same time.
>
> The leases are generally shorter term and therefore leave a better ability to respond to inflation.

FIGURE 13–1   Anaconda Tower, a 40-story office building located in the Denver central business district. This 820,000-square-foot building has 596,999 square feet of usable area. The developer, Oxford Ansco Development Company, completed the building in 1978. Photo courtesy of Landis Aerial Photo, Englewood, Colorado.

Special Use Buildings

The special use office building generally commands a higher rental rate per square foot than other office buildings in the same area. This is due to higher construction and operating costs. The most common type of special use building is the medical-dental office building.

The construction costs are typically higher because of the additional cost of special purpose facilities and equipment. The operating costs may be higher for a variety of reasons:

Typical six-day operation of the building

Higher cleaning costs

Higher plumbing and electrical maintenance because of additional fixtures

Higher building maintenance due to greater number of visitors or clients entering the building

Substantial alterations of individual suites for new tenants

Higher personnel loads (occupants/square foot)

The investor should be aware of the higher risk inherent in special use office buildings. When a doctor ceases his practice, for instance, the investor runs the risk that the doctor's operation may also cease, causing increased leasing expenses. In a commercial operation, however, the demise or retirement of a member of a firm does not usually interrupt the operation of the firm.

Condominium Buildings

Condominium ownership of office buildings comprises the smallest market of the four types discussed in this chapter. While seemingly popular during the late 1970s and early 1980s, the acceptance and use of condominium office buildings has not been widely embraced by the development community recently.

In general, the occupant of an office condominium has fee simple ownership of the office space. The corridors, elevators, lobby, grounds and parking areas are considered common areas. Each owner pays a fee to the association to cover the expenses and management of the building.

Several factors have made the office condominium attractive to the small businessperson:

1. Lenders recognized that office condominiums were another means of real estate ownership and subsequently committed long-term financing to the purchaser of such property.
2. The Economic Tax Recovery Act of 1981 allowed condominium owners to recover the cost of their asset over a 15 year period, which is ordinarily before the mortgage is paid off.
3. Office condominiums could be used as a hedge against inflation.
4. All of the advantages of investment real estate are available to the condominium owner.

There are some disadvantages with the condominium alternative:

1. The capital investment required may inhibit the owner's ability to expand their business operations.

2. Ownership responsibilities are generally more time consuming than the responsibilities of tenant positions relative to space occupancy requirements.
3. Ownership tends to be a comparatively longer-term commitment than leasing, and may limit flexibility relative to expansion or relocation requirements.
4. Recent changes in the tax code may prove to be a deterrent regarding condominium office ownership when compared to leasing.

THE OFFICE LEASE

A lease is a conveyance of an interest in a property for consideration. It is very important for the lessor and lessee to be aware of the essential elements of an office lease. An office lease should include:

> The date of the lease
> The names of the lessor and lessee
> The description and location of the premises
> The area in square feet
> The amount of consideration (rental rate)
> The method of escalating the base rent (Consumer Price Index adjustment, etc.)
> The lessor's obligations
> The lessee's obligations
> The rights of the parties in the event of casualty loss, condemnation, or negligence
> The rights of the parties in the event of default
> How and where notices shall be served
> Subordination provisions
> A "successor" clause
> Special clauses (for example, subletting, assignment, attornment, and renewal options)
> Signature of the lessor and lessee

A well-written office lease should be clear and concise. The lessor and the lessee should fully understand the terms of the lease. If litigation occurs, the courts should easily see the elements of the lease and be able to make a judgment.

The lessor should be aware of the following pitfalls when preparing an office lease:

> Describing the use that the lessee may make of the premises as "general office purposes"—the description should be more specific.
> Failing to provide that improvements, including those made by the lessee, belong to the lessor
> Failing to document work to be done and by whom
> Agreeing to the lessee's request that the lessor may unreasonably withhold consent to or approval of all matters in the lease that require the lessor's approval or consent
> Failing to place a time and use limit on the lessee's consumption of utilities
> Failing to take into consideration the fact that the lessee's special use may increase the lessor's maintenance or insurance costs

Giving the lessee an "exclusive" (it is immaterial whether or not this is an unconstitutional restraint of trade)

Providing for an abatement of rent if the lessor is not covered by insurance

Giving the lessee the unrestricted right to assign or sublet

Not restricting the rights of the lessee to make improvements or alterations

Failing to provide for rental escalations

Failing to define the exact basis for determining rental rates during a renewal period

Granting the lessee broad expansion privileges or rights of first refusal on adjacent space

Leasing Office Space in an Inflationary Economy

In an inflationary economy where office space is in short supply, owners should try to maintain a flexible position. Long-term leases should contain provisions that will permit the escalation of rental rates and the pass-through of expenses. There should be a clause that requires the lessee to offer space to the lessor before subletting or that allows the "profit" from subletting to flow to the lessor. The lessor should avoid the use of a clause that requires the lessee to obtain the lessor's consent before subletting but that also provides "which consent shall not be unreasonably withheld." If the lessee can present a sublessee with a good background and excellent references, the lessor's refusal can be called "unreasonable."

Future Payment Clauses in Leases

Leases containing rent escalation clauses are used by lessors to protect themselves against the erosion of the dollar. In a soft rental market they can also be used as an incentive for a prospective lessee. A lease written for a relatively low initial rental rate that escalates in the future may be currently attractive to a new tenant.

Most rent escalation clauses are dominated by two methods: the formula method and the reevaluation method. The formula method for escalation clauses is generally based on the Porter's Wage Index, the Consumer Price Index, or a defined increase by time period.

Porter's Wage Index. The Porter's Wage Index is an index developed by the Building Service Employees Union, AFL-CIO. The union negotiates with the Realty Advisory Board on Labor Relations, which is a landlord's trade association in New York City. The maintenance contract negotiated between these two parties is observed by most landlords in New York City, so the contract produces a formula or index that reflects maintenance costs related to real estate. In essence, the Porter Wage Index is directly related to the increases in wages to the workers who maintain and operate office buildings. Under this formula, generally for every increase of 0.01 cent per hour in the hourly wage rate index, the rental rate is increased by 0.015 cent to 0.0175 cent per square foot per year.

Consumer Price Index.   The Consumer Price Index formula is a means of basing adjustments in the rental rate on the performance of the economy in general. Usually the year the lease is signed becomes the base year. The CPI for that year is noted, and any increase in the CPI is directly applied to the base rent. Most leases specify that decreases in the CPI can never reduce the rental below its base amount. Usually the CPI adjustment is made on an annual or semiannual basis. Some leases stipulate that the base rent is to be adjusted at 100 percent of the CPI increase; other leases specify adjustments at a smaller percentage.

Step-up formula (defined escalations).   This formula provides for an increase in the base rent in a defined amount at specified intervals. It may be used to compensate the lessor for predicted increases in expenses or erosion in the value of the income stream from inflation. It may also be used as an inducement for a lessee who is starting a new business and can afford only a small rental initially.

In a soft office market the step-up lease can be used to undercut existing rental rates. The lessor offers an initial rental rate that is lower than other rates in the area. This lures tenants away from other buildings. Actually, however, over the life of the lease the rental rate, which is raised annually, may equal the average rental rate charged in comparable buildings.

Reevaluation method.   Under this method at specified periods of time the rental rate for the property is increased on a fair market rental value basis. The new rental rate may be fixed on the basis of the appraised market value of the land and improvements, at a defined or to be determined rental rate; or on the basis of the rental value of the area occupied by the tenant, as determined by market comparison. This task is generally handled by an MAI (Member, Appraisal Institute).

Reimbursement Provisions

In addition to being able to use various methods for escalating base rent, the lessor can make use of various reimbursement provisions to cover increases in operating expenses. Such reimbursement provisions are of critical importance in ensuring that there is no erosion in the net rental income stream.

Typical operating expense provisions in office building leases fall into two categories: (1) the direct pass-through, on a pro rata basis, of any operating expense increases over the operating expenses for the base year of the lease or (2) operating expense increases over a defined figure specified in the lease.

When defining escalations, it is preferable not to list the various expense items. Instead, a definition of operating costs should be inserted, such as "Operating costs shall be deemed to mean all costs which for federal tax purposes may be expended rather than capitalized." This avoids arguments with tenants about what should or should not be included. A clause should also be inserted that gives the lessor the right to collect from the lessee any sales or gross receipts taxes levied as a result of the collection of rent.

In an attempt to simplify the various lease provisions on operating expense increases and to avoid the danger of misinterpretation of expense categories, many lessors are now using net leases (sometimes referred to as pure net or triple net leases). In this form of lease, the base rent is lower than the base rent in comparable gross leases that include an allowance for operating expenses. Any expenses of operating the building are then the obligation of the lessee on a pro rata basis.

The most important step in drafting a lease is to make sure that it is clear, concise, and complete. If this is done, there will be very small chance of any misunderstandings between the lessor and the lessee.

LEASE OPTIONS

A lease option is a means by which the optionor grants for consideration to the optionee the exclusive right to lease a specified space at a specified price for a specified period of time.

Remember the adage that options are for "takers" and not for "givers." If the option does not benefit the taker, he will not exercise it; but if the option does benefit the taker, he will exercise it. Either way, the giver is at a disadvantage. Since the granting of options provides a one-way benefit that may have no reciprocal advantage to the optionor, the counselor should advise that options be carefully scrutinized. The property owner's ability to bargain on a lease option is governed by market conditions. It may be desirable to grant options in order to secure the tenant in a soft market or to ensure that the owner receives sufficient compensation for doing so.

The following are some disadvantages of options:

1. Options for renewal and expansion hinder the lessor's planning for the building.

2. Options hamper the development of an effective public relations–oriented leasing policy. Prospective tenants do not care to sign leases, even for five years, for space that may be taken away from them if the option holder exercises his expansion option.

3. Assuming that the tenants are generally responsible, options create a discrimination problem. Granting more options to more tenants would not solve the problem; on the contrary, it would only create a state of uncertainty and chaos.

4. The owner's control over the building is weakened by tying up merchandise—office space—that may or may not be sold at some future date at prices that cannot be properly established years in advance. Future negotiation of rents is not the answer to a present one-way commitment whereby the tenant has nothing to lose and everything to gain. The optionor simply ties up space "that should be left available" for future choice.

If an option must be granted, it should be negotiated according to the following principles:

The right to lease additional space in the future should apply to space on the same floor or, if possible, a contiguous floor.

The lessee should give at least six months' written advance notice of its intent to exercise the option. If large spaces are involved, one year's notice should be required.

The lease expiration date of the optioned space must coincide with that of the original lease.

The quantity of the space to be made available should be stated as a range—for example, "at least 5,000 but no more than 7,000 square feet."

The rental rate to be paid should be specified, and this should be qualified by stating that the rental rate will be that rate or the then prevailing rate for similar space in the building, whichever is greater.

The expansion space should be leased on an as is basis, with the lessee paying for all tenant finish. This is especially important for the lessor where the optioned space has been previously finished and occupied.

The lessee being granted the option must not be in default on the original lease when the additional space is taken.

Care must be taken to ensure that unusable modules of space are not left by expansion options.

A long series of consecutive options should be avoided. These only further complicate the lessor's ability to make long-term plans for the building.

Since an option to lease expansion space may also entail a renewal of the original lease, the preceding principles should also be applied to the renewal.

MARKET ANALYSIS FOR PROSPECTIVE OFFICE BUILDINGS

The need for comprehensive and accurate market studies dealing with office space has never been greater. Many cities in the United States are the scene of unprecedented office building construction. Some are experiencing boom levels of construction activity. There is potential for a "bust" even greater than the one that occurred in 1974–75. The real estate counselor must meet the challenge of accurately assessing the factors that drive demand in his or her region. Sophisticated developers and major tenants recognize the need for expert counsel; lenders are demanding it.

How does one approach the problem of preparing an office market study? The primary objective is to define a specific market or submarket area for study and to place the supply and demand characteristics for office space in that study area in proper perspective over the forecast period. Each study area should be closely analyzed for the individual factors affecting its future growth potential and that of competing areas.

A proper and comprehensive market study should address the following questions:

What is the right amount of office space?
How should the entry of a building into the marketplace be timed?

At what annual rate will the proposed supply be absorbed?

How long will it take for the entire proposed supply to be absorbed?

How effectively can a specific building compete for occupancy?

How long will it take for a specific building to achieve stabilized occupancy?

Office market studies generally require an analysis and investigation of seven general areas:

The current balance between supply and demand

The magnitude of the proposed supply over the projection period

The amount of office demand over the projection period

The relationship between supply and demand for each year of the projection period

The average occupancy rate in competitive office space for each year of the projection period

The time required to absorb all existing vacant office space, all office space under construction, and all proposed office space

The competitive position of each building that will be vying for tenants over the projection period

These areas of investigation can be organized into four sections of a report under the following general categories:

1. Inventory and analysis of competitive office space supply
2. Analysis of office space demand
3. Absorption rate conclusions
4. Application of the findings to a specific location and property

Data in these areas must be assiduously collected and thoughtfully analyzed, and the final opinions must be expressed clearly and concisely. The client then can apply this information to his building and obtain an accurate understanding of the probable performance of his investment.

The details of each step and the methodology to be employed are explained below.

Inventory and Analysis of Competitive Office Space Supply

The first step is to identify the current condition of the market. This requires a comprehensive survey and inventory of both existing and proposed buildings. Also, comparing the current and near-future projected growth rates with the growth rate of office space additions in recent years allows current activity to be brought into historical perspective.

Supply analysis methodology. Not all of the office supply is equally competitive. For this reason, it is necessary to classify the existing office supply into groupings.

What groupings should be used will depend on the specific product type that is the subject of the market study and on the unique characteristics of the study area. The counselor's job is to properly identify these groupings.

The following groupings are useful for the analysis of high-rise office buildings in a central business district:

Group I: Modern high-rise buildings constructed from 1950 to 1970
Group II: Modern high-rise buildings completed from 1970 through the date of the survey
Group III: Major office buildings that are under construction or have been proposed

Buildings constructed prior to 1950, which, for the most part, are pre–World War II buildings, are generally considered to be noncompetitive and are therefore not included in the survey. However, they should be included in the tabulation of the total inventory. The special characteristics of the study area should be considered carefully at this stage. Some older buildings may be very competitive with newer buildings due to remodeling or historic significance.

Each building of each group should be analyzed on a chart on the following basis:

1. Date of building completion
2. Gross building area
3. Total leaseable area
4. Number of stories
5. Percentage occupied as of survey date
6. Space available as of survey date
7. Rental rates
8. Parking (number and rental rate)
9. Comments

The "Comments" heading concerns general information about the building, explaining such features as unusual characteristics, expense "stop" provisions, rental escalation provisions, degree of preleasing for buildings under construction and proposed buildings, and major tenant identification.

The buildings included in the Group I category should comprise all of the major high-rise office buildings in the study area that were constructed between 1950 and 1970. It is important to extend the survey to include these buildings because space in them is competitive with space in the high-rise office buildings constructed subsequent to 1970.

There is probably, however, a rental differential between the buildings in Group I and the buildings in Groups II and III. Thus, any measurable amount of vacant space within the Group I buildings would have an effect on the absorption rate in the new and proposed buildings.

The buildings in the Group II category constitute the most important sector of the supply analysis because their condition of occupancy and level of rental achievement are most indicative of the probable performance of the proposed buildings.

The Group III buildings include all of the buildings currently under construction or currently proposed for construction. It is important to obtain accurate estimates of the expected date of completion of these buildings, and special effort must be expended to ensure the most inclusive information possible.

The most difficult task that confronts the counselor is separating casual announcements of proposed buildings from the buildings that will actually be constructed. This determination is critical to the validity of the projection. In-depth investigation and great care must be exercised in this regard.

Analysis of Office Space Demand

The next step is to quantify the effective demand for office space in the study area over the projection period. The factors that are generally considered to have an effect on demand for office space are

1. Population changes
2. Employment trends
3. Local and national economic factors
4. Actual historical levels and trends of office space absorption
5. Special community factors

Population changes.   The population growth and demographic characteristics of an area are pertinent to the demand for office space because it is a well-supported general rule that the larger a city, the more office space per capita it contains. Consequently, the historical and projected population changes of an area can be used to support projections of future office space demand.

Employment trends.   The rate of growth in employment has a considerable effect on the amount of office space within an area and is a more direct indicator of office space demand than is the more general population growth characteristic. The composition of the work force also has a direct effect on office space demand. A very high percentage of the work force of nonindustrial cities is employed in office space. The number of employees has a smaller impact on office space demand in industrial cities than in nonindustrial cities.

Employment growth projections for specific geographic areas are usually available from local planning offices. Employment in office-intensive industries combined with the use of office worker ratios can be used to yield office employment estimates. These figures can then be used to estimate office space demand by application of ratios on office space per employee. A word of caution: the ratios must be proved to be valid for the specific study area.

National and local economic factors. The status of current and projected general national economic factors, both actual and perceived, can have a substantial effect on the demand for office space. Changes in the national economy bring about changes in the local economy.

These economic factors are general indicators and do not translate directly into estimates of demand for office space. It is important, however, to consider the trend, direction, and strength of national and local economic forecasts to determine whether they are consonant with specific projections of office space demand. A mismatch could indicate an erroneous demand projection or identify a trend that, being counter to other projections, is likely to represent a special purpose or short-lived demand.

Each locale should be scrutinized for the economic factors that influence its growth. For example, the central business district of Denver is unique because of the degree to which it dominates its surrounding region. As the largest city within a 600-mile radius, Denver is the distribution center and financial hub for the entire Rocky Mountain Region.

Special community factors. In any specific area special factors that create demand should be taken into consideration. These could include

1. The nature and composition of the existing economic base
2. Regional in-migration modes
3. The emergence of a new industry or unusual expansion of an old industry
4. Exceptional specialized facilities

Growth is dramatically affected by the presence of such operations as corporate headquarters, medical centers, recreational facilities, specialized industries, and governmental offices. Such operations generate support industries and increase employment. Technological changes in existing industries can also influence the type of employment in an area.

Each city should be analyzed carefully to identify catalysts of growth or decline that may be indigenous to the area.

Absorption Rate Conclusion

The purpose of this section of the study is to analyze and process into general absorption rate estimates the data obtained in the supply and demand sections of the study.

The principal tool in projecting absorption rates is an analysis of historical absorption rates. Any analysis of historical absorption rates must fully account for the fact that the forces which are currently driving office space demand may be substantially different from the forces which historically provided impetus to office space demand in the study area. For this reason, a detailed analysis of the factors that create demand for office space is pursued.

Absorption is defined to occur when space is actually occupied, not when preleasing has occurred. The date of absorption is the year in which occupancy actually occurred. In the case of some of the smaller buildings, for which historical detailed information may not be available, absorption can be averaged over a period of years or lumped into the year in which the major portion of the space was occupied. Where the necessary data are available, absorption should be logged in the period when the space was actually occupied.

Other factors that influence the absorption rate are:

1. *Space vacated by tenants moving to other quarters.*   If the occupancy rate in existing competitive buildings is essentially 100 percent, the vacated space has been reabsorbed within the time period under study. Therefore, the measure of space absorbed in new buildings is equivalent to true absorption.

If the occupancy rate in existing buildings is not 100 percent, an adjustment for vacancies must be made.

2. *Demolitions.*   The counselor is required to identify true net absorption figures when aggregating historical data. For this reason, absorption figures must be adjusted downward by the amount of office space that has been demolished, converted to other uses, or otherwise removed from the study area.

Unless there are unusual circumstances, space in demolished office buildings is generally found to be noncompetitive, so it may not be worthwhile to make adjustments to absorption figures for this item if its quantity is nominal.

3. *Demand as a function of supply.*   It is important to consider the available supply, as well as the demand, when analyzing absorption.

Sporadic historical absorption rates may be attributable to a mismatch between supply and demand. An unusually high absorption rate in one year may be the result of a pent-up demand from a previous time period and not a true reflection of demand for that year. Conversely, a low absorption rate in one year may be the result of excessive supply in that year rather than low demand.

A meaningful interpretation of historical absorption rates requires an understanding of changes in the factors that have created demand for new office space and of the effect that adequate supply of office space has on absorption. Many statistical tools for processing historical data into estimates of future performance are available to the forecaster. If, however, the factors that are currently creating demand are different from the factors that historically created demand, and if those differences are not accounted for, the projections will be inaccurate. Therefore, a simplistic averaging or straight-line projection of historical absorption can be dangerous and must be tempered by judgment.

The absorption rate figure obtained by examining historical data is a helpful base from which to understand how the market is likely to react over the projection period. What the characteristics of the local office market are likely to be in the next few years is a question that must be answered. Another question that must be answered is how those characteristics will be affected by the availability of an uninterrupted supply of modern, attractive, first-class office space.

Absorption can be stimulated by the availability of such a supply because

1. Major companies contemplating relocation and requiring large quantities of contiguous space will not be lost by default because of the lack of a competitive supply of first-class space.
2. The physical attractiveness and full complement of amenities available in modern buildings encourage tenants to upgrade and expand their facilities.
3. The higher volume of aggressive promotion by developers and leasing agents promoting new buildings is effective.

The foregoing discussion of historical absorption rates, the factors that create demand, and the effect of supply on absorption rates would be incomplete without the consideration of the following collateral items:

1. *Did the absorption rates occur because of rental concessions?*   In order to answer this question, it is necessary to know whether rental rate concessions are being made in order to achieve leasing. This requires an analysis of the performance of rental rates over a period of time.

The data should be secured for the earliest dates obtainable, and the trend of rental rate increases must be analyzed. If the conclusion is that absorption has occurred without rental rate concessions, additional insight into the strength of the demand is provided. It most likely indicates that developers have been able to offset increased construction costs through higher rental rates. If it appears that concessions have been made, the figures reflect a softness in demand or an excessive supply.

In addition to analyzing historical rental rate increases, the prudent counselor will interview developers and leasing agents of under-construction and newly completed office buildings to determine whether scheduled economic rentals are being obtained. In a soft office market the published rental schedule for an office building may remain unchanged but the effective rental rate being obtained may actually be substantially less due to concessions that are made in other aspects of the lease transaction such as

1. Increased tenant improvement allowances
2. Periods of free rent
3. Generous (high) expense "stop" provisions
4. Deletion of escalation provisions
5. Assumption of tenants' lease obligations in other buildings

2. *What effect will competition from other areas have on absorption rates in the study area?*   Although the presence of an adequate supply of office space within the study area enhances office space absorption rates, an abundance of office space in competitive locations could have an adverse impact on absorption rates. The degree of trade-off between different areas must be assessed to measure the effect of the alternative locations. To accomplish this, we must understand the condition of the marketplace for office space in other areas that compete with the study area.

When the data relative to office markets outside the study area have been accumulated and analyzed, the following questions should be asked:

1. Is there a difference between rental increases in the study area and rental increases in the competing locations?
2. Is there a difference between the availability of office space in the competing areas now, or will there be in the future, as compared with the past?
3. If rental rates are escalating in one area, what is the status of supply in the other areas?
4. Has the impact of the competing areas been fully established?
5. Is the study area experiencing a period of revitalization or decline?
6. What is the pattern in the relationship between the study area and the competing areas?

Generally, the decision to locate in one office submarket versus another is dependent on many criteria, a good portion of which are highly subjective. However, the majority of companies that opt to locate in the higher-priced or prestige area are committed to that location and are not potential users for the alternative location. There is, of course, some trade-off between areas. The existence of a substantial supply of office space in the suburbs generally has some effect on the demand for central business district office space; there is generally a price advantage for suburban space over CBD office space, and suburban parking may be provided free.

FIGURE 13–2   Citicorp Building in New York City. Photograph by Martin Barkan, courtesy of James Felt Realty Services, New York, New York.

If there was at all times an abundant supply of competing space, then the historical absorption rates demonstrated for the study area include the effect of the competing office space supply and are therefore "net" absorption rates. If there is a substantial change in the ability of one submarket to compete with another, the counselor must consider this change when making absorption rate projections.

Statistical applications of data to predict future performance. In order to bring estimates of absorption into sharper focus, statistical applications of historical data may be utilized. Linear and curvilinear regression analyses can be applied to the historical data in order to make projections.

Linear regression is a statistical tool for projecting historical information into the near future. It is a system for mathematically drawing a straight line graphed through a series of known historical data points that may be extended to forecast future observations.

In applying this method of forecasting, it should be noted that atypically high or low observations in the historical data series may unreasonably distort the forecast. Such atypical observations may be judgmentally eliminated from the series in order to produce a more reasonable resulting forecast.

For nonlinear growth phenomena, several curve-fitting functions are available to the analyst. These result in growth projections that would be graphed as a curved line.

In addition, an extensive body of knowledge is applicable to multiple regression forecasting of cycles and various other forecasting situations.

It is important to select the forecasting technique that is most applicable to the problem being solved. Judgment is almost always necessary because changes in real estate markets often will not fit any of the theoretical curves.

Forecasting is most accurate within the limits of the spread of the smallest to the largest time variant. Therefore, forecasting five years into the future is not reasonable if only four years of past experience are available, whereas a three- to five-year forecast may be very reasonable with ten to twelve years of reliable past data.

In order to gain more insight into probable absorption rates in the near-term future, extensive interviews should be conducted with the agents responsible for the major portion of the leasing that has occurred in the study area. These interviews provide insight into current levels of interest and activity in office space leasing and provide the leasing agents' prognoses for the future.

The final conclusion is a synthesis of all the accumulated and properly analyzed data. It should be expressed as a range of demand estimates for each year.

Application of the Findings to the Subject Area

The next step in the study is to aggregate the potential supply of new office space that will be added to the study area during each year of the forecast period.

It is now possible to contrast or compare the available supply figures, by year, with the estimates of yearly absorption.

The data should be summarized in chart form and should include

1. Established data for the base year
2. Identification of all new office buildings that are to be added to the inventory over the projection period
3. An estimate of the year of completion of each building
4. The total amount of leasable space that will be added each year
5. The cumulative total of the leasable space contained in all buildings
6. The annual and cumulative estimated absorption rates for each year (low and high estimates)
7. The unabsorbed space remaining at the end of each year and cumulatively for the time periods (low and high estimates)
8. The average occupancy in new space for each time period

Although absorption rate estimates may be established, the actual absorption that will occur in any particular year will vary depending on the available supply in that year and on the carry-over of unabsorbed demand from previous years.

The unabsorbed space at the end of each period is calculated by subtracting the estimated absorption per year from the total supply that will be added for each year. This total is expressed cumulatively over the projection period.

The "average occupancy in new space" figure is computed by contrasting the average unabsorbed space at the end of each year (cumulative) with the cumulative available new supply each year. This statistic does not relate to the specific performance of any individual building. It is, however, an indication of what the average occupancy rate might be at that point in time if all buildings were able to compete equally for new tenants. This, of course, is generally not the case. Nevertheless, the "average occupancy in new space" figure is a data point that is useful in predicting the performance of a specific building based on differences in location, quality of construction and design, and leasing expertise.

Office market study conclusions.   Some of the principal conclusions that can be derived from an office market study are as follows:

1. The quantity of the existing and new supply, assuming that all proposed buildings are constructed
2. The current level of demand for office space in the study area
3. The magnitude of historical demand
4. The estimated annual absorption rate over the projection period
5. Whether absorption has occurred at economic rental rates or whether rental concessions have been required
6. Whether or not the availability of office space in competing locations will adversely affect the projected absorption rates for the study area
7. Whether there are periods of mismatch between supply and demand for new buildings

8. The year that total effective absorption of all space in new buildings is likely to occur
9. The prognosis for a specific development project

The implications and value of these conclusions should be apparent to all real estate professionals. The office market study provides a basis for thoughtful, cogent decision making.

TYPES OF OFFICE MARKETS

There are two basic types of office markets: strong markets and soft markets. Historically, a strong office market has been a one-tiered market. In such a market the developer who constructs a building leases it directly to tenants and any space that the tenants may vacate is quickly reabsorbed by the expansion needs of other tenants in the same building or the same market area.

A soft market results from a reduction in demand or an increase in office space supply that may be excessive relative to the level of demand. During a period of soft demand there is a four-tiered market. The tiers are as follows:

1. A tenant moves into new space in the same market area and offers its old space for sublease, creating new supply.
2. With expansion in mind, a tenant leases more space than is needed and has a portion of the space available for sublease.
3. A tenant migrates to new space outside the metropolitan area.
4. A tenant migrates to new space in a different submarket area.

The four-tiered market results in the following:

1. Lower market rents—hardest hit are the most recently completed buildings and the buildings under construction
2. Less demand for prime space
3. Greater effects on fringe locations than on central locations
4. A new underground rental market created by the substantial amount of subleased space
5. Concessions—free rent, relaxed escalation clauses and expense reimbursements, enhanced tenant remodeling allowances, and so on
6. Curtailment or postponement of new development plans

SUBJECTIVE ELEMENTS OF THE OFFICE MARKET STUDY

An often overlooked aspect of the office market study is the evaluation of subjective factors that distinguish various office submarkets within a metropolitan area from one another. This type of analysis may be especially pertinent for large space users, for example, large companies that will put several operating departments, with various locational needs, under one roof. In such cases, the needs and convenience of employees as well as the needs of the functioning departments are considered. Different weights may be assigned to each of the variables depending on their importance as perceived by the tenant. Alternatively, the variables may not be weighted, so that the various operating departments of the tenant can assign their own weights to them.

The subjective elements that may be included in such an analysis include, but are not limited to, the following:

1. Driving time
2. Public transportation
3. General office support facilities
   a. Restaurants
   b. Hotels
   c. Office service facilities
   d. Hospitals
   e. Personal convenience facilities
4. Airports
5. Parking
6. Cost of office occupancy
7. Safety
8. Physical environment

The above-listed elements may be analyzed on a purely subjective basis and described narratively in the counseling report, or an attempt may be made to rate each of these items on, say, a ten-point rating scale.

SELECTED REFERENCES

BUILDING OWNERS AND MANAGERS ASSOCIATION INTERNATIONAL. *The Office Building Experience Exchange Report* (annual). Washington, D.C.: BOMA International, 1982.

CLURMAN, DAVID. *The Business Condominium: A New Form of Business Property Ownership*. New York: John Wiley & Sons, Inc., 1983.

FARBER, JOSEPH. "Preparing an Office Space Demand Study and Rate of Absorption Study." In *Office Buildings: Development, Marketing, and Leasing*, pp. 15–22. Chicago: American Society of Real Estate Counselors, 1981.

INSTITUTE OF REAL ESTATE MANAGEMENT. *Income/Expense Analysis: Surburban Office Buildings* (annual). Chicago: IREM.

———— *Managing the Office Building*. Chicago: IREM, 1981.

McMAHAN, JOHN. *Property Development: Effective Decision Making in Uncertain Times*. New York: McGraw-Hill Book Company, 1976.

NATIONAL ASSOCIATION OF INDUSTRIAL & OFFICE PARKS. *The Development of Speculative Buildings*. Arlington, Va.: National Association of Industrial & Office Parks, 1980.

URBAN LAND INSTITUTE. *Office Development Handbook*. Washington, D.C.: Urban Land Institute, 1982.

CHAPTER FOURTEEN
COMMERCIAL PROPERTY
COUNSELING

Commercial properties are defined as properties where (1) things are sold (for example, retail stores) and (2) services are rendered (for example, office, restaurants, and service stations). This chapter excludes office buildings since these have already been covered. After discussing the classifications of commercial property, the chapter considers the steps involved in selecting or analyzing commercial sites and how the counselor assists in lease negotiation. Finally, a case study illustrates the counselor's role in commercial property transactions.

CLASSIFICATIONS OF COMMERCIAL PROPERTY

Some definitions of the different classes of commercial property are offered at the outset:

> *Neighborhood center.* Typically has 30,000 to 40,000 square feet. Its anchors will be a drugstore and a small food store, which can be of the 7–11 type. Its trade area will typically be on the order of 3,000 households. Its tenants center will provide goods and services that people want within easy reach. They will go to the neighborhood center to pick up the cleaning, to fill a prescription, or to buy a half gallon of milk.

Community center. Typically has 120,000 to 150,000 square feet. A food store and a drugstore will still be the anchors, but both will be large. In many ways, a community center, often called a convenience center, is an oversized neighborhood center. A community center probably needs a 10,000 household trade area; typically, a two-mile radius is about the maximum. The trade area will consist of several identifiable neighborhoods and will be the neighborhood shopping center for the nearby households.

Regional center. It is possible for a regional center to have 300,000 square feet, but most regional centers have in excess of 500,000 square feet. The major anchor will be one or more department stores. The maximum trade area is a five-mile radius; the center needs 50,000 households. A regional center will often have a food store, a drugstore, laundry and cleaners, and the like in a somewhat separate area on its perimeter. In other words, the regional center may have a community or neighborhood center adjoining it.

Superregional center. Usually has more than 1,000,000 square feet. There will be at least three major department stores with 100,000 square feet each.

The above definitions are intended to be general guidelines. Therefore, one should not be too concerned if a parcel of real estate or a proposed use does not fit these definitions. The seat of a small rural county may easily provide most of the retailing of the entire county. Thus, it is a regional shopping center even though it may only have 50,000 square feet of retail space. The central business district in a city may lose its department stores and become, in effect, a huge neighborhood center for a daytime neighborhood. Small strip commercial developments in older neighborhoods are neighborhood centers without parking. Denver's Colfax Avenue is fifteen miles of almost uninterrupted retail uses, including almost every conceivable commercial (and other) activity. It is basically a series of neighborhood, community, and regional centers with fuzzy trade area boundaries.

STEPS INVOLVED IN SELECTING A NEW COMMERCIAL SITE

The Objective

There are a multitude of reasons for studying retail potential. The counselor may be seeking a site for a given use, a use for a given site, tenants for a given building, or combinations of these. The problem tends to break down into who lives in the trade area and what and how much they buy. In selecting a site for a particular store, the necessary type of prospective consumers is probably known and the task will be to identify them. If a particular site has been selected, this process is reversed. The problem in any event is to determine the number of buyers and to forecast how much money they will probably spend for certain goods or services.

The Local Economy

An urban area will have people who are engaged in the production of goods and services both for local consumption and for export. These goods do not have to be coats or cars. For instance, the "goods" produced by a ski area is recreation that is exportable in the sense that some of the skiers come from outside the area—and bring money into the local economy. A bowling alley, on the other hand, produces recreation that is consumed locally. A bank in a large financial center produces "goods" that are essentially for export, whereas a bank in a small rural town prdocues "goods" primarily for local consumption.

All "goods," either exportable or local, are sensitive to some degree to events elsewhere. The "goods" of Colorado's ski areas may serve as an example. In the 1980–81 season the snow was poor—the Colorado ski areas were unable to get the raw materials necessary to produce their product. In 1981–82 the snow was excellent, but the consumers of the ski areas' product were suffering from unemployment and generally unfavorable economic conditions elsewhere. Detroit competes with imports, rail competes with trucks, skiing competes with other recreation, and so on. They can all fall on hard times.

From an employment point of view, some fields are fairly well insulated against boom-and-bust cycles. High-tech employment tends to keep going in hard times. Information handling is reasonably secure against downturns. Financial services may be reduced, but the reductions will not be traumatic, as they are when manufacturing plants close down completely.

The level of unemployment, the level of education, and the percentages of jobs in various classifications can all assist in depicting the nature of a local economy. There is no cookbook recipe that will replace experienced judgment in this analysis. Perhaps the most important item to remember in analyzing economic conditions is that if they are good they will eventually get worse and that if they are bad they will eventually get better. The question is when and to what extent such changes will occur.

Demographics

Much of what was studied in the local economy will be repeated in the study of a trade area. The level of unemployment, the types of employment, the educational level, and household incomes will all help to reveal the retail potential.

Remember that the analysis must involve more than just numbers. The buying habits of a sport with newly coiffed hair, a crew neck sweater, perfectly straight teeth, and a squash racket in the back of his Mercedes are very different from those of a good ol' boy with a Harley-Davidson belt buckle, a western shirt, and a rifle rack in the back of his pickup truck. Yet the household incomes of both types of consumer *can be, and often are, the same.*

It is possible to generate accurate trade area data by going from door to door and interviewing the occupants. Unless you have a huge staff that includes a mathematician and a year or two to finish the assignment, this approach is unlikely to be feasible. However, there are other, much quicker ways to develop demographic generalizations about your trade area. For instance:

1. Interview local schoolteachers. They are likely to have a pretty good idea regarding the educational level of the parents, the types of jobs the parents have, family activities, and so forth.
2. Underwriters for local savings and loan associations have a feel for the income level of the families moving into an area. Contacts within the S&Ls are fairly typical of the contacts of people in the real estate business.
3. Much can be learned by just driving up and down residential streets. Look for signs of small children (tricycles, big wheels), teenagers (flamed automobiles, well-used basketball courts in the driveways), anything that might tend to tell you who is living there.
4. It may be useful to classify automobiles on the collector streets (do not try this on arterials). The cars that come by will be family, sports, or working-type vehicles (that is, station wagons, Mercedes, or pickup trucks). Note the general age of the drivers. A sample taken during rush hour will yield some idea of white-collar versus blue-collar employment. A midday sample will give something of a profile of the people who are at home during the day.

Census data, information provided by local chambers of commerce, economic studies commissioned by banks, and bank charter studies can all yield helpful information. Asking questions in the area will invariably produce useful results.

Transportation and Access

The transportation system has a tendency to control the trade area and to define how people get around within the trade area. It has different effects on different sizes of retail facilities. An interstate highway will bring people to a regional center; therefore, an interchange can be a good place for this type of shopping center. The same highway will eliminate households from the trade area of a community center by forming a barrier. The community center typically does a higher business volume when it is more centrally located. The location of a retail facility within the transportation system is much more complicated than simply making a traffic count. For instance, a small restaurant might easily be better off next to a commuter rail stop with a nominal number of people afoot every day than it would be on an arterial street with 80,000 vehicles per day passing at 40 miles per hour.

Access to a retail outlet must be perceived as being easy. The word *perceived* is significant here. We see instances of people who go to a regional shopping center, spend a half hour in a traffic jam that makes one wish for the peace and quiet of Iwo Jima, and park far from the store to which they are going. Most of these customers will say that they do this because it is convenient, but they will not go to that much trouble to get to a small retail outlet.

Essentially, the necessary ease of ingress and egress is more or less inversely proportional to the size of the facility. A regional center may be visible for miles;

FIGURE 14–1   Northwoods Mall in Peoria, Illinois. This enclosed mall has a gross building area of nearly 775,000 square feet on a 48-acre site. Note the expressway and arterial street access to the mall. Courtesy Harold J. Carlson Associates, Inc., Mount Prospect, Illinois (managing agents).

a small shop, a fast-food outlet, or a strip store may be visible for only a few moments. In the latter cases, traffic signals, turn lanes, and other devices are needed to make entry convenient.

Ideally, a facility will be easily accessible to four directions of traffic. This is as true for the store at the bus stop as it is for the suburban center. If a neighborhood store is reached by customers on foot, it does not need to be very far away to miss the traffic altogether.

The necessity of easy and short access is to some extent a function of the number of dollars that are likely to be spent by the customer. A person who is buying a car is likely to go to more time and trouble getting to a destination than is a person who is shopping for a loaf of bread.

An appropriate location can be different for each type of retail facility. It should be repeated that there is no cookbook recipe for this type of site selection. Relevant data compiled for this purpose must be analyzed carefully, with the counselor's judgment being a principal ingredient in the selection of a successful site.

Competition

It will always be necessary to know how many other facilities are, or can be, competing with yours within the same trade area. Evaluating the effect of existing competition is fairly straightforward. Judging the impact of potential competition can be more difficult. Potential competition may be found at vacant land zoned for retail, at undeveloped sites, and at badly utilized existing space. The existence of competition is not necessarily detrimental. Frequently, two nearby competing stores each do better than either one would alone. However, a problem arises when there are not enough consumer dollars to support all of the competing businesses. Any trade area has a limited quantity of money available to support drugstores, grocery stores, department stores, or anything else. Most trade areas cannot attract the potential customers unless there are enough conveniently located facilities. As soon as the optimum number of outlets is passed, everybody's sales tend to decline.

If there is no competition and a particular business succeeds, there will soon be competition. Also, if there is vacant ground to be developed, somebody is going to develop it. All vacant or underdeveloped commercial ground represents sources of potential competition.

New retail centers often go after the trade of badly managed competitive facilities. This strategy is fine, but it must be remembered that those facilities can turn their management around and recapture much of their original trade. Generally speaking, a business has a higher likelihood of succeeding when there is enough trade for all merchants.

Recommendations

The counselor's job is not to tell the clients what they want to hear but to tell them the truth. For example, expensive, high-fashion women's clothing will not sell in neighborhoods occupied by people whose predominant employment is in the building trades. Do not make the mistake of thinking that this is intuitively obvious; if it were, there would be no counseling assignment in the first place.

The essence of the study is to present a series of well-founded statements and numbers that your client can use to make decisions. The recommendations can include:

Do not do it at all.
Do not do it here.
Do not do it here now.
Do it now but somewhere else.
Do it here and now, but do it differently.
All is well; go for it.

One hundred pages of real estate buzzwords will not suffice. Clients are entitled to have specific, documented recommendations that are stated briefly and are expressed in a clearly worded manner.

LEASE NEGOTIATIONS

There are some consistencies in tenant negotiations that are worth listing. Prospective tenants have several standard remarks that they usually make. The list includes, but is not limited to, the following:

1. "I don't like your center."
2. "I don't like the location."
3. "I don't like you."
4. "I can't afford the rent."

5. "The rent is cheaper at better locations."
6. "I should not have to pay percentage rents."
7. "I am doing you a favor by considering your facility."
8. "I will provide traffic that will help your center."
9. "Business is terrible anyway, and I really shouldn't be considering another store."

It should be noted that in some cases one or all of the above statements may be true. As is the case in any negotiation, it is best to know which, if any, of them are true *and* which of them the prospective tenant knows to be true. If there *are* cheaper and equal locations, you will have to cut the rent or do without the prospective tenant. If the prospective tenant does not know about the alternatives, you will not have to make as many concessions. If there *are not* cheaper and equal locations but the prospective tenant thinks there are, he or she must be educated.

The counselor must do homework. A lease negotiation is an adversary situation. The better-prepared opponent will have the advantage. The negotiator who fully understands his or her strengths *and* weaknesses will have the advantage. And finally, the negotiator who fully understands the opponent's strengths and weaknesses will have still another advantage.

Tenant Selection

Getting a shopping center fully leased is in many cases easier than keeping it full. If the counselor is convinced that the trade area is wrong for a tenant, the center or building is usually better off without that tenant. A tenant that attracts no traffic, fails in business, and leaves a vacancy can make a whole shopping center look bad. Be wary of fads. Running shoes, tanning centers, and country and western clothes shops may be short-lived. In summary, exercise caution in tenant selection. It is not heroic to fill a building with tenants that will eventually fail.

Percentage Leases

The small specialized shops will usually pay higher percentages. The large stores are the anchor tenants and pay very low percentage rentals, if any. Percentage rentals may vary from 1 percent to 18 percent and often are in the range of 5 percent to 7 percent.

Dollars and Cents of Shopping Centers, published by the Urban Land Institute, contains some good information on the subject of percentage leases. This publication cannot replace localized research, but it provides a starting point in retail counseling.

The base rent in most shopping centers does not usually make the center look too good economically. The overage (percentage of gross sales) collected above the base rent is often the factor that determines whether a center is viable. It must be remembered that the percentages are a means for helping the income of the real estate rise in inflationary times or when sales rise and a means for allowing the merchant some breathing room if sales are less favorable. The percentages are *not* a means for enabling the landlord to get in the tenants' pockets.

Tenant Improvements

The most typical tenant improvement situation has the landlord providing demising walls and the tenant making his own leasehold improvements. The landlord must retain control over improvements; the quality and type of interiors must conform to the image of the center. However, the financial burden of improvements is generally on the tenant.

Most of the tenants (but not most of the square feet) will not have particularly strong financial statements. However, a high proportion of the tenants are likely to sink everything they have into improvements; even though the actual dollars may be small, the commitment is substantial for such tenants. Mom and pop retailers will work extremely hard to protect their investment, and they are often the most productive tenants in a center.

CASE STUDY

It is sometimes difficult to see how a narrative discussion, such as the preceding part of this chapter, relates to an actual study with real income, expenses, and profits or losses. The case presented below—the definition of the problem, the graphics, and so on—is taken directly from a counseling assignment. As with most such assignments, the information available was imperfect, and some analysis was omitted, and perhaps other analysis was unnecessary.

The study property was a shopping center that contained about 800,000 square feet and was built in an excellent location roughly ten years too early. The owners had been perfectly capable of carrying the years of losses, though it had never been their intention to do so. At the time of the study, even though the center showed a positive cash flow, for all practical purposes it had failed. However, it was financed at an interest rate that was then highly desirable. The center was on a ground lease with a fixed term that extended well into the twenty-first century and had no renewal options. There was excess land at the site. The counselors had these six major tasks to perform in this assignment:

1. To find out what was going on within the center at present.
2. To project the future income and expense of the center.
3. To work with agents for the owners in determining how much the center was worth to the owners' portfolio.
4. To identify the logical buyer or buyers.
5. To determine an affordable market price to those buyers. Obviously, if this price equaled or exceeded the amount arrived at in task 3, a sale would probably take place.
6. To assist the agents for the owners in selling the property and closing the sale.

1. Finding out what was going on was not particularly complicated, but it was messy. It required roughly 150 working hours to produce the schedule of tenants, of which part is shown in Figure 14–2. A large proportion of the tenants

FIGURE 14–2 Partial Schedule of Tenants.

TENANT	R	SQUARE FEET	LEASE TERM FROM	TO	RENEWAL OPTIONS
Allen's Shoes	R	3,665	03/10/66	07/31/81	2–5 yrs.
American Family Insurance		759	07/15/66	07/14/76	—
American Loan (AVCO)		1,056	03/01/76	02/28/81	—
Baublemart, Ltd.	R	741	04/01/74	03/31/79	—
Bed and Bath Fashions	R	1,024	08/01/71	07/31/77	—
Benson Optical	R	744	11/01/72	10/31/76	—
Bombay Shop	R	150	07/15/66M	07/14/69	—
Bombay Shop Stg.					
Borg's Childrens Cottage	R	2,004	03/10/76	02/28/86	—
Burke Marketing Research		1,210	09/01/75	08/31/78	1–2 yrs.
Calandra Card & Camera	R	3,234	03/10/66	03/09/76	1–5 yrs.
Carnation Ice Cream	R	4,428	03/09/74	03/09/81	—
Charlie Chan	R	2,400	06/05/76	09/30/79	1–3/1–4 yrs.
Cinderella Shoe Repair	R	512	07/01/73	06/30/78	—
Colo. Lace & Dry Cleaning	R	1,191	12/01/75	11/30/80	—
Conrad's Mademoiselle	R	8,320	03/10/66	03/09/81	1–5 yrs.
Crafty Cook	R	820	06/01/75	05/31/78	1–3 RN
Cricket, Ltd.	R	1,617	03/10/76	03/09/81	—
Crow's Nest	R	1,138	03/01/75	02/28/77	—
Dairy Queen	R	225	08/01/74	07/31/84	—
Dairy Queen					
Dardano's	R	1,536	03/01/66	04/30/79	—
Dave's Villa Tobacco	R	429	11/01/74	10/31/76	—
Dine-Out, Inc. (Forum)	R	17,376	10/15/69	10/14/79	1–10 yrs.
Dine-Out, Inc. (Gladiator)	R	6,164	10/15/69	10/14/79	1–10 yrs.
Double Up	R	1,452	03/10/66	03/09/81	—
El Chico Corporation	R	6,525	08/01/71	07/31/86	2–5 yrs.
Farmers Insurance		272		05/31/76	—
Flagg Shoes	R	1,560	03/10/66	03/09/81	2–5 yrs.
Florsheim Shoes	R	1,139	12/01/69	01/31/85	1–10 yrs.
Florsheim Shoes	R	800	05/01/71	01/31/85	1–10 yrs.
Florsheim Shoes		467			
Fontius Shoes	R	5,456	03/10/66	03/09/86	—
* * *	*	*	*	*	
Walgreen Drug	R	17,305	03/01/66	02/28/95	—
Woolworth	R	53,320	07/21/64	01/31/86	4–5 yrs.
World of Sleep (Red Owl)	R	19,800	03/10/66	03/09/86	—
Wyatt's Cafeteria	R	11,554	03/10/66	03/09/86	4–5 yrs.
Zale Jewelry	R	1,914	03/10/66	03/09/81	2–5 yrs.
Brendan Diamond	R	1,579	04/01/76	03/31/86	—
One-Hour Optical, Inc.	R	514	02/15/76	02/28/79	—
Total Retail		781,943			
Total Nonretail		41,889			
Total		823,832			

were paying no common area charges, and there were limitations on these charges for a number of the remainder. The leases showed clear signs of deals having been made in a tenants' market.

Getting all of the appropriate pieces of paper in the proper files took many of the hours spent. There were instances of leases that were apparently signed by a national credit, but in fact the national credit had been released by separate agreement. One of the retail anchors had an option on some space that was leased as offices; this was about to cause a $200,000 annual decline in gross income. In any event, completion of this compilation and lease review function permitted the counselors to go on to step 2.

2. It was appropriate to identify a subarea within the total trade area. Some interviewing in the mall, a sample of the checking accounts used at one of the anchors, and a consumer report that a local newspaper published at that time all suggested that this smaller trade area was of crucial importance to the center. This comparatively small trade area was relatively more affluent than the total trade area (see Figures 14–3 and 14–4). However, the household sizes of the two areas were not significantly different. The single-family residences tended to be the second or third home purchased by the families; homeowner turnover was moderate; and the families tended to be older than average. The apartment projects in the area were generally occupied by younger versions of the same people who occupied the single-family residences.

There was a pretty good match between housing costs and household income. In other words, this was not an area where families tended to make themselves house poor in order to climb socially. The trade area was developing—it had been roughly half-developed ten years earlier, and it was 82 percent developed at the

FIGURE 14–3.   Household income in trade area.

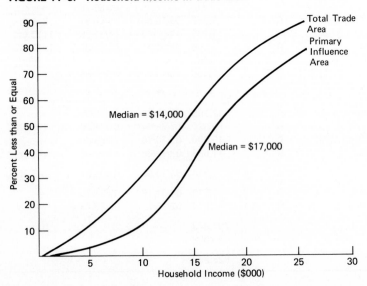

FIGURE 14–4.   Comparison of primary and total trade areas.

	TOTAL TRADE AREA	PRIMARY INFLUENCE AREA
Land area (square miles)	79	28
Percent urbanized	93	82
Median household income	$14,000	$17,000
Retail sales per household	$ 9,700	$11,000
At full urbanization		
Population	275,000	70,000
Households	92,000	23,000
Total retail sales	$892 million	$253 million

time of the study. Retail space in the trade area was slightly overbuilt, but this excess would disappear as the remaining residential ground developed. Not much vacant ground was either zoned or planned for more retail space, so the potential for significant increases in retail space was limited.

It was concluded that the area was stable. It was fairly well insulated from economic cycles. The proportion of total sales captured by the subject center was not as high as desirable, but it was substantial and growing slightly. The stability of the future income to the property was excellent.

The projections for the future income behavior of the center are shown in Figures 14–5 and 14–6. A check with the owners five years after the completion of the assignment confirmed that the projections were reasonable. The increasing net income stream shown in this figure became the basis for the yield calculations to the owner and the proposed sales price.

3. Determining the value of the shopping center to the owners turned out to be a wasted effort. They preferred to be involved in ventures with a significantly

FIGURE 14–5.   Shopping center income projections.

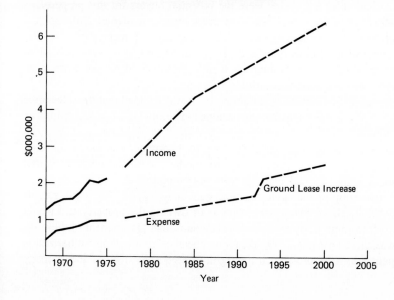

FIGURE 14–6. Shopping center income projections.

YEAR

	1977	1985	1993	2000
Sales/square foot in 1976 dollars	$ 95	$ 125	$ 125	$ 125
Sales/square foot in inflated dollars	$ 100	$ 181	$ 231	$ 275
Gross sales (000)	$78,600	$142,300	$181,600	$216,200
Income (000)				
Retail	$ 2,100	$ 3,984	$ 5,085	$ 6,053
Common area	160	182	213	240
Fixed	172	172	172	172
Expense (000)				
Ground Rent	$ 209	$ 241	$ 683	$ 808
Other	830	1,146	1,462	1,738
Total	$ 1,039	$ 1,387	$ 2,145	$ 2,546
Net	$ 1,393	$ 2,951	$ 3,325	$ 3,919

higher earning potential than is typically offered by a shopping center. They lacked the expertise to do any additional development with the center, and they had no desire to develop such expertise. Essentially, the excess land was worth nothing to the owners. It also became clear that they were tired of the center and really wanted to dispose of it.

4. In this case, potential owners were not difficult to identify. The net income was conservatively projected and safe. The property needed improved management but not a dramatic turnaround. There was potential for some additional development. The center was leveraged but still required substantial amounts of cash. The center had "institutional investor" written all over it. Major life insurance companies such as Prudential, Equitable, and Aetna were the potential buyers for this property.

5. Establishing a sales price often becomes more a matter of philosophical agreement between the seller and the counselor than a matter of mathematics. Asking $100 million for $50 million worth of real estate can be a perfectly valid procedure if the potential purchaser is an Arabian oil sheikh. However, if the purchaser is an American insurance company, that attitude will simply cause you to spend several months in unsuccessfully marketing the property. It was decided that the sales price should be based on the most sensible projections that could be made and on proper marketplace yields.

The yields sought by institutions are easy to determine, and they tend to be relatively consistent from one organization to another. With the projections that had already been made, the calculations were not complicated.

6. The marketing of the center became genuinely bizarre. Six organizations had been identified, all of which were capable of owning the property and would want to do so. It became fairly evident that the counselors' assessment of these six institutions was shared by others. The center had been offered without authorization to all six organizations by brokers. It had been offered at least twice and as many

as fourteen times. The eventual buyer had been offered the property three times. In total, twenty-five brokers had offered the property. Several were local brokers; the most distant one was in London. The prices the brokers were using ranged from 60 percent of the actual asking price to double the asking price, and the broadest conceivable range of terms of sale had been offered.

One unanticipated aspect of this counseling assignment was that the counselors had to spend several days contacting brokers and telling them to discontinue their sales efforts. First, the brokers were not going to be paid. Second, they were ruining some potential buyers (two organizations said that they refused to consider a property that apparently had such a hashed-up marketing program). Third, many of the brokers were representing themselves as agents of the owners, which raised the real possibility that the owners would initiate legal action.

The eventual buyer was brought on track. As is often the case, he wanted a six-month $1 option to study the real estate. The counselors thought that forty-eight hours was sufficient. Eventually a mutually agreed-upon option period was set. The final purchase price was off by less than 2 percent of the asking price.

Closing a shopping center sale can be an agonizing process. Tenants may pay their percentage rents and/or their common area fees at different times—monthly, quarterly, semiannually, or annually. The seller may attempt to get a pro rata share of the upcoming Christmas season income. The buyer will attempt to keep it all. Common area fees will often reimburse substantial expenditures made before the sale. The seller will try to get it all back; the buyer will attempt to give the seller only a pro rata share. Reasonable parties can usually agree on what is right and proper, but the agreement must be reached before the property transfer closes. In effect, the seller is going to be involved in the real estate for up to a year beyond the closing, and the buyer and seller must not be arguing later over who gets how much of the percentage rentals and common area fees. This closing took roughly twenty hours over three days, but it did close.

Getting this deal organized and made was a 350- to 400-hour assignment spread over an eight-month period of time. The hours were well spent. None of the effort was expended on routine matters. Every step required concentration. The final result was a sale that was fair to both the buyer and the seller.

SELECTED REFERENCES

CARPENTER, HORACE, JR. *Shopping Center Management* (2nd ed.). New York: International Council of Shopping Centers, 1978.

GARRETT, ROBERT L., HUNTER A. HOGAN, JR., and ROBERT M. STANTON. *The Valuation of Shopping Centers*. Chicago: American Institute of Real Estate Appraisers, 1976.

GRUEN, CLAUDE, and NINA J. GRUEN. *Store Location and Customer Behavior*. Washington, D.C.: Urban Land Institute, 1966.

LION, EDGAR. *Shopping Centers: Planning, Development, and Administration.* New York: Wiley-Interscience, 1976.

LUKENS, REAVES C., JR.   *The Appraiser and Real Estate Feasibility Studies.* Chicago: American Institute of Real Estate Appraisers, 1972.

McKEEVER, J. ROSS.   *Merchandising and Promotions—Shopping Center Operations.* Washington, D.C.: Urban Land Institute, 1958.

NELSON, RICHARD LAWRENCE.   *The Selection of Retail Locations.* New York: F. W. Dodge Corporation, 1958.

URBAN LAND INSTITUTE.   *Dollars and Cents of Shopping Centers.* Washington, D.C.: Urban Land Institute, 1977.

——— *Parking Requirements for Shopping Centers.* Washington, D.C.: Urban Land Institute, 1965.

——— *Shopping Center Development Handbook.* Washington, D.C.: Urban Land Institute, 1977.

CHAPTER FIFTEEN
INDUSTRIAL PROPERTIES

Real estate is one of the most interesting and complex assets used in the world's commerce. This chapter deals with the most specialized and variable type of real estate—industrial property. The importance of industrial property in the economic activity of all countries is immense. The basic function of all industrial properties is to provide space for activities involved in the production, storage, and distribution of tangible economic goods. To the industrialist, real estate (the land, the land improvements, the buildings and attached building equipment) is part of the ingredients needed for the industrial process. Without the types of activities and functions performed at industrial facilities, the ability of an economy to support a complex society would be severely diminished. Industrial production accounts for over a third of the national employment and the gross national product.

The variability and specialization involved in industrial properties present extensive opportunities for counseling. The purpose of this chapter is to present, via an overview of industrial property, the places where these opportunities occur and to point out certain pitfalls to avoid. The chapter will also suggest methods of analysis and types and sources of information to acquire and analyze.

COUNSELING AND
INDUSTRIAL PROPERTY

Generally speaking, counseling for industrial properties does not differ significantly from counseling for other types of property. Many of the same general types of reports and studies are required. These include appraisals, investment analyses, location studies, property utilization studies, cost-benefit studies, negotiation counseling, operations analysis, feasibility analysis, highest and best use studies, management studies, engineering studies, market research, trend analysis, development planning, zoning studies, environmental impact studies, and the presentation of expert testimony. Many of the methods of data analysis are the same as the methods used with other types of property. Dilmore's *Quantitative Techniques in Real Estate Counseling* provides an excellent compendium of such methods (see Selected References).

The characteristics and the market motivations of industrial real estate are different from those of other types of real estate. Because of these differences, many of the real estate principles of the single-family home, the apartment, the shopping center, and the office building cannot be transposed to the industrial real estate market. All successful real estate counselors must be researchers at heart, but because of the complexity and variability of industrial properties this is especially true for the industrial property counselor. Industrial property counseling seems to require long-range analysis more often than do other types of real estate counseling. Long-range analysis attempts to forecast situations that may face the client several years from now, whereas short-run to intermediate types of analysis that arise from an immediate problem facing the client. One of the reasons for the greater use of long-range analysis in industrial property counseling is that the limited life cycle of most products means that changes in manufacturing facilities will be required several years hence.

TYPES OF INDUSTRIAL
PROPERTY

Industrial property encompasses several types of buildings. These are generally classified into three types. They are (1) general-purpose properties, (2) limited-purpose or special-purpose properties, and (3) single-purpose properties.

General-purpose properties are properties that can be adapted to a wide range of alternative uses with minimal expense and difficulty. Such properties are often constructed on a speculative basis and are usually adequate for office and service uses, light manufacturing, general storage, and/or assembly. Properties that have special or custom features to accommodate an original or a subsequent user, such as craneways, elaborate power distribution, or large offices will be regarded as general-purpose properties if the special features are easily removable or do not hinder other general uses.

Limited-purpose or special-purpose properties are properties whose physical characteristics restrict their use to a small range of industrial activities. They are designed with a particular process or function in mind. Examples include some chemical plants, steel mills, freezer storage facilities, and heavy manufacturing facilities. Because these buildings are so process related and even customized for the original user, they may represent a more difficult problem of disposal. Frequently, because of the heavy original investment and the high cost of construction for modern replacement, such functionally deficient facilities are kept in operation beyond their "normal" life. Innovative alternative uses of such facilities might result from real estate counseling. For instance, many of the abandoned large facilities in New England and other areas have been converted into multitenancy spaces by investors (see the "Single-Tenant versus Multitenant Buildings" section of this chapter).

Single-purpose properties are useful for only one industrial activity. Examples include some chemical factories, dairies (processing units), refineries, grain storage silos, and railroad yards. Some convertibility to alternative uses is always possible at a price. Grain silos have been transformed into hotels and chemical factories have been transformed into general use facilities, but the conversion cost is extremely high. The cost of conversion is an important attribute of feasibility since the converted facility must compete with similar facilities in the marketplace. Other properties in competition for the same clients define the market.

Counseling assignments often arise from an attempt to convert single-purpose buildings to other uses or from the loss of a major tenant from a general-purpose building. Both cases require market research surveys and cost-benefit studies on conversion or subdividing. Every empty industrial building is a counseling opportunity, but many occupied industrial facilities can also present counseling opportunities—particularly those that are distressed.

PROPERTY LOCATION
SELECTION PROCEDURE

The selection of the appropriate site or finished facility for a company is a decision that is extremely important for the future success of the firm, as well as a very complex decision. Due to these factors, this selection procedure is a common counseling situation. Corporations want expert advice on this aspect of their business decisions, and because many corporations do not have such capability on their staff, they often hire the outside consultant (real estate counselor) for guidance. Even when corporations have staff property location specialists, a counselor will often be hired as a "local expert." The matching of company needs with the attributes of an industrial property is a process that requires tremendous amounts of data. As

FIGURE 15–1   General Property Selection Checklist.

Community Factors
1. Economic trends
   a. Macro market
   b. Micro market
   c. Demographic
   d. Housing
2. Transportation
3. Education and vocational training programs
4. Governmental attitudes
   a. Taxes
   b. Environmental controls
   c. Land use controls
5. Level of public services
   a. Police and fire protection
   b. Hospitals
   c. Utilities
   d. Zoning
   e. Building codes
6. Local and state taxes
7. Supporting services
   a. Labor skills
   b. Suppliers
   c. Raw materials
   d. Machine shops

Site Considerations
1. Physical features of site
   a. Terrain
   b. Drainage
   c. Subsoils
   d. Size and shape
   e. Floodplain
2. Location
   a. Access to related services
   b. Proximity to workers' neighborhoods
   c. Land uses and zoning
   d. Rail, truck, and airplane access
   e. Parking
3. Property acquisition costs
   a. Site
   b. Building
   c. Construction costs

Building Analysis
1. Size
2. Type of construction
   a. Roof
   b. Floor load capacity
3. Layout and design
   a. Expansion potential
   b. Fire protection and safety systems

    c. Plant efficiency
    d. Ceiling weight and bay span
4. Electric service
5. Elevators, lifts, and conveyors
6. Inside and yard storage
7. Truck and rail loading facilities
    a. Dock height
    b. Truck turnaround area
    c. Turnaround area paving

---

many as a hundred variables are sometimes considered in an industrial property decision. The attributes to be considered are usually divided into three major categories. They are (1) community factors, (2) site considerations, and (3) building analysis. Figure 15–1 is a general property selection checklist.

COMMUNITY FACTORS

There are numerous community factors that should be considered when selecting an industrial property. Among the major factors that must be considered are economic trends, available transportation, education and vocational training programs, governmental attitudes, the level of public services, taxation (local and state), and supporting services. In order to correctly evaluate all of these community factors, the counselor should prepare or have prepared a community survey for the client. Figure 15–2 contains a detailed checklist of community factors to include in a community survey. The client may have much of this work done by its own employees, but the final product, or at least an evaluation of the community survey, can best be done by the counselor. The counselor is the procedural and local expert and is aware of the numerous specific items that are critical to the success of such an evaluation. Therefore, the counselor can assume the role of coordinator or orchestrator.

    The community factors that should be considered are not equally important to different firms. The local economy may be less important than broader economic trends if the site is to be developed for an assembly plant for a national corporation. However, transportation facilities would be of paramount importance for receiving parts and shipping out finished products. Depending on the skills required for the work force, educational or vocational training may or may not be of concern, except as a fringe benefit to employees, whereas state and local taxes are of concern to all businesses. Taxes are paid directly out of profits. Some states seem to have low tax rates, but individual localities may impose income taxes in addition to real estate and other taxes. The total tax burden to the client is the relevant information, and the counselor should be sure that this information is assembled for the client. Environmental and land use controls must also be considered since they add costs

FIGURE 15–2   Detailed Checklist of Community Factors.

Community Checklist for Industrial Site Selection

1. Are the attitudes of state and local government favorable to a new industry and generally conducive to community progress?
    Tax rates and structure
    Assessment practices (residential and agricultural versus business and industry)
    Right-to-work legislation
    Zoning legislation and practice
    Incentives
    Extent of business representation on local government boards and councils
    Workers' and unemployment compensation programs
    Strong nonpolitical local leadership

2. Will the school system be acceptable to management employees transferred into the community?
    Public schools
    Parochial schools
    Technical schools
    Colleges—community (two years)
    Colleges—liberal arts (four years)
    Colleges—engineering
    Adult opportunities for continuing education and advance degrees
    Condition and sophistication of school facilities and equipment
    Teacher-pupil ratio
    Percentage of teachers holding degrees
    Average expenditure per pupil
    Curricula

3. Is the community structured to furnish an acceptable level of services to a new industry?
    Police (performance during labor disputes)
    Ambulance service
    Fire protection
    Water
    Sanitary sewers
    Storm sewers

4. Are the social, cultural, recreational, and shopping facilities adequate to support a quality of life that will attract employees to the community?
    Shopping—downtown and suburban
    Recreational facilities
    Social and fraternal organizations
    Cultural and athletic activities
    Wide choice of religious facilities
    Hospitals and special care facilities
    Hotel and meeting accommodations
    Attractive, viable central city
    Strong special service organizations
    Good support of community service fund(s)
    Social acceptance of "outsiders"

5. Are there aspects of the community that might interfere with the industry's minority employment objectives consistent with federal and state laws and policy?

FIGURE 15–2   Continued.

Is there evidence of unusual racial tension or failure by the community to deal realistically and appropriately with minority grievances?
> Identification of significant ethnic and/or minority groups in the community
> Leadership of above groups
> Reaction of community and group leadership to volatile or potentially volatile situations
> Representation of ethnic groups and/or minorities in local police, fire, school board, and community leadership
> Community acceptance of equal opportunity employment

6. Does the community contain or have convenient access to the supportive services required for day-to-day plant operation?
> Material suppliers (new as well as traditional sources)
> Machine shops
> Tool and die shops
> Plastic and metalworking
> Cleaning services and employment agencies
> Maintenance services

7. Are there residential neighborhoods of the quality normally desired by the levels of technical and management personnel who will staff the plant? Does the community have the capacity—contractors, mortgage lenders, developed land, etc.—to supply housing to the industry's incoming employees in a reasonable time and at reasonable prices?
> Number of homes (by price range) in multiple listing service
> Is speculative residential construction common?
> Availability of developed residential sites
> Comparison of prices with "benchmark locations"
> Typical architecture and type of construction
> Availability of home financing
> Rental units and apartments—cost per unit, age, condition

8. Does it appear that the proposed plant can conform to its hiring schedule and build a labor force without compromising its skill and productivity requirements?
> Size of labor market, SMSA
> Commuting patterns of labor force
> Unemployment and underemployment
>>   Skilled
>>   Unskilled but trainable
> Entering labor force from local school system
> Number and composition of registrants with employment security office
> Acceptable attitude
>>   Absenteeism
>>   Turnover
>>   Productivity

9. Does the community offer vocational and industrial training programs which will be beneficial to the proposed plant?
> Local vocational and technical schools
> State funding of vocational training progams
>>   State vocational school system
>>   In-plant training programs

10. Proprietary question(s) relating to specific employee relations considerations.

FIGURE 15-2   Continued.

---

11. Are there union practices, chronic shortages of material, an inadequate number of general contractors or subcontractors, or similar problems peculiar to this community which might adversely affect the design and construction phase of the project?

    Experience of several recent major construction projects

12. Is the community served by transportation and utilities adequate to support the industry?

    Natural gas (interstate, intrastate)
      Assured
      Interruptible (historical frequency of interruptions)
    Electric power (generation source, reliability, and rate structure)
    Motor freight
    Commercial airlines
    Railroads
    Access to deepwater port or maintained barge channel
    Facilities for private aircraft
    Interstate highway system
    Typical shipping time to customer and supplier locations
    Availability of containerized or piggyback facilities
    Water (availability and chemical analysis)

13. Are wage rates and benefits at a level which will enhance the industry's competitive position in the marketplace?

    Rates and benefits of other industries
    Union contracts of other industries
    Relative cost of living for the community
    Incentive programs or historical aspects which place other industries in a preferred position when competing for labor

14. What governmental economic development incentives are available?

15. How will state and/or local environment considerations affect site selection, cost of plant construction, and operating cost?
    (See following list of environmental questions.)

Some Environmental Questions for Community Profile

1. General
   What major industries are located in the area?
   What is the nature of their operation (chemical manufacturing, metal fabrication, metal finishing, textiles, etc.)?
   What is the status of the state implementation plan (SIP)?
   Does the community have an environmental commission? Who is the primary contact person?
   Does the state or community require an environmental impact statement (EIS) for new projects?

2. Liquid waste
   What receptors are available for receiving plant wastewaters?
     Sanitary sewer, storm sewer, river, stream, lake, other
   Does the community have a publicly owned treatment works (POTW)?
   a. What is the name of the authority?
   b. Has the authority issued a sewer ordinance?

FIGURE 15–2   Continued.

---

   c. Are there numerical limitations imposed on specific pollutants discharged to the POTW?

   d. Does the POTW have an NPDES* or state discharge permit for the wastewaters?

   e. How many industries discharge wastewaters to the POTW? What are the magnitude and nature of these discharges?

   f. How much can the POTW now accept?

   g. Does the POTW plan to expand its treatment capacity in the next five years? How does it plan to recover its capital investment from industrial users—that is, does it have an accepted industrial cost recovery (ICR) plan?

3. Air

Does the community or state limit the nature and composition of fuels burned by industrial plants, or any other emissions?

Have there been any citizen complaints related to odors, visible emissions, or other environmental impacts from industrial plants?

Do you know of any publicized air pollution incidents in this area?

What is the status of the community with respect to the attainment of each of the six national ambient air quality standards? Are trade-offs available?

4. Solid waste

What types of facilities are available for solid waste disposal (for example, open dumps, sanitary landfills, incinerators)?

   a. Are any of these landfills designed for proper handling of chemical sludges, solvents, oil, and other hazardous liquid wastes?

   b. Are these landfills publicly or privately owned or operated?

   c. Is suitable land available for landfill expansion?

   d. Does the proposed plant site include enough suitable land for landfill construction on the premises?

Has any regulatory agency imposed limits on what materials may be incinerated, or on the emissions from the incinerator(s)?

   a. Are any operating under state or local permits?

   b. What happens to incinerator residues or sludges?

---

*National Pollutant Discharge Elimination System.

Source: *A Guide to Industrial Site Selection* (Washington, D.C.: Society of Industrial Realtors and National Association of Industrial and Office Parks, 1979), pp. 21–23.

and perhaps time delays to construction. The level of public services is important for conduct of the business.

Other community factors that should be reviewed are police and fire protection, hospitals, utilities, zoning, and building codes. Parks, golf courses, theaters, and other entertainment and leisure facilities are important, especially if the business needs to attract skilled workers from other cities and regions. Before deciding to relocate, prospective employees from other areas will consider not only the standard services of the city but other cultural, leisure, and educational facilities as well.

The importance of various community factors changes over time. Figure 15–3 contains results of a survey on the most important factors in the location of corporate headquarters. According to the survey, productivity of workers, proximity to cus-

FIGURE 15–3   Most Important Factors in Locating Corporate Headquarters.

1981 RANK (Figures in parentheses are 1976 ranks.)	1981	1976
1. Productivity of workers (4)	38%	33%
2. Proximity to customers (2)	35	36
3. Efficient transportation facilities for materials and products (1)	34	41
4. Availability of unskilled or semi-skilled workers (2)	28	36
4. Community receptivity to business and industry (6)	28	28
6. State and/or local attitude toward taxes on business and industry (9)	26	23
6. Availability of skilled workers (11)	26	17
8. Proximity to raw materials, components, or supplies (7)	23	26
9. Availability of energy supplies (4)	21	33
9. A growing regional market (7)	21	26
9. Costs of property and construction (10)	21	22
12. Ample area for future expansion (11)	17	17
12. Quality of life for employees (N/A)	17	N/A
14. Financing inducements (14)	16	11
15. Proximity to other company facilities (13)	15	13
16. Availability of technical or professional workers (17)	14	10
17. Water supply (14)	13	11
17. State and/or local posture on environmental controls and processing of Environment Impact Reports (14)	13	11
19. Adequate civic waste treatment facilities (19)	5	4
20. Calm and stable social climate (19)	4	4
20. State and/or local personal income tax structure (24)	4	2
22. Proximity to services (18)	3	8
22. Fiscal health of state and/or city (19)	3	4
22. Efficient transportation facilities for people (23)	3	3
25. Personal preferences of company executives (24)	2	2
26. Availability of clerical workers (26)	1	1
N/A Style of living for employees (19)	N/A	4
No answer	7	5

N/A: Not asked.

Source: *Why Corporate America Moves Where: A Fortune Market Research Survey of Facility Location Decisions*, 1982.

tomers, efficient transportation facilities for materials and products and community receptivity to business and industry have become important in location decisions. Greater emphasis during the five year period between surveys was assigned to availability of skilled workers. This change underscores the importance of technology in industry. The counselor must be careful to keep informed of the current preferences and needs of clients.

Much of the material necessary to complete a community evaluation survey is available from public sources. Census information and tax and employment statistics are usually obtainable at little expense and with relative ease and reliability. In addition, large amounts of relevant information can be obtained from numerous governmental or quasi-governmental organizations—planning commissions, chambers of commerce, local and regional development groups, industrial development commissions, utility companies, and local colleges or universities. Many bibliographies and discussions of research and information sources are also available. However, care must be exercised not to confuse the collection of relevant facts with the integration, analysis, and interpretation of those facts. A clerk can acquire and summarize the necessary information, but the integration, analysis, and interpretation should be done by an expert in industrial property. These should be functions of the counselor.

SITE CONSIDERATIONS

The physical features of the site are paramount to the client. The major site considerations are listed in Figure 15–1. If the physical features of the site do not meet the requirements for the given industrial use, the site must be rejected immediately. Problems with financing or similar matters can be negotiated, but physical shortcomings can rarely be adequately alleviated. One consideration that has become an important factor in recent years is site size. A site that does not allow for expansion at a later date will force a growing client to move earlier than might be appropriate. Poor economic conditions have recently forced many companies to sell off extra land that they no longer need for expansion, but in general it is better to have too much land than too little.

Location studies have become one of the major areas of interest in real estate and regional-urban economics. Accordingly, numerous studies have been done on how site location should proceed and what should be considered. Location studies are also one of the more common assignments of industrial real estate counselors. Often the counselor will be hired to perform only part of a location study instead of the entire study. Sometimes the counselor simply coordinates the efforts of numerous other persons who are performing specific functions. For example, the client firm may do part of the work in-house before engaging the counselor. The counselor then hires specific professionals (engineers, accountants, etc.) for narrowly defined tasks and integrates the results of their work into a coherent analytic report useful for making the decision originally postulated by the client. The selection of a location should proceed in stages. First, a general geographic area should be selected. This choice is dictated by the requirements of the client. A preliminary study should be done by the client or the counselor to determine what problem this industrial property is to solve. Is the problem one of distribution, or is additional product required? Perhaps general geographic location is unimportant if specific site needs are satisfied. If so, the counselor can proceed immediately to the specific locational attributes required. The selection of a specific community will then be necessary.

Numerous surveys have been conducted in recent years to determine the most important locational attributes desired by industry. The results are largely what a person would expect for a business. Always included are availability of workers, availability of raw materials and supplies, inexpensive utilities, transportation facilities (usually rail, truck, and air), growing regional markets, and proximity to customers. Of course, these desired attributes are in addition to acceptable physical features of the site and acceptable acquisition costs. Again, the counselor plays a pivotal role. The obvious requirements of the proposed operation (transportation, utilities, workers, etc.) must be integrated with the market factors such as growing markets and proximity to customers. The counselor should do this work with the appropriate industry personnel or other independent consultants to integrate these considerations into the decision-making process. The counselor obviously cannot be an expert market analyst for many different industries but must blend his or her expertise with the knowledge of the client and others in order to achieve an optimal location decision. A checklist of site factors should include at least the following main topics:

1. Location
   a. Surrounding areas
   b. Specific site
2. Utilities
   a. Sanitary sewer
   b. Storm water management
   c. Water supply—community
   d. Water supply—from rivers or lakes
   e. Water supply—from wells
   f. Electric power
   g. Natural gas
   h. Propane or L.P.G.
   i. Fuel oil
   j. Other fuels
   k. Telephone
   l. Waste disposal—liquid
   m. Waste disposal—solid
   n. Waste disposal—gaseous
3. Transportation
   a. Air
   b. Water
   c. Railroad—freight
   d. Railroad—passenger
   e. Highway—trucks
   f. Highway—automobiles
   g. Public[1]

Property acquisition costs are of major importance. Often land has to be acquired for special-purpose and single-purpose buildings, which have to be constructed when existing facilities fail to meet space requirements. Existing general-purpose buildings can more often be purchased and are ready for occupancy. Since acquisition costs are a major factor, an effort should be made to locate more than one potentially acceptable site or building in the preliminary stages of search and

[1]This list was taken from a more detailed "Site Selection Checklist," found in *A Guide to Industrial Site Selection* (Washington, D C.: Society of Industrial Realtors and National Association of Industrial and Office Parks, 1979), pp. 25–27.

negotiation. If one property should not qualify because of high acquisition costs or unacceptable physical features, the counselor then has other sites or buildings that are potentially acceptable and does not have to start from the beginning of the decision process again.

BUILDING ANALYSIS

Notice that the analysis of property selection has moved from the general to the specific. First the community factors are considered, then the site, and now the building itself. Building analysis is the most specific part of property selection and concludes this service provided by the counselor. The general major building considerations are listed in Figure 15–1. Building analysis reflects the factors required for site selection to a great extent.

Property size is a major consideration, regardless of the type of industry. Appropriate floor space and storage space must be present for performance of the desired function in the required volume. The type of construction will be important for some industries but less important for others. Layout and design for special-purpose and single-purpose properties will be critical considerations. However, for general-purpose properties adjustments can be made quite easily. Internal transportation (elevators, lifts, and conveyors) is important, but it is often supplied by the occupant. Appropriate storage facilities (inside and outside) are essential and are a consideration of size (site and building). Transportation is critical for all industries, and the need for truck, rail, or air service must be defined. In addition, the counselor should be aware of certain unique requirements of the client. Perhaps the client needs a large supply of hot water or natural light. Does the building satisfy these requirements? The satisfaction of the unique requirements of various industries and the successful integration of these requirements into the building selection process (especially if an existing building is involved) are important services provided by the real estate counselor. A single error at this stage can be very costly to the client.

SINGLE-TENANT VERSUS MULTITENANT BUILDINGS

A variety of challenging assignments relating to the complexity of single-tenant versus multitenant buildings are available to the real estate counselor. The development of modern single-story, multitenant or "incubator" buildings has increased enormously in the post–World War II era, but the same period has also experienced the continued construction of buildings designed for the single tenant and frequent conversions of multistory, single-tenant facilities to multitenant properties.

In the case of older multistory buildings, subdivision has taken place, with separate tenants occupying different floors of the building. Assisting a property owner in such a conversion can be a great challenge to the counselor, and in this area real estate counselors have provided valuable services to their clients. Many functionally obsolete buildings have been successfully and profitably converted to multitenancy, particularly in the urban areas of the nation's older industrial communities. Floor load, elevators and vertical transportation, column size and spacing, ceiling height, parking, security, ingress and egress, and shipping and receiving are among the areas of critical concern. Although older multitenant buildings present some problems, they can be very functional and successful, and they are often available at a lower rental than that of newer facilities.

New multitenant industrial buildings are rarely designed as multistory structures. They are mostly single-story structures that have been designed with maximum tenant leasing flexibility, so that each tenant has individual shipping, parking, and entrances. There are many such buildings in the numerous planned industrial districts and parks that have been developed since the mid-1950s. In such parks, there is commonly a combination of buildings built for specific single occupancy (often built to the tenant's specifications) and general-purpose properties built and designed for more than one tenant. Often these buildings are built on a speculative basis, with little or no preleasing.

In an industrial park, utilities, transportation facilities, and access to markets, labor, and supplies are available to all equally. This, combined with the economy of scale obtained from the construction of larger multitenant facilities, can provide the tenant with better services and possibly lower rent than would be provided by a freestanding single-occupancy property located elsewhere.

The real estate counselor should examine carefully the many factors determining a single-tenant versus a multitenant facility. The tenant's type of use of the property is most important. In some cases, the tenant's use and process are not compatible with those of adjacent tenants, and vice versa. Compatible use can be far more important than the occupancy cost. If the company cannot produce, assemble, distribute, or store its goods in an acceptable manner, it will have to either relocate or operate inefficiently.

The need for expansion can also be an important factor in determining the choice between single-tenant and multitenant buildings. In a single-tenant facility,

FIGURE 15–4   A freestanding, single-tenant industrial building suitable for light manufacturing, distribution, or light assembly. Courtesy of Adler Galvin Rogers, Inc., Cleveland, Ohio.

provided there is ample land, expansion can be planned and executed without having to move. In a multitenant facility, expansion normally comes from taking over adjacent space when it is available. Unless the tenant has specific options for additional space at given terms and conditions, it may not be able to obtain the required space. The counselor should carefully evaluate both the present and the future needs of the client before making a recommendation.

INDUSTRIAL REAL ESTATE
AS AN INVESTMENT

Investment in industrial real estate has become much more popular in recent years. This is at least partially due to the increase in available information about risks and returns in real estate in general and in industrial real estate in particular.

There are three basic categories of equity investors in industrial property:

1. User-investor
2. Nonuser-investor
3. Combination of user and investor

The *user-investor* is simply the industrial tenant that chooses to own rather than lease a property. The counselor should be familiar with the primary factors in advising a client to buy or lease, which are discussed in Chapter 9. Assuming that the desired facility can be either purchased or leased, the primary consideration will be the alternative uses of capital and return on capital investment. Every "for profit" industrial enterprise requires a return on its invested capital. In general, if a higher return can be realized through investment in equipment or product development than through ownership of real estate, it may not be advisable for the client to own the real estate as an investment. A careful analysis of the proposed use and availability of capital should be made in arriving at an investment-purchase versus lease decision. Part of the return analysis will include comparison of the tax considerations—that is, fully deductible rent payments versus depreciation and mortgage interest deductions and cash flows. Figure 15–5 contains a sample comparative analysis of operating costs for use in cash flow estimation. Another important consideration in the analysis should be the potential effect of capital gains for the client if real estate is owned and sold in the future at a book profit.

Owning-investment versus leasing can also affect the company's balance sheet. Direct mortgage indebtedness can have undesirable effects on the balance sheet as compared to leasing obligations and can unnecessarily impair a company's ability to create further leverage. This subject is also discussed in detail in Chapter 9.

There are a number of other considerations involving the degree of flexibility that affect the decision to own-invest or lease, and the degree of flexibility in one versus the other depends on the client's needs and requirements. For example, companies often choose to own the facilities where they are making a large in-

FIGURE 15–5   Comparative Analysis of Operating Costs (000s).

	SITES*					
	A	B	C	D	E	F
Transportation	$ 20	$ 60	$ 55	$ —	$ 30	$ 75
Labor						
Direct						
Indirect						
Benefits						
Total labor	75	95	80	—	50	100
Plant overhead						
Depreciation						
Building	—	—	—	—	—	—
Machinery and equipment	—	—	—	—	—	—
Maintenance	—	5	—	—	—	10
Taxes						
Real estate	16	(7)	10	—	5	16
Personal property	—	—	—	—	—	7
State income	2	10	14	—	7	(10)
Utilities						
Electric power	4	7	6	—	2	5
Gas and oil	(1)	(1)	(1)	—	2	17
Water	(6)	(5)	(5)	—	3	(4)
Wastewater disposal	—	2	2	—	—	14
Total utilities	$ (3)	$ 3	$ 2	$ —	$ 7	$ 32
Total comparative annual operating costs	$110	$166	$161	$—	$99	$230

*Over (under) site D, used as base.

Source: *A Guide to Industrial Site Selection* (Washington, D.C.: Society of Industrial Realtors and National Association of Industrial and Office Parks, 1979), p. 30.

vestment in leasehold improvements in order to protect that investment rather than have it become part of the residual value of a property owned by the nonuser-investor. In such cases, control of the real estate may be essential and may be more easily accomplished through owning than through leasing. A lease with an option to purchase (future investment) may also solve the problem.

The *nonuser-investor* basically includes institutions, REITs, individuals, and groups of individuals (partnerships and syndications), both domestic and foreign, that consider industrial property desirable and find that it provides an adequate rate of return on investment (the details of investment analysis are discussed in Chapters 6 and 7). Industrial real estate has historically been a popular and successful investment property vehicle. Among the reasons for this situation is the fact that there has been an ample availability of this type of product in most market areas. In addition, industrial real estate historically has been less management intensive than apartments, hotels, office buildings, and shopping centers. In general, industrial property does not require custodial service or a high degree of "common area" maintenance and building operations.

Until the mid-1960s most investors sought long-term leases in industrial property because they were not concerned with inflation and wanted to limit their leasing risk. Today most investors, both domestic and foreign, are seeking leases of no more than five years unless they have full inflation protection. However, the trend is moving back towards longer leases because of lower inflation and higher vacancy rates. Leases that were more commonly "gross" in the past are now more desirable if they are "net" because net leases give more protection to yield for the investor. At a minimum, gross leases should provide for "pass-throughs" on most expenses. These trends are the result of a highly inflationary economy and a desire on the part of the investor to minimize fixed income streams and maximize control over operating expenses.

Return on investment and methods of analyzing yield in industrial property are constantly changing as a reflection of the short- and long-term economy, a process that also affects alternative types of investment property. The industrial economy in the market area in which the investment is taking place must be studied very carefully. What is the absorption rate of industrial space? How much vacant space exists? In particular, industrial real estate relates heavily to trends in technology, location, user preference, and current standards. In advising his or her investor client, the real estate counselor should have a thorough knowledge of local market trends and their interrelationship with these factors.

Like the user-investor, the nonuser-investor must decide whether it is best to purchase a single-tenant facility or a multitenant facility. There is obvious risk to an investor in buying a single-tenant facility because the entire income stream then depends on one tenant. The multitenanted facility offers some protection as to vacancy, particularly if the lease expiration dates are staggered. On the other hand, a nonmanagement, intensive single-tenant property can be an excellent investment, particularly if it is located in a well-planned industrial park and there is general market demand for a building of that size. The counselor should incorporate these facts into the investment analysis.

The final category—*combination user-investor*—is the company that invests in industrial real estate for use as well as *independent* investment. Quite simply, this is the user that buys a property with excess space, which it then leases to another tenant. All of the considerations that apply to the investment analysis of both the user-investor and the nonuser-investor, as well as the key occupancy questions pertaining to the user aspects of the property, should be applied to the combination user-investor. The combination of use and investment can be very beneficial if the two purposes do not conflict with each other. The counselor providing advice in this situation must have a thorough knowledge of both property use and investment analysis factors in order to help the client make its decision. The investment analysis factors would include all present value techniques (present value, net present value, profitability index, discounted payback period), the internal rate of return, probability distributions, the effects of leverage, and risk-return considerations.

SELECTED REFERENCES

BROWN, ROBERT KEVIN.   *Corporate Real Estate*. Homewood, Ill.: Dow Jones-Irwin, 1979.

DILLON, JOSEPH G.   "Industrial Real Estate Brokers Entering Era of Super-specialists." *Industrial Development*, March–April 1976, pp. 16–17.

DILMORE, GENE.   *Quantitative Techniques in Real Estate Counseling*. Lexington, Mass.: Lexington Books, 1981.

EVANS, SAMUEL.   "Industrial Park Development." *The Appraisal Journal*, April 1972, pp. 235–45.

GAINS, JAMES P.   "Industrial Land Valuation." *The Real Estate Appraiser and Analyst*, Winter 1981, pp. 5–9.

GRDEN-ELLSON, NANCY.   "Industrial Real Estate in the 1980's." *Business & Economic Review*, November 1981, pp. 27–35.

HARTMAN, DONALD J.   "Industrial Property." In *The Real Estate Handbook*, ed. Maury Seldin, pp. 1037–53. Homewood, Ill.: Dow Jones-Irwin, 1980.

HAYMES, A.   "Real Estate Dealing: Increasing Cash Flow in an Industrial Investment." *Real Estate Review*, Summer 1976, pp. 18–21.

————.   "Real Estate Dealing: Making the Most of an Industrial Investment." *Real Estate Review*, Fall 1976, pp. 14–17.

KINNARD, WILLIAM N., JR., STEPHEN D. MESSNER, and BYRL N. BOYCE.   *Industrial Real Estate* (3rd ed.). Washington D.C.: Society of Industrial Realtors, 1979.

KYLE, ROBERT C.   "Evaluating Industrial Properties." *Journal of Property Management*, November–December 1979, pp. 321–23.

POLLINA, RONALD R.   "Industrial Parks: Site Selection, Development, and Promotion." *American Industrial Development Council Journal*, July 1977, pp. 7–29.

————.   "Industrial Parks: What Firms Look For." *American Industrial Development Council Journal*, April 1977, pp. 33–57.

SOCIETY OF INDUSTRIAL REALTORS.   *Industrial Real Estate—An Annotated Bibliography*. Washington, D.C.: Society of Industrial Realtors, 1982.

THORNE, OAKLEIGH J.   "Industrial Park Cash Flow Analysis." *Industrial Development*, March–April 1971, pp. 2–9.

TROXEL, JAY C.   "Functional Analysis of Industrial Property." *The Real Estate Appraiser*, January–February 1974, pp. 35–38.

URBAN LAND INSTITUTE.   *Industrial Development Handbook*. Community Builders Handbook Series. Washington, D.C.: Urban Land Institute, 1975.

WEBB, JAMES R., and C. F. SIRMANS.   "Yields and Risk Measures for Real Estate, 1966–1977." *The Journal of Portfolio Management*, Fall 1980, pp. 14–19.

————.   "Yields on Commercial and Industrial Real Estate versus Other Assets." *Real Estate Issues*, Fall–Winter 1982, pp. 28–33.

CHAPTER SIXTEEN
RECREATIONAL AND RESORT PROPERTY COUNSELING

Resort properties have unique characteristics that need to be identified immediately. The most important of these characteristics is that resort properties are often seasonal operations. If a resort is on the seashore and caters to summer vacationists, then its potential income streams peak during the summer. On the other hand, if a resort is at a winter ski slope, then its income is generated principally during the winter. Most resorts have made very strong efforts to lengthen the season and to find alternative attractions that will justify keeping their doors open during the off-season. Some of these efforts have been successful, but others have not. It is therefore imperative that the counselor initially recognize the duration of a resort's seasonal business.

Other important characteristics of resort properties include their location relative to population centers and the ease with which they can be reached. The term *recreational property* is often overused and it means different things to different people. A desert, for example, may provide a fine recreational experience to a person who lives on a foggy seashore, yet that same foggy seashore may provide an enjoyable recreational experience for a person who resides in an arid region. Before a proper analysis of the recreational and resort property can be made, the counselor needs to quantify the probable use of the recreational property, the duration of the season, and the probabilities of economic success.

The range of recreational and resort properties includes tennis developments, oceanfront projects, and even mixed use developments. In some parts of the country, retirement developments have been quite successful. Their recreational activities are often centered on indoor activities such as bowling, painting, pottery, and handcrafts. Skill is needed to determine the optimum mix of such recreational amenities.

CHARACTERISTICS OF RECREATIONAL LAND

Timber is often a ground cover on recreational property. Many times, the standing timber (which is considered part of the real estate) provides the aesthetic beauty that makes the property attractive for recreational development. At other times, however, some of the timber can be cut and sold off without adversely affecting the recreational potential of the property. If the counselor suspects that this latter condition is the case, it is recommended that a professional timber cruiser be retained to work with the counselor in determining the local forest practices, assessing the merchantability of the species located on the property, and estimating the quantity, quality, and value of the timber crop. A decision needs to be made as to whether the harvest would be a "clear-cut" of all the timber or a "selective-cut" of only those trees that can be spared without adversely affecting the recreational potential of the land. In the western states timber is usually considered saw timber, that is, as timber that can be cut into the lumber used for construction. In the eastern states much of the timber is considered pulpwood and is used in paper products.

Minerals can sometimes create conditions that adversely affect highest and best use for recreational purposes. This is particularly true in areas where the exploitation of minerals can create noise, air, or water pollution conditions more closely akin to the conditions of large industrial communities than to the pristine conditions of recreational areas.

At other times, however, mineral rights present no major obstacle to recreational development. Often oil or geothermal exploration can be done in such a way as to minimize the adverse impact on adjoining properties.

Proximity to water is a major attribute of recreational property. The water may be an ocean, a lake, a river, or a stream, but the size, the reputation, and the recreational experiences available from it provide invaluable recreational opportunities to the adjoining lands. The opportunities for fishing, swimming, sailing, water skiing, wind surfing, or even just sitting and looking at the water enable residential and commercial ventures to thrive on nearby land. Of paramount importance, especially in the western states, is the availability of domestic water.

The counselor should spend adequate time in researching the characteristics of the water body. This research should cover trends in pollution levels, specific regulations prohibiting use of the water surfaces, the monthly cycle of water levels, the reputation of the area for water sports, and likely competing uses for the water such as its use as a source of water for a major population center.

Some lakes are operated primarily for hydroelectric purposes. In these lakes water supplies build up during the spring runoff and are depleted prior to the winter rains. The water level of such lakes is therefore constantly changing unless other factors are present. These other factors include the interrelationship of the dams at several connecting lakes, the influence of use of the lake for recreational purposes, unseasonal water flows, and contractual agreements between the operators of the lake and other upstream or downstream users regarding the timing and the amounts of releases from the dam. All of these factors need to be analyzed in order to properly evaluate the amount of water that will be available in the lake during the recreational period.

Soil condition affects the stability of adjoining lands and the development costs that might be experienced by a subdivider or a builder. In some areas layers of peat or other very porous soils are layered into the soil. This type of condition creates a problem that will undoubtedly add to construction and development costs. Usually such soils must be removed and replaced with gravel or other solid material to provide a foundation for construction. Sometimes it may be necessary to build on piling.

Some areas, particularly in the West, have developed a recent notoriety because of their potential for earthquakes or because of their location near a fault or an active volcano. The U.S. Geological Survey maps and local forestry offices can usually provide necessary information regarding the geology of the area in question.

POPULARITY OF AREA

The popularity of an area obviously determines its drawing power for a purchasing public. Many large recreational areas scattered across the United States draw visitors from all parts of the nation.

Other recreational areas attract a more regional clientele. For example, many of the smaller ski slopes in the West are used primarily by westerners who drive a few hundred miles to take a skiing vacation. Due to the size of this market area, its reputation is concentrated within a few adjoining states.

There are many major terminal resorts in the Rocky Mountain states which have focused regional and national recognition on the area. The success of such resorts often enhances the development potential of adjoining lands. As noted earlier, the main characteristic of recreational and resort property is the cyclical nature of its business. There is an on-season and an off-season. During the on-season there is usually a lot of business. During the off-season there is rarely any business, or at best it is spotty.

Some of the more successful resorts have been able to partially stabilize their business volume throughout the on-season and off-season cycle. Generally speaking, these resorts are located in areas whose temperate climate can be enjoyed on a nearly year-round basis. In some cases, conferences or special vacation packages have encouraged greater use of facilities during the off-season.

Access to the area is another major attribute that needs evaluation by the counselor. It would be difficult for a major ski area to develop a national reputation unless there were airports nearby that could handle the incoming tourists. Admittedly, highway access will provide business from population centers that are within a couple of hundred miles, but it soon becomes difficult to entice a sufficient number of users into the area if driving distances are more than a weekend trip away.

KEY CONCERNS WITH RECREATIONAL AND RESORT PROPERTIES

The real estate counselor can provide a most valuable service to developers of prospective recreational or resort projects. Specifically, he or she can alert the developer to the unique constraints of such projects and to marketing quirks that can be learned only through previous experience with or research of an area. The counselor will invariably provide the client with essential information on such matters as obtaining required permits, identifying a specific submarket, and preparing a marketing strategy to capture a particular segment of that submarket. Other matters that the counselor deals with include project design, amenity staging, and facilities management.

Ski Areas

Snow skiing came into prominence as a popular winter outdoor activity in the post–World War II era. Although downhill skiing started in the early part of this century, the major upswing in the popularity of this sport began in the mid-1940s. Since that time hundreds of new ski facilities have been developed in areas that can provide a winter snow cover of reasonable duration and that are accessible by vehicle and within reasonable proximity to a large body of population. The time distance from major airport and rail facilities is an important consideration in the probable success of a given facility. This is perhaps more important for ski resorts than for other types of recreational developments.

The ski slopes must have reasonable accessibility to a population center. Many smaller ski areas have been developed within a hundred miles of large urban centers, so that the skier can visit them on a one-day outing. Such facilities provide limited overnight accommodations and have after-hour night spots.

Major ski areas attract both the weekend skier and the vacation skier who will spend a week or two in the area. Such facilities require extensive overnight accommodations and dining and entertainment centers.

Both types of successful ski areas enjoy good road access through the ski season, accessibility to a large "skiing market," slopes of varying degrees of difficulty that can provide a challenge to the beginner and the expert alike, sufficient lifts to carry the skiers up the hill, skiing instructors, and an equipment shop that rents and sells skis, skiing gear, clothing, and the other accessories that are necessary to make the skiing operation work.

The selection of a potential ski area requires a detailed historic study of snowfall characteristics. The most popular areas in the West are those that have early snows and are able to retain a snowpack well into the spring months, at least until Memorial Day. Many of the established ski areas have acquired snowmaking equipment that is used to maintain a snow cover on the slopes during warm winters and early springs. Snowmaking machines to touch up the slopes are invaluable in this type of area because they enable the ski season to go on uninterruptedly or even to be extended a few weeks.

The counselor must evaluate a ski area on the whole by its historic performance, its current reputation, and its possibilities for further development. All the technical ingredients of the supply (the facilities available or potentially available at the area) and demand (the likelihood that skiers will want to use the area) equation remain much the same for an evaluation of this type of property as they would be for an evaluation of other types of property. The area must be able to compete with facilities that handle large crowds; it must provide a challenge to all levels of skiers; it must offer accommodations and shopping for the weekender; and in addition, it is desirable that nearby areas be available for private residential developments. In recent years condominium projects have gone a long way toward stabilizing winter ski areas as a second home community.

FIGURE 16–1   Aspen, Colorado, as seen from a chair lift ascending Aspen Mountain. Photograph by Michael Kennedy, courtesy of Aspen Skiing Company.

Some ski areas, particularly in the western states, have been developed on government-owned land. In such instances, the U.S. Forest Service often acts as the administrative agent for the government and issues a permit for private developers to develop the ski slopes based on agreed master planning of the area. The law and the politics of the permit process should be understood. Mammoth Mountain on the eastern slopes of the Sierra Nevada in California is a good example of this type of development. All of the ski slopes have been developed on government land, while Mammoth Village, at the foot of the mountain, has been developed on private land.

It is again important for the counselor to recognize the seasonal nature of most ski areas. Sometimes their location in mountainous country is such that summer boating, fishing, hiking, and camping are sufficient to carry an area through a twelve-month recreational experience.

Marinas

A marina is defined as a boat basin that has docks, moorings, storage, supplies, and other facilities for boats. Marinas come in all sizes, shapes, and design, and in many sections of the United States they are a commodity that is in short supply. In areas that have a large number of visiting boats—for example, Florida—there may be an abundance of dry storage but a shortage of wet berths.

In recent years the steadily increasing use of recreational boats has increased the demand for facilities to service their needs. There appears to be an ever-growing need for new slips and boat ramps to service boats of all sizes, ranging from the small fishing boats that are trailered to the boat ramp closest to the favorite fishing spot up to the large oceangoing sailboats and powerboats that are increasing in number in our coastal communities.

Most of the marinas on inland lakes and waterways have been designed for use by trailerable boats. At a marina of this type the facilities are usually oriented toward boat rentals and fishing, with summertime uses for water skiing, sailing, picnicking, and just plain messin' around with boats. This type of marina is often limited to summertime operation. In the South, however, year-round operations can be developed quite successfully.

Most marina construction seems to be along the creeks, rivers, bays, and ocean entrances that are identified as being navigable bodies of water. Boats that are 25 feet and larger in size, which are fairly cumbersome to trailer, are usually stored in the water year-round in the southern latitudes. In the colder northern areas, such boats are often put in dry storage for the winter. However, along most of our continental shoreline, yachtspersons are able to keep their boats in the water on a year-round basis. This means that moorings, berths, or slips must be available on a continuous basis. The newer marinas today are often quite large, usually in the 300- to 500-slip size. There is a harbor master, and the onshore support facilities typically include rest rooms, showers, a marine store, a large paved parking lot for automobiles, a dry storage yard, and often a nearby restaurant. Some of the marinas have installed cranes instead of a boat ramp, so that the trailerable sailboats and powerboats can be lifted off the trailer or cradle and lowered directly into the water. Upon completion of the day's use of the boat, it is loaded back onto the trailer and placed in a dry storage lot. In this manner, the capacity of the marina can be greatly enlarged even though there is no more room for berths and slips.

Many of the marinas were built and are owned by private yacht clubs. The site may be owned by the club, or leased from a municipality. In the latter instances, the club often has to make berth space available for both members and nonmembers.

In some parts of the country much new marina construction is being built by municipalities and through government ownership or subsidy. The two- to three-year permit process that is required to get a marina approved, the high cost of mortgage funds in the private investment market, and the high cost of construction (a recently built 400-slip marina in California cost $5,500 per slip), make it very difficult for a private investor to tie up a site, pay for the experts needed to get approval by the 300 to 400 groups that must be environmentally satisfied, build the marina, and then pay for it with present-day revenues. Since municipalities, on the other hand, are able to obtain low-interest loans and sometimes grants from government agencies, they are able to justify building in today's economy.

There are, of course, many exceptions to this current problem of revenue shortfall, the most prominent of which is the marina that is constructed as part of a new residential community with water orientation. The facilities required for such a marina development can be used by the other phases of the project, with the marina development becoming a good profit center for the overall project.

The valuation of a privately owned marina is essentially the same as the valuation of most other business ventures. The counselor must look at the basis of tenancy on the land, the cost of that tenancy, the size and condition of the operation, the present and probable future annual operating costs, and the costs of special repairs (breakwaters, docks, riprap, parking lots, etc.) and then decide whether the current expenses are likely to continue at a reasonable level. The counselor must then undertake a market study to determine the probability of new competition in the area and the probable trends of rental rates for slips. The problem then becomes an extension of normally accepted valuation and counseling techniques. A market study may be required at this point.

Before leaving the subject of marinas, it is most important that the counselor realize the difficulties entailed in the permit process required to build a new marina. On navigable streams it will be necessary to eventually deal at length with the U.S. Army Corps of Engineers, which has jurisdiction over most navigable waterways and wetland areas. The corps's jurisdiction stems from several laws. Section 10 of the River and Harbor Act of 1899 requires a permit for any structure of work in or affecting navigable waters of the United States; Section 404 of the Clean Water Act requires a permit for the discharge of dredged or fill materials into the waters of the United States; and Section 103 of the Marine Protection Research and Sanctuaries Act of 1972 requires a permit for transporting dredge material in order to dispose of it in ocean waters.

The permit process should be planned to cover two to three years, and a potential marina developer is well advised to undertake early discussions with personnel at the Corps of Engineers to see what steps need to be taken to meet existing requirements. The corps usually becomes aware of a new privately planned marina project from the city or county public works department where the first application is made. It is important to meet with public agencies as early as possible to find out what they want and what they are going to require. Then, by the time the application goes to the corps for public notice, most of the problems should have been anticipated and answered. In the California area the corps will notify some 300 to 400 groups that have an "interest in" any new projects involving wetlands. The most active group is the U.S. Fish and Wildlife Service. The corps's permit process involves a number of matters, including public access to the water or the project, public interest, water quality, fish and wildlife protection, historical preservation (burial grounds, etc.), the conservation of resources, better control of flood damage, desirable land use, the availability of recreational facilities, food protection, bulkhead protection needs, and the probable economics of the new project.

The counselor should realize that although obtaining a permit for a new marina is not an easy matter such permits can be obtained since marinas are generally considered desirable by most government agencies. Sometimes a properly designed and constructed new marina is a more than acceptable trade-off against the loss of marginal wetlands.

GOLF COURSE DEVELOPMENTS

A golf course can be a significant asset to a residential community, but it is not something to be entered into lightly or without proper counseling. The two basic types of golf courses are the nine-hole course and the eighteen-hole course, each of which has a variety of configurations. A nine-hole course is typically about 3,000 yards long, and an eighteen-hole course is about 6,500 to 7,000 yards long. Nine-hole courses are not as prevalent in private developments as the full-size courses. Just as important as the length of the course is the amount of acreage that must be set aside for it. A nine-hole course will usually need from 50 to 80 acres; an eighteen-hole course generally requires from 110 to 160 acres; and 200 acres is not uncommon for championship courses.

Demand

A key question in providing a golf course in a development is whether the cost of the course and the land "lost" for it are more than offset by the increased demand and sales revenue for the lots, homes, hotels, and so on adjacent to the course. In this connection, there are some fundamental demand factors that should ordinarily be considered carefully by the counselor before work on the development is begun.

FIGURE 16–2   Brandermill, a residential community built on a reservoir near Richmond, Virginia. Note that the houses in the background have both a fairway and a water view. Courtesy of Morgan and Associates, Richmond, Virginia.

A basic question is what type of development is being planned. The following four types of communities are frequently developed with golf courses: (1) first-home communities, (2) semiretirement communities, (3) second-home recreational communities, and (4) resort communities.[1] The nature of the development will influence the course design.

In addition, various demographic characteristics of the prospective occupants must be analyzed to judge the probable success of a golf course. A rule of thumb, which of course is insufficient to determine the demand for a particular golf course, is that it takes 15,000 to 25,000 people to support a course. Demographic factors should be studied to determine whether the personal income of prospective purchasers is adequate to support the golfing facilities as well as to afford the residential or resort development planned for the area or the specific property. Age can influence the design and the eventual success of the proposed development. Young people may be unable to afford the property. On the other hand, older persons who are able to afford the property may require an interesting but not overtaxing golf course.

As with other types of real estate developments, the consultant must take into account such factors as location, accessibility, and present and probable future competition. Terrain and soil conditions are perhaps even more important for the golf course community than for other types of developments. The presence of high

---

[1]Rees L. Jones and Guy L. Rando, *Golf Course Developments,* Technical Bulletin 70 (Washington, D.C.: Urban Land Institute, 1974), pp. 36–42.

winds can adversely affect the popularity of a golf course and thus impair property sales or income from transient facility uses.

Design

Assuming that the market analysis reveals sufficient demand in the target market, then a community enhanced by a golf course must be designed skillfully by a golf course architect. The counselor can provide invaluable guidance for the

FIGURE 16–3   Woodmont, a private country club community in Tamarac, Florida. Courtesy of Von Hagge & Devlin, Inc., Houston, Texas.

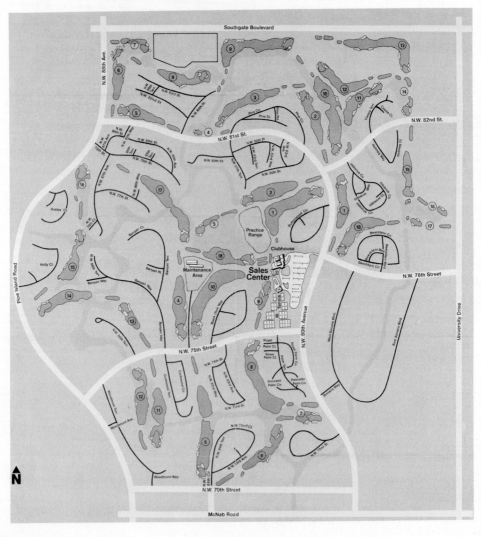

design by supplying information from his or her market analysis. Some key design considerations are to have the greens large enough and the fairways wide enough to prevent the players from becoming backed up and to prevent the greens from lacking sufficient interest because the location of the holes cannot be changed. The residences will need to be set back far enough and the exteriors designed and painted so as not to negate the open and natural sensation of the course. At the same time the terrain will have to be utilized so as to produce the optimum level of challenge for the golfers while maximizing the monetary yield to the developer.

Effects of Golf Course on Project Success

A golf course is not an end in itself, but it can be a very attractive amenity to the community of which it is an integral part. Even nongolfers are attracted to an address on a fairway or near "the" country club. The history of golf courses in residential communities reveals that they not only sell homes but that they cause homes overlooking the course to sell at a premium. Such premiums may vary from 10 to 50 percent over the prices of interior lots of similar size. In short, a well-designed course properly integrated into a residential community creates a highly desirable prestige address. Similarly, people will come from long distances to stay at resorts with courses that have earned outstanding reputations.

There is an important distinction between development-type golf courses and clubs and those that relate to real estate developments. The development-type golf courses and clubs are usually owned by the developers and are used for promotional purposes while homesites and surrounding housing are being sold. After the sales campaign has been completed, the members usually take over. The property owners can usually run their club more profitably than the developer since they are willing to give up many of the extra flourishes that are provided during the marketing period.

There is no standardized approach to setting club membership fees. Three frequently used methods are

1. Clubs with regular golf dues only
2. Clubs with regular golf dues and initiation fees
3. Clubs with regular golf dues, initiation fees, and equity membership cost

Maintenance

A key consideration in designing a golf course is to minimize its maintenance costs. To achieve this objective, the architect will try to minimize grades and will space trees far enough apart to facilitate machine mowing. Also, pine trees are generally preferable to hardwood trees that necessitate frequent leaf cleanup. A balance must be struck between the amount of the initial capital expenditure for such items as an automatic irrigation system and the cost of manual watering later. Whenever possible, there should be an on-site source of water.[2]

A final category of maintenance—more properly called management—is the operation of the clubhouse. This one component, according to Hunter Moss, CRE, can either make or break a golf course development. The greatest single mistake is to have too many golfing members for the golf course. (A rule of thumb is that there should be 350 to 400 golfing members per golf course.) This error, in turn, can adversely affect the sales of the surrounding real estate.

TIMESHARE HOMES

Timeshare, or interval ownership, is not a new concept. However, its popularity has grown tremendously in recent years, mostly because developers have worked hard to broaden the buyer market for second homes in resort areas. Many more families can afford a two-week timeshare purchase than can afford full ownership of a vacation home. By dividing the ownership expense among several owners, the number of potential buyers for a particular property is greatly expanded.

The interval ownership concept is rather simple: instead of buying a house or condominium for fifty-two weeks a year, you buy a share of the property for the period during which you wish to use it. Timeshare is therefore a "vacation" concept. For this reason, the amenity package is very important. Projects with golf, tennis, fishing, and swimming and other water sports reach a broader market than is reached by developments that lack a wide range of vacation activities. Some notable exceptions are located in ski areas, campgrounds, and wilderness areas.

The counselor must address the issue of off-season weeks at an early stage in the timeshare planning process. A developer cannot afford to sell all in-season weeks without properly planning the marketing of the less desirable intervals. Price differentials among the intervals can partially alleviate the problem. However, a better strategy is to package a good week with a poor week in the sales program. In this way, the seasons sell out on a uniform basis.

Typically, the developer will sell fifty-one weeks, leaving a week for unit refurbishment. Even though the units are occupied by "owners" most of the year, they still suffer wear and tear. Management will clean and inspect each unit between users so that major repairs may be charged back to the interval owner. Nonetheless, the yearly rehabilitation period is necessary to ensure that furnishings and equipment remain in good condition. Management's role is a difficult one. It is not easy to satisfy the varying wishes of interval owners with respect to the level of desired maintenance. The continuing success of a timeshare development is greatly depen-

[2]Cecil McKay, Jr., and Karla L. Heuer, *Golf Courses: A Guide to Analysis and Valuation* (Chicago: American Institute of Real Estate Appraisers, 1980), pp. 24–25.

dent on the ability and efforts of the management group. Management must also work with the owners' association, collect and invest the reserves for major replacements, and handle the annual refurbishments.

Ownership in timeshare units can take many forms. Most often, the buyer purchases a fee simple interest for the time span of his or her purchase. Other ownership forms include

1. *Fee simple.* This is perhaps the best understood form of ownership from the buyer's standpoint. It is also the safest from the standpoint of avoiding legal complications.
2. *Right to use license.* This is in effect a contract between the developer and the buyer that is set for a specific term of years.
3. *Club membership with right to use.* Where this is used in connection with an interval, the buyer combines the benefits of club membership with a right to use the property for the interval period.
4. *Vacation lease.* Where a lease for a term of years is used, the relationship is simply that of landlord and tenant. Typically, these arrangements are for periods of twenty to forty years. At the end of the lease term the developer recaptures the property. At this time he can renew leases, change the use of the property, or make such other disposition as might be appropriate.

Of the various forms of ownership, fee simple will probably prove to have the best resale value. This is particularly true when the remaining term of rights to use or leasehold interests is relatively short. In addition, it is usually easier to finance a fee simple interval than the other forms of interval ownership. Although one would expect fee simple intervals to be priced significantly higher than vacation leases or right to use intervals, there has not been a notable price differential.

The form of ownership affects not only demand but also unit pricing. The pricing of a timeshare interval is at best difficult. In addition to the usual physical, locational, and supply and demand factors, the counselor must consider the form of ownership and segment the weeks of the year into values that reflect buyer demand. With proper pricing the sales agent should be able to sell shares in all seasons even if the "good-bad" package system is not used.

The ability to sell "off weeks" has been enhanced materially by the success of the exchange networks. A timeshare owner whose unit is a member of an exchange network may swap his interval for one of equal seasonal value at his choice of hundreds of other units around the world. It is important for all parties to remember that an owner will rarely be able to swap his off-season interval for an in-season period. This flexibility has been a great help in selling intervals throughout the year.

In addition to its profit benefit, timesharing benefits the developer of resort areas by greatly increasing the resident population at the project. An owner of a two-week interval will rarely leave it vacant, usually renting it or lending it to friends if he does not use it himself. This increased population naturally has a favorable effect on the utilization, and hence the profitability, of the golf courses, restaurants, and other project amenities. This aspect is particularly important in new resorts where the carrying cost of the recreational amenities is very great.

RESORT CONVERSION

When lot or home sales are slow at a private recreational community, the developer may consider converting the project to resort rentals. Typically, a resort conversion is prompted either by financial distress or by the recognition that a rental approach may prove more attractive financially. Slower than anticipated sales may result from unsound market analyses, an upward shift in mortgage interest rates, a lack of discretionary family income, inadequate promotional effort by the developer, poor timing, or a combination of factors.

When the developer cannot generate enough site or building sales to cover his operating costs and mortgage debt service, he must consider converting some of the unsold inventory to resort rentals. The role of the counselor is to weigh the financial feasibility of such a conversion because it is neither without costs nor without risks.

Some of the problems related to the resort conversion are

1. Dealing with and being fair to those persons who have already purchased homes or sites in anticipation of living in a private development without tourists. Handling this problem requires diplomacy, tact, and time.
2. Granting favorable treatment to the permanent property owners while allowing the transient guests reasonable access to the same amenities, such as the golf course or tennis courts.
3. Obtaining qualified staff to handle reservations, maintenance, room and food service, linen, maid service, security, and possible internal transportation.
4. Providing an equitable and economically appropriate rental system—both for the developer's unsold inventory and the individual property owners' homes.
5. Properly promoting the resort properties. It is generally easier to resolve this problem than to resolve the problem of promoting a private community since travel agents and travel writers with newspapers can be enlisted to promote the resort. Such free outside assistance would not be available for a private development.[3]
6. Providing a variety of fairly diversified activities. Whereas nominal activities are required for a private development, people paying to visit a resort expect continuing activities that appeal to different age groups. Additional staffing is needed to carry out this expanded activities mission, and care must be taken to avoid offending the permanent property owners.

There are some potential advantages to a resort conversion. Before considering such a move, a study of the property's marketing potential is needed. It may be that the property lacks the location, weather, amenities and overall appeal as a prospective resort. However, if it has this potential, among the advantages of the resort conversion are

1. Generating revenue from unit rentals, food service, and recreational facilities. This revenue may be insufficient to generate a profit, but it will be beneficial in reducing the negative cash flow of the private development/resort.

[3]David Pearson, Gary Sandor, and Fred Schock, "Resort Conversion: A New Response to a Developer's Dilemma," *Urban Land,* September 1975, pp. 8–9.

2. Attracting prospective property buyers to the development. Once a person has visited and enjoyed a resort, he or she may seriously consider buying a property to ensure continued enjoyment at the same location.

CASE STUDY

A developer is presented with the opportunity to acquire a partially developed resort subdivision. The property is offered by a bank that recently foreclosed after the initial development effort failed. The subdivision has been designed to yield 300 single-family lots oriented around an eighteen-hole golf course. The following work was completed before construction was halted:

1. Main entrance and 600 lineal feet of roadway
2. Installation of sewer, water, and natural gas lines—the capacity of these utilities is more than sufficient for the entire development
3. Rough clearing of fairways for an eighteen-hole golf course

The developer asks his real estate counselor to examine the property and development plan in light of current market conditions to determine whether he should undertake this project. The developer has an agreement with a private golf club to build and operate the golf course and a small clubhouse on the property. The present club membership is so large that an additional eighteen-hole golf course is needed. The developer will deed to the club at no cost the land required for the course and the clubhouse. The club in turn will agree to accept as members those persons who buy homes in the proposed subdivision. The agreement also provides for a reduced initiation fee for such new members. This arrangement will permit the developer to concentrate on the development of lots and yet assure the successful construction and operation of the golf facilities. The developer's expertise is in building subdivisions and selling lots to a group of five home builders. The lot inventory in his existing subdivisions is running low, so he is poised to start a new project. The market for homes in the proposed resort subdivision appears very strong, and the five home builders express definite interest. The only problem is that the project is not financially attractive based on the bank's asking price for the project "as is." Since the price is firm, the counselor decides to study the development plan and the lot pricing to determine whether a higher yield can be obtained.

The counselor's preliminary findings are as follows:

1. Sufficient market demand exists for the 300 lots to ensure full absorption within a designated time frame.
2. The original developer's projected average lot price of $15,000 is obtainable based on a careful market analysis.
3. The development cost estimate is realistic based on the cost experience of comparable subdivisions.
4. The arrangement with the golf club for the golf facilities is favorable for the developer.

Although the counselor's research supports the revenue and expense projections of the client developer, the acquisition cost effectively eliminates any potential profit. The counselor notes that the land plan shows several parallel and adjoining fairways, thereby limiting the number of lots actually adjoining the golf course. He suggests that the project be redesigned to maximize the number of lots with fairway views. A new site plan is drafted that separates the adjoining fairways and rearranges the street system, thus increasing the number of lots on the golf course.

The counselor calculates revenue and expense projections based on the new lot configurations. The revised plan still yields 300 lots, but the increased number of lots with fairway views raises the average lot price to $17,500, with little change in development costs. This increase in revenues, with costs essentially constant, appears sufficient to make the development feasible. However, a realistic discounted cash flow of all forecast development costs (both hard and soft) and sales revenue over the development-marketing period provides more assurance as to the financial feasibility of the project.

The developer purchases the property and completes the subdivision. Lot sales occur faster than originally projected because of the strong demand for lots on the golf course. The shortened absorption period and increased lot prices provide the developer with an attractive return on his investment.

SELECTED REFERENCES

AMERICAN LAND DEVELOPMENT ASSOCIATION. *Resort Timesharing: An Analysis of Three Nationwide Surveys.* Washington, D.C.: American Land Development Association, 1979.

BOSTER, ALYCE. "Marketing the Time Share Unit." *Real Estate Review,* Spring 1975, pp. 104–8.

CLOSSER, BRUCE M. "Appraising the Ski Area." *The Appraisal Journal,* July 1980, pp. 325–37.

CONROY, KATHLEEN. *Valuing the Timeshare Property.* Chicago: American Institute of Real Estate Appraisers, 1981.

DAVIS, THOMAS J., JR. "Time-Sharing Exchange Networks." *Real Estate Review,* Fall 1978, pp. 42–45.

———. "Time-Sharing Ownership: Possibilities and Pitfalls." *Real Estate Review,* Winter 1976, pp. 49–54.

DOWLING, WILLIAM Q., and RICHARD F. MARR. "Timesharing and 'Condotels': Valuable Additions under the Right Conditions," *Urban Land,* March 1983, pp. 12–15.

DRIVER, B. L., ed. *Elements of Outdoor Recreation Planning.* Ann Arbor: University of Michigan Press, 1974.

GOELDNER, C. R., and T. A. BUCHMAN. *Economic Analysis of North American Ski Areas, 1981–82 Season.* National Ski Areas Association. Boulder: University of Colorado, 1981.

GOELDNER, C. R., and KAREN DICKE. *Bibliography of Skiing Studies* (6th ed.). Boulder: University of Colorado, 1982.

HART, CHRISTOPHER W. "A Method for Valuing Time-Sharing Intervals." *Real Estate Review,* Summer 1980, pp. 107–13.

JONES, REES L., and GUY L. RANDO. *Golf Course Developments.* Technical Bulletin 70. Washington, D.C.: Urban Land Institute, 1974.

LUSTECK, JOSEPH A., and JACK K. MANN. "The Feasibility of Recreational Land Development." *The Appraisal Journal,* January 1978, pp. 7–19.

McGRATH, JOHN WILLIAMS, and PATRICK S. MULLIGAN. "Future Golf Courses: Economic Realities." *Urban Land,* December 1975, pp. 5–16.

McKAY, CECIL, JR., and KARLA L. HEUER. *Golf Courses: A Guide to Analysis and Valuation.* Chicago: American Institute of Real Estate Appraisers, 1980.

MALLERIS, LEONIDAS C. "Five Legal Hurdles in Time-Share Ownership." *Real Estate Review,* Summer 1978, pp. 97–101.

PEARSON, DAVID, GARY SANDOR, and FRED SCHOCK. "Resort Conversion: A New Response to a Developer's Dilemma." *Urban Land,* September 1975, pp. 3–12.

TROWBRIDGE, KEITH. *Resort Timesharing—How You Can Invest in Inflation-Proof Vacations for Life.* New York: Simon & Schuster, Inc., 1982.

CHAPTER SEVENTEEN
COUNSELING FINANCIAL INSTITUTIONS

Real estate is widely recognized as being a major segment of the nation's wealth, somewhere in the range of 60 to 65 percent. It consists of land as well as its various improvements, such as buildings, roads, and utilities. Investors are willing to pay substantial sums of money to acquire rights in real estate. Financial institutions on their own or as managers for depositors and other clients control great amounts of investable capital. These organizations are frequently called on to invest in a broad assortment of realty interests. They are often referred to as intermediaries because they receive funds as deposits or, in the case of insurance companies, as policy premiums and invest them in a "legal list" of opportunities. They then return a substantial portion of realty net earnings to their customers in the form of interest or dividends. These organizations also have capital of their own that is similarly employed, but wholly for their own benefit.

With financial institutions serving as important managers of our nation's vast real estate wealth, there is a constant interfacing of the realty industry with commercial banks, mutual savings banks, savings and loan associations, life insurance companies, and other types of financial institutions. On a daily basis the financial institutions are active in creating the two prinicipal real estate investments: debt (or mortgages) and equity positions.

In the usual debt situation the investment is for a specified, limited time and it provides a benefit in the form of a fixed interest rate. During recent inflationary periods new investment vehicles have been created that combine debt and equity characteristics. For example, mortgages have been arranged with "kickers" in the form of participations in gross or net incomes. Other types of mortgages have been introduced that offer the usual debt protection and include rights to convert all or part of the loan to equity. Currently, the availability of debt capital is being greatly enhanced and its cost ameliorated by a process known as "securitization." In this arrangement, pools of mortgages serve as collateral security for bond issues underwritten by investment bankers and sold to the general investing public. The securities are referred to as CMOs (Collateralized Mortgage Obligations).

Equity situations differ from debt in that they provide no contractual right to a fixed *return on* or *return of* the investment. The investor naturally hopes for these benefits, and to be induced to take action, he must believe that he has good prospects for realizing a competitively attractive yield, including full investment recapture. An equity investor's claim to project earnings is subordinate to operating expenses and debt service. The equity investor assumes a venture's greatest risks, and he is at the mercy of the pressures of volatile or declining economic conditions. The characteristics of debt and equity positions are the same for both individual and institutional operations. "Securitization" of the equity investment has occurred on a massive scale and has been referred to as Syndication. The investment arrangements outlined above are the functional background against which one considers the problems and practices of real estate counseling for financial institutions.

BUY OR LEASE
HEADQUARTERS

The first contact between a financial institution and real estate comes from the universal need for a "roof over one's head." Where and how to arrange this are problems requiring real estate expertise for satisfactory solutions. The needed talent may exist in the organization, but more probably it must be sought outside. Doubtless, some organizations prefer to make do with insiders, such as officers and directors, but the decision to use these people is very often unfortunate. They are usually eminently qualified in their own business specialties, but real estate must be recognized as having its own peculiar training requirements and knowledge demands. In most instances, the investment required for a headquarter's facility is substantial, so it is hard to believe that in selecting or developing one, an institution would not seek the same quality advice that it customarily obtains to assess any other major investment. Yet the selection is often handled by unqualified in-house personnel. It has often been said—and probably truly—that in the securities field, the legal arena, and assorted other business activities experts are identified and their services are sought but that in real estate *everyone* is an expert. No doubt this overrating of one's ability occurs because most people are homeowners and have had the experience of buying at least one property. One may recall that the "expert" has been defined as "a person who has done it *once*." The selection of institutional headquarters is generally most satisfactorily solved by professional real estate counselors.

Location for Optimum Business Development

The first decision to be made is the selection of an appropriate location. For a financial institution, the choice is frequently limited by laws or regulations restricting the organization's operational area. Within these confines, however, there are usually multiple opportunities. Which location should be selected?

As in all other commercial operations, the customers of a financial institution are its lifeblood. A desirable location is one that makes it convenient for customers to use the organization's services. Site selection should be based on a thorough understanding of an institution's functions and clientele. A location desirable for a thrift institution might be a central site in a heavily populated residential area. Such a location might not, however, be desirable for a commercial bank servicing business entities. For that purpose, a site in the heart of a city's established commercial area would be best. A life insurance company handling most of its business by mail should be free from most of the locational constraints experienced by banking institutions. All organizations are affected by the parking needs caused by the extensive use of private automobiles by employees and customers. Given the variety of factors involved, a real estate counselor serving financial institutions must combine an understanding of their operations with a thorough knowledge of market supply-demand conditions for usable real estate. So equipped, he can recommend the appropriate match-up of his client's locational needs with available real estate.

Working Capital Needs

Since the stock-in-trade of financial institutions is capital, they must have locations facilitating their dealings in that commodity. It is clear that continuing progress in computerization is bringing the marketplace into each and every office. Geography has lost some significance, and its importance as a barrier to doing business will doubtless erode further. It is a fact, however, that location still has importance. Witness the congregation of financial institutions in and around the New York Stock Exchange in New York City and the similar concentrations in other major cities. A commercial bank clearinghouse exemplifies a powerful locational influence in the banking industry. Today, notwithstanding advanced computerization and communications systems, major money center banks feel constrained to locate their operations centers near the facility. This creates intricate problems in the proper location of office facilities that are best handled by professional counselors having special expertise and in-depth market information, rather than by in-house personnel.

To sum up, an institution's paramount need is a location affording optimum convenience for transacting business with its present and prospective customers. This is a fundamental requirement for its successful development and expansion. To serve financial organizations competently, a real estate counselor must have a good grasp of the principles of their businesses as well as their future plans. This is true whether the institution is a commercial bank, a savings bank, a savings and loan association, a life insurance company, a securities dealer, or any other type of financial service organization. This is no simple requirement, but it is a must for a counselor guiding clients in the location of financial institution headquarters facilities.

Short- and Long-Term Business Plans

Real estate advice to financial institutions should take cognizance of both their short- and long-term business plans. With the benefit of hindsight, one might today criticize the location of existing, monumental banking buildings in neighborhoods long since commercially dead because of urban decentralization. But in not a few cases, the facilities served profitably for many years and should not now be classified as mistakes. In other cases, however, buildings were erected when area decline trends were already evident, and neighborhood demise should have been foreseen.

A site selected for the headquarters of a financial institution is usually intended for long-term use. Therefore, the facility's planning and development should be based on extended forecasts of the area's economic potential, particularly its desirability for financial service activities. On no other foundation can an organization feasibly invest the amounts of capital typically required. It is still an accepted belief that financial institutions should strive for "image" by being housed in buildings that convey a sense of permanence. Hence, elaborate and expensive improvements

FIGURE 17–1 A savings and loan association headquarters. Courtesy of SAVINGS AND LOAN NEWS, Chicago.

are often considered appropriate, but if improperly located, they can be very costly mistakes.

There are locations where the long-term outlook is not favorable but where a profitable business experience can be anticipated for a period of ten years or so. A real estate counselor, with awareness of this general economic prospect, as well as the specific institution's business potential, can guide the organization to a location and a facility that will serve its short-term earnings goals but avoid the costly overimprovement of a facility designed for long-term use. Problems of this type are not unusual, and they present counselors with important service opportunities.

Since financial service organizations are in intense competition for the acquisition and control of capital, they are very "bottom line" conscious. If they are publicly owned, a common ambition is to have their stock trade at improving price levels. To achieve this goal, they cannot afford the financial drain of costly and inefficient business facility development programs. A counselor is certain to be knowledgeable in these aspects of financial organization operations. Therefore, he can use his real estate skills most effectively in solving their problems.

Comparative Analysis of
Prospective Space Arrangements

A decision that institutions frequently have to make is whether to own or lease real estate facilities. The question arises because a real estate investment *is* money. A financial organization's business is to deal with this commodity in such ways as lending, investing, managing, and exchanging. To the extent that its funds are tied up in real estate, they are unavailable for these profitable uses. This is plainly disadvantageous because it results in a diminution of potential business volume. An obvious alternative is to lease the real estate. It might be argued that rent payments also involve the use of money. But the amount, in any one year, is far less than that required for property acquisition. Funds devoted to property ownership are not removed from an institution's customary business for just the year of purchase; their unavailability continues until the property is sold.

A real estate counselor may be engaged by an institution planning new headquarters or by one dealing with an existing property. In either case, the organization will want to handle its housing problem in the most economical manner. In the former situation, a review of the institution's balance sheet and business experience, particularly its capital requirements, should answer the question of whether it is better to own or lease. If the decision is to own, the real estate counselor will use his talents to help the client develop an efficient facility. If the decision is to lease, other problems require his attention. The selected lease arrangement may be a simple rental of an existing facility, but perhaps a sale-leaseback of a building erected by the institution may be regarded as more favorable. In either case, the counselor draws on his general real estate experience to advise the client concerning lease terms, such as duration, rental, mode of payment, options to renew, operating expense arrangements, and real estate tax payments. Since the sale-leaseback mode is essentially a financing plan, its use will be recommended only when current capital market conditions justify the client's participation. For example, an institution would not pay an amount of rent that represented 15 percent of the sales price at a time when it could acquire the funds as a mortgage loan at 10 percent. This is a basic cost constraint that may be subject to some modest changes. The purchaser, in fact, may occasionally take a significantly lower rate of return, provided he gets full tax shelter benefits of ownership.

The "image" problem also influences decisions on owning or leasing. Institutions hope that they will be perceived by the public as durable, steady, and substantial, and they tend to believe that a prestigious appearance will be helpful in achieving the objective. Speculative commercial builders are not interested in these items because extra building features involve added costs but not greater profits. To achieve a desired image, an institution should participate in the planning process, and its builder should probably receive additional compensation in the form of either an initial subsidy or larger rent provisions. The problem described is often solved by the sale-leaseback procedure.

In view of the numerous considerations involved in choosing between an existing building and a new facility, a counselor serving a financial organization must fully understand its business functions and operations. Existing buildings often have desirable locations and excellent appearances, yet in some cases their space layouts and mechanical equipment are not desirable or efficiently adaptable for an institution's operational processes. On the other hand, although there are prestige factors that flow from occupancy of a sparkling new, impressive structure, the actual cost may be not only substantial but far greater than the original estimates on which the occupancy decision was based. These additional construction costs are usually accompanied by higher operating expenses.

Financial institutions are generally not in the real estate business per se. They are dealers in financial services and are interested primarily in the "bottom line" results of these activities. Most are publicly owned and are constrained to be responsive to stockholder demands for attractive dividends. Because it can greatly affect the financial results of an organization's operations, the decision on location and type of headquarters is critically important. Research and study are required to develop a proper choice that accords due regard to the importance of appearances but gives equal attention to economic considerations. The handling of a headquarters selection problem highlights the importance of counselor services to a financial institution. He is well equipped to analyze alternatives and provide realistic assessments of the consequences flowing from them. His counsel will include clear, objective pictures of the different situations, rather than the subjective and often erroneous views that a layperson can so easily develop. History demonstrates that improper property selection can cause unfortunate financial results, particularly for organizations emphasizing "appearances." The excess costs of overelaborate facilities are likely to impair the institution's earnings performance.

Impact of Accounting Rules

An apt description of a counselor is that he is an economic generalist. His concerns cover many fields, and he is obliged to stay well informed in all. A good example is accounting. The rules and procedures employed in reporting the results of business activities have far-reaching effects. They shape the public's perception of the profitability of a business, which, in turn, influences the price at which the stock of the business will trade. Although this is undeniably true, the public's view, ironically, often differs substantially from the picture that accountants seek to communicate. In reporting their business results, banking and other financial organizations must comply with the difficult "generally accepted accounting principles" (GAAP). This complicates efforts to portray true conditions. Armed with a working knowledge of an institution's financial operations, as well as general accounting practices, a counselor is particularly well equipped to help solve its various problems. For example, a headquarters' selection may involve the application of Financial Accounting Standards Board Statement No. 13. Formerly, institutions were inclined to lease headquarters and branch facilities, simply because the arrangement did not affect their balance sheets. Instead, they were merely required to account for the rent involved by showing it in operating or profit and loss statements. This was particularly important to banks because their balance sheets did not show scarce capital tied up in owned real estate. Instead, they reported these equity funds as fully available to support the lending activities that constituted their business lifeblood. This and other factors promoted many sale-leaseback situations. Recently, however, the Financial Accounting Standards Board promulgated a rule entitled FASB No. 13, which, like all similar rules, has the force of law for a publicly owned organization. The regulation provides that long-term lease arrangements must be capitalized and carried on balance sheets, eliminating the previous accounting advantage. There is much more to this rule, and the above describes only a small part. It is sufficient, however, to demonstrate how accounting rules and practices can influence and change an institution's outlook, operations, and financial reporting. In headquarters and branch planning, effective real estate counseling entails a working knowledge of the instutition's functioning and accounting practices as well as general real estate market conditions.

Branch Site Locations

Financial institutions, such as banks, savings and loan associations, and insurance companies, have a number of characteristics in common, and the most important of these characteristics is that they all deal with large groups of people. It follows that to be located near heavy concentrations of eligible customers is a very desirable situation. Further, capable business management looks beyond the acceptability of current conditions and gives equal, or more, attention to future growth. Although present population levels are important, expansion trends are really the prime consideration. The selection of a successful branch location hinges largely, then, on the proper understanding and use of demographics. Financial organizations, however, are often not at liberty to pursue their carefully developed judgments and locate in what, apparently, is the most favorable spot. Their branching actions are usually circumscribed by laws and regulations. In effectively guiding an institution in site selection activities, a counselor will employ extensive knowledge of demographics as well as an awareness of regulatory constraints.

Identification of Growth Areas

Each segment of the population has a different significance to different financial institutions. Obviously, a residential concentration of people is far more beneficial to a thrift institution than to a commercial bank. A site in a well-established and growing residential area should prove ideal for savings banks, savings and loan associations, and insurance company branches. History has demonstrated that certain age and income groups unquestionably save more than others; that some prefer conservative investments, such as savings accounts, whereas others look for more venturesome outlets; and that some tend to be especially sensitive to financial market trends and will readily shift investments, whereas others are uninterested in competitive considerations. An institution's counselor will factor these elements into his or her branch location recommendations.

Accessibility of Site

Commercial banks, investment advisory groups, and, to some extent, insurance companies transact their most important business with commercial organizations. For them, a desirable branch location is one that is in close proximity to concentrations of business enterprises. Future area development is a major concern since an obvious institutional objective is growth. Business groupings such as New York's Wall Street area, Chicago's Loop, and San Francisco's Market Street represent a particular type of important commercial concentration. They contain principally headquarters facilities for large organizations and secondarily a variety of branch offices. There are smaller versions of this sort of concentration in all medium-size communities, and the regional commercial institutions tend to locate and prosper in such districts.

Over the past twenty years the real estate industry has produced a multitude of large office parks and research and development areas. A typical project comprises a substantial group of office and industrial buildings used for high technology, research, or light manufacturing, and on the park's perimeter there are often one or more commercial bank branches. Although these banking situations frequently produce favorable business results, their future growth is limited by the size of the park. When fully developed, it offers no potential for further expansion, and the surrounding area might be zoned to prohibit commercial improvements.

All financial service organizations need customers, and the more available customers there are, the better; therefore, being readily accessible to population concentrations is a business asset. One can readily appreciate the critical importance and benefits of good vehicular facilities, such as easy approach routes and ample parking. There are, of course, many successful institutions in locations where business is still transacted with a pedestrian clientele. These businesses are found in downtown locations close to subway stations or other mass transit stops. A counselor familiar with an organization's business patterns can locate and recommend suitable, efficient real estate facilities.

The massive development of suburbs experienced throughout the post–World War II years was possible because of the availability of automobiles and the development of extensive, excellent road and highway networks. The growing areas generally lacked mass transit, except for a few scattered bus lines. Businesses of all kinds had to depend on customer use of the new highway systems. The more the highway networks extended, the greater became the commercial potential of abutting properties. It soon became clear that for retail businesses nothing was more important than ample on-site parking and easy highway approaches. Inadequate parking space is an obvious detriment to business, because it generates customer frustration and limits business activity. Clearly, these general vehicular requirements are important considerations in the selection of sites for branches of financial institutions. This is true whether the branch is situated in a shopping center or is freestanding. The need to accommodate a clientele oriented to automobile use has strongly influenced real estate development patterns. Real estate counseling skills are, therefore, the most effective tools for choosing business locations that are properly related to customer support.

The day of the urban business centers is not over. Their health has been promoted and maintained through the construction of and improvements to mass transit, such as subways, elevated lines, and bus routes. Financial institutions have invariably prospered at locations convenient to such transit facilities. This fact has had, and continues to have, a dramatic impact on urban real estate values and use trends. A real estate counselor cognizant of these facts of life is capable of advising on downtown branch locations.

Competition

In selecting institutional branch locations, no consideration is more important than competition. This is true even though financial organizations are in what has been regarded as a "regulated business" in which competition is subject to legal limitations. Recent legislative trends, however, have moved toward deregulation, and competition is now becoming increasingly intense. The depository institution deregulation committee, recently created by Congress, is now attempting to equalize the powers conferred on the various institutions. Certain localities are described as "having a bank or savings and loan association on every corner." Judging the influence of existing discernible competition is not a difficult task. Becoming aware of newly developing competitive elements and judging their impact on financial industries is a much more formidable task. It requires the development of reliable data on the planning activities of organizations permitted to have a presence in the area. The ability to compile such information is a typical skill of the real estate counselor. By identifying and properly factoring competitive forces into the decision-making process, he can save a financial institution from costly error.

Legal and Regulatory Constraints

Financial activities, particularly banking, are usually closely regulated and subject to several layers of governmental supervision. For example, a commercial bank may have looking over its shoulder (1) a state banking department, (2) the comptroller of currency, (3) the Federal Reserve Board, and (4) the Federal Deposit Insurance Corporation. This supervisory straitjacket has often been quite limiting, particularly in the matter of branching. In some states institutions are permitted to open offices only in the county in which they were organized. In other localities more liberal branching rules are in effect, but these may still impose some degree of limitation. In still other situations, such as that of Illinois, branching has been completely forbidden. To avoid delays, added expense, and frustration, supervisory constraints should be carefully investigated before commencing real estate arrangements for a new branch. Successful branch site selection entails an awareness of existing and probable industry competition, as well as an adequate understanding of legal and supervisory limitations.

A new banking era is about to commence. Over many years a ban against crossing state lines was the industry's most limiting constraint, and until very recently prospects for its elimination were virtually nonexistent. Curiously, that sort of restriction did not affect insurance companies. However, Congress has put in motion a program for deregulating the banking industry and the start of interstate banking appears imminent. Ironically, it was not a philosophical shift that brought about change; rather, it was distress of the banking system caused by persistently high interest rates. To rescue weak institutions, supervisory agencies have urged stronger banks to take them in hand through merger arrangements. This need has become so great that pressure to find a solution to the critical problems of the banks has overcome the force of reasoning and prejudices about the sanctity of state lines. When the breakthrough finally occurs, in addition to takeovers of existing institutions, there will be a scramble for new banking locations and additional branches. Farsighted organizations are now planning for these future moves. This is a probable industry growth opportunity, and a progressive bank will exploit it through effective use of real estate counseling services.

Other banking innovations are occurring, and lending organizations are now engaged in new real estate activities. In some states, even though branch banking laws are still restrictive, loopholes have been found and used. For example, the establishment of a small facility in a supermarket or a department store has met with approval, even though strict interpretation of branch regulations would not normally permit this action. This is putting banks into a large new field of real estate activities in which they can profitably employ advisory services.

TRUST DEPARTMENT OPERATIONS

The traditional trust department functions of banks and insurance companies involve the handling of both testamentary and inter vivos trusts. Among the assets normally found in these trusts are various real estate interests, including both mortgages and equity positions. Thus, the proper discharge of the trust department's fiduciary responsibilities mandates the acquisition of real estate counsel. For financial organizations, this is a business area with enormous growth potential. This potential is apparent when one considers the present magnitude and growth rate of pension trusts, which so frequently engage banks and insurance companies to manage their investment portfolios. Traditionally, pension funds were invested almost exclusively in securities, but in recent years there has been a significant move to real estate. The management of pension trust accounts has been largely the province of substantial insurance companies and commercial banks, but smaller advisory groups are now penetrating the market. Some pension organizations have handled the management problem by employing in-house personnel with both securities and real estate investment skills. The "extraordinary degree of care" responsibility imposed on fiduciaries, however, has prompted many to seek outside, independent expert advice. This growing demand has promoted the growth of existing investment counseling organizations and encouraged the creation of new entities. It is said that pension trusts now have assets totaling about $1 trillion. The current real estate investment position of pension trusts is estimated at no more than 2 to 3 percent of assets, but many observers believe, and the real estate industry hopes, that they may expand their holdings to 10 percent. Such an enormous increase, amounting to more than $50 billion, should generate a huge volume of real estate industry activity, including development, trading, financing, and management. The competent handling of these matters will demand high-quality skill and judgment.

Review of Selected Properties

There are many ramifications in the handling of trust real estate assets. The investment objectives spelled out in a trust indenture may make it clear that real estate is not considered a desirable holding. If any real estate is in the account, it must then be liquidated and the funds received must be allocated to approved uses. In selling, a trustee's responsibility is to obtain the best possible price and terms. Clearly, his most prudent course of action is to engage a counselor to manage the marketing. This experienced professional will identify the market (individuals or organizations), gather and interpret recent transaction data, organize salient information concerning the property, create an offering memorandum, communicate that memorandum to the market, and develop a group of buying proposals for the trustee's consideration. Finally, he can participate, to the extent requested, in the sale decision.

Recommendations to Trust Department

In some instances, it may be clear to a trust department that certain owned real estate should be retained. The investment benefits of the real estate are perceived to coincide with the objectives of the trust account. For example, properties acquired for pooled accounts, containing funds of a group of pension trusts, are not ordinarily turned over rapidly but are regarded by the participants as long-term investments. They are held to realize the benefits of future income and valuation growth. The increased investment time frame does not lessen a trustee's obligation to achieve optimum investment performance. Real estate does not prosper when neglected; it must be actively attended. There are continuing leasing, management, and financing problems. To attain desired objectives, all functions must be competently handled. A trustee's role is substantially passive; he does not usually get involved in active management. It is his responsibility, however, to seek and engage the experts who will handle investment servicing operations. This is another trust function in which a real estate consultant can play an important role. Through his broad experience in the real estate industry he can identify and assist in engaging competent leasing and management organizations. In view of ongoing pension trust expansion, this should prove a growth field for real estate counselors.

A trust department must also make decisions concerning major alterations to the properties it controls; for example, it should examine and act on proposed structural changes that can be expected to create more profitable property uses. Changes in neighborhoods, architectural styles, functional standards, tenant mixes, and other factors may point to the need to change a property's physical makeup to meet new market demands. In these situations, the major issue is to determine the economic feasibility of the alterations.

To develop a reliable conclusion, a host of skills are required. Market analysis and demographics must reveal the existence of demand for the facilities as well as indicate probable rental levels. Management studies should indicate the expected costs of operations. Architectural and engineering skills are needed to plan physical changes and estimate construction costs. Financing experts are required to arrange appropriate project funding. Finally, a competent brokerage organization should be engaged to manage space marketing programs.

A trustee confronted with this multitude of problems may well be dismayed, but he cannot evade responsibility for optimum investment performance since by law he must take only those actions that a well-informed, prudent person would take in similar circumstances. He is accountable for damages resulting from any actions that he takes outside the scope of legally defined prudence. Surely, the trustee's safest course of action is to engage an independent, experienced real estate counselor. This expert's talents can be employed to organize a team of specialists capable of handling a property alteration's many problems. A "prudent" trustee would not regard a quick "as is" disposition of a property as an escape from the difficulties outlined. Moreover, he would not give away future benefits but would stay with the situation, and with the aid of adequate counsel, he would properly discharge his responsibilities.

At present, trust departments face many leasing problems that previously did not exist. In the past it was appropriate for trustees to purchase properties that were fully rented to satisfactory tenants on long-term leases, thus eliminating early renewal problems and minimizing vacancies. The investment would be substantially passive. Because of inflation in the 1970s and 1980s, lease practices have changed drastically. Instead of prizing long-term contracts, a trustee is obliged to shun them in favor of short-term tenancies in order to be able to adjust rents frequently. If longer-term leases are considered, they should contain newly developed arrangements, providing variable rents indexed to the Consumer Price Index (CPI) or some other objective standard. New leases also require tenants to pay varying percentages of real estate taxes and operating expenses. These clauses are called "pass-through" or "expense stop" arrangements. All such provisions are attempts of lessors to protect themselves against inflationary expense escalations. Notwithstanding a landlord's compelling reasons for seeking new and favorable lease terms, there must be market supply-demand pressure to create tenant willingness to go along. In a rapidly changing economic era, a trust department controlling real estate assets must be alert and must react appropriately. Since trustees typically lack real estate expertise, they are obliged to seek help, and a logical source is a member of the real estate counseling profession.

Mortgage Lending Activity

The real estate industry experiences great market activity, most of which is made possible by mortgage financing. A typical investment consists of a large portion of mortgage money and a much smaller amount of equity funds. The total investment *is money,* and debt capital is considered the lifeblood of the real estate industry. Financial institutions are major participants in real estate markets, as they supply most of the mortgage capital utilized. Traditionally, mortgages were long-term at fixed interest rates. Recent inflation has prompted contract changes, including shorter terms and variable interest rates. Because mortgages offer lien protection and claim priority, they are an attractive investment vehicle for many financial institutions.

Construction Supervision

The two major types of mortgage loans are construction loans and permanent mortgages on existing properties. In the construction loan field, mortgage contracts involve staged fundings as construction progresses and loans are usually made only against another institution's "takeout" or long-term permanent mortgage commitment. Thus, upon the completion of a project, the construction lender expects to be paid off through the funding of a permanent mortgage by another lender.

The real estate counselor's training and experience make him well equipped to advise lending institutions through all phases of construction lending. The real estate counselor can provide guidance in the development of a project's plans and specifications. These should lead to and facilitate the construction of desirable improvements at the most economical costs. The counselor can arrange to engage expert engineering personnel whose efforts will ensure compliance with plans and specifications. These engineers (or architects) also estimate dollar amounts of construction in place at various stages of the project. This is a very necessary control in making interim construction loan advances. The counselor, above all, can ably handle valuation and feasibility issues. By employing counseling assistance, a financial institution can participate in profitable building loan financing with a comforting sense of security.

The best-laid plans of men and mice often go bad. Although an unfavorable outcome should not be highly probable, such an outcome is always possible in construction lending. When trouble arises, a lender must take prompt, effective protective action. He should preserve the priority of his lien and vigorously move to compel his borrower to correct defaults. Absent a quick solution, the lender must diligently prosecute a foreclosure action or press the borrower for a deed in lieu of foreclosure. If he has an uncompleted project on his hands, he must be prepared to finish construction, since that will create the best value and the most favorable conditions for marketing the real estate. Each of these steps is a specialized action requiring particular talents. A counselor who can organize and direct a real estate investment "work-out" team is worth his weight in gold. These difficult situations highlight the need for a counselor to be a highly skilled economic generalist. During the real estate debacle of the mid-1970s numerous financial institutions had serious real estate problems. They had to scramble to secure expert assistance from a limited number of available professionals.

Appraisal Review

Whether a mortgage loan involves a construction project or an existing completed property, its amount generally has to conform to legal or regulatory limitations. For example, conventional mortgages have been restricted by various state laws to 75 to 80 percent of appraised value. Insured and guaranteed mortgages, such as FHA and VA mortgages, have more liberal regulations permitting loan to value ratios of 97 percent and even higher. In all cases, the mortgage is by far the largest portion of the investment and the purchaser's equity is relatively small. These conditions emphasize the need that institutions have for reliable appraisal services. Poor valuation judgment can change an intended 75 percent loan to 100 percent or more of true value. Although the counselor may have some appraisal background and skills, he is often not a valuator per se, but he has excellent review capability that enables him to judge competently the quality of appraisals performed by others. He will surely be able to assist a mortgage lender in the acquisition of qualified appraisers—whether they are in-house personnel or outside, independent professionals. By reason of his broad market experience and his varied real estate skills, he is eminently qualified to advise on valuation problems. His services will ensure the making of quality mortgage loans by the institution.

Underwriting Counseling

Underwriting mortgage loans involves more than just the real estate appraisal function. The credit of the borrower is a key consideration, even though he or she may have no personal loan liability. It is some indication of his or her ability to keep a project going to completion in spite of time delays and unforeseen expenses. Mortgage loans are usually long-term contracts; hence, future expectations are important. The prospective health of a mortgage is inextricably tied to probable future conditions in the neighborhood and community surrounding the pledged real estate. Forecasts of future money and capital market conditions are also important. In periods of inflation, when interest rates escalate, portfolios of long-term, fixed-rate mortgages are not salable except at prohibitive discounts. This can create serious liquidity problems for banking institutions at times when deposit withdrawals are above normal. Portfolios should be structured to achieve the best possible match between the repayment terms of the institution's assets and the repayment terms of its liabilities.

The terms and conditions of mortgage loans should be arranged to harmonize with perceived future financial conditions. For example, if considerable inflation is expected by well-informed economists and bankers, long-term mortgage loans should be avoided or should be made only with variable interest rates. It is also advisable to have the contract include arrangements for the lender to share in the future growth of income and property value. Similarly, a prudent mortgagee would lend only on properties with leases that provide income variability or that have short terms affording frequent opportunities for inflation adjustments. Interest rate volatility normally impels lenders to develop only short-term portfolios. In the recent past mortgage underwriting was considered to be a function with relatively few component parts. The economic "roller coaster" experience of the late 1970s and early 1980s has dispelled the myth of simplicity.

Staff Personnel versus Outside Counselor

Given the value of a real estate counseling service to a financial institution, a pertinent question is whether the most favorable results will be realized by using employees or by engaging outside independent professionals. There is no pat answer. Each case must be judged separately in the light of its individual circumstances. This question can be better understood by considering a few situations and identifying possible solutions.

First, an institution surely has more and closer control of in-house real estate personnel than of outside independent experts. The chief advantages of using staff personnel is the timeliness and certainty of services. An independent counselor has a clientele to serve, and he must spread his attention over the entire group. He may, to some extent, favor his larger customers, but he cannot give absolute assurance of immediate performance to any of them.

Objectivity

The element of objectivity also enters the picture, and it is an important consideration in making a decision between staff services and an independent adviser. Although a real estate professional who is an employee is usually quite independent, there are constraints on independent judgment in any employer-employee relationship. A typical loyal staff member will invariably attempt to fit his activities and thinking into the framework of organizational policies. This is not to say that he is subservient but that as a normal human being he will react to the pressures of surrounding circumstances. It would be an extraordinary individual who could totally resist such influences and function as though he were in a vacuum. The outside independent counselor, of course, is free from employer-employee constraints. On the other side of the coin, however, staff personnel are likely to be more familiar with an organization's problems and needs. They are living with the particular business on a day-to-day basis; their insights should be clearer, and they should be most responsive to the employing organization's concerns. The outside independent adviser must devote substantial time to acquire organizational knowledge and background equivalent to that of the staff member. Because of the pressures of serving the balance of his clientele, he may be hard pressed to find the time needed to do this.

Market Knowledge

The scope and depth of real estate knowledge of the parties involved will strongly influence the decision between staff and outside real estate talents. The element of employment by itself should have little impact on the choice. This selection will hinge more on the abilities and experience possessed by the individuals. The only possible limiting influence that employee status may have on a staff person's knowledge is that his full time is devoted to a particular institution's business affairs. This necessarily entails his concentration on a limited sector of the real estate market—the portion that relates to his organization's business. The outside independent, with a varied clientele, will have exposure to a greater number of market segments. This should give him more diversified experience and a broader knowledge of market conditions. Deciding between staff and outside services is a difficult matter, and there are no conclusive guides, because individual capacities are involved, and these vary greatly.

Business Volume as a Determinant

Business volume is a customary economic element that influences the selection of real estate advisory services. Many business organizations lack sufficient real estate involvement to warrant employing full-time staff personnel. In the financial institution field, however, it is hard to think of an organization that could not profitably use in-house services. In a previous section of this chapter, a multitude of real estate financing functions were discussed, and it should be plain that all but very small institutions will have continuing real estate operations that require expert advice and guidance. Business trends of the past twenty-five years clearly reveal a continuing expansion of real estate investments by financial institutions. Therefore, the business volume generated by these investments is likely, in most cases, to be adequate to support staff real estate advisory personnel, and failure to engage such personnel could well be false economy. With proper organization, however, an institution's real estate business, whether large or small, can be handled satisfactorily by either in-house staff or outside personnel. It is in "overflow" situations that institutions find the use of outside advisers especially attractive.

Speed of Service

Speed of service in a dynamic industry is always a major concern. Financial institutions are handling growing volumes of transactions in increasingly diversified investment fields. Since real estate is a major element of the total economy, it will be a key field of activity. In it, timing will always be a critical factor. An institution with the ability to move aggressively and to make good investment decisions quickly will not only gain a lion's share of the available business but will also realize favorable financial results. In no other field is this more evident than in real estate. To act expeditiously in this field, an organization requires prompt real estate advisory services, and this seems to indicate some advantage in having full-time in-house personnel. In response to the press of competitive business conditions, in-house personnel can be available at all hours of the day or night. However, when an outside adviser is needed, the institution must fit its needs to the schedule of the adviser.

Cost of Services

Not least among the elements in the selection process is the cost of services. Obtaining inadequate, inferior assistance, merely to save expense, will prove a disastrous economy. But spending that is out of proportion with an institution's business volume could be equally damaging. Cost may be the determining factor in a choice between in-house personnel and outside professional advice. A relatively small organization might be unable to bear the cost of full-time top-quality real estate personnel, but it can, and often does, engage people capable of handling its routine real estate business. If that institution decides to participate in a large, complex real estate venture, it should realize that it must accept the expense of engaging an outside expert, a counselor. The cost theme has many variations, and it will always influence the choice of services.

Staff Cooperation

Whether an institution selects in-house or outside services, their effectiveness will depend on cooperation from the institution's staff. Real estate investment activities embrace a multitude of functions in widely diversified fields, such as accounting, law, engineering, and architecture. Various organizational officers and departments of financial institutions generally specialize in one or more of these functions. Such officers and departments have at their disposal important information and data needed for the investment decision-making process. Making this material readily available to the counselor will speed and enhance the quality of his or her performance. This is an action requirement that cannot be ignored by the institution's top management. A real estate counselor is entitled to expect and receive the fullest degree of cooperation. With efficient interaction between the institution's staff and the counselor, the organization will improve its prospects for superior real estate investment performance.

SELECTED REFERENCES

ALEXANDERSON, K. W.   "Bank Branch Location Feasibility Analysis." *The Real Estate Appraiser,* July–August 1969, pp. 43–48.

BEATON, WILLIAM R., and THOMAS H. HALL III.   "Apraisal Analysis of Branch Bank Sites." *The Appraisal Journal,* July 1965, pp. 336–44.

BENZER, SHIRLEY L.   "Real Estate Doctors to the Banks." *Institutional Investor,* May 1977, pp. 67–68.

BRUCE, FRANK E.   "How to Size Up a Business Location: Land Use Patterns, Traffic Studies, and Trends in Community Development All Help in Site Selection." *Burroughs Clearing House,* December 1974, pp. 26–51 + .

FINANCIAL INSTITUTION SERVICES.   "Strategies for Profitable Growth: A Comprehensive Approach to Facilities Planning." *Real Estate Report,* Second Quarter 1976, pp. 6–8.

HUBLER, GEORGE W.   "Branching in Supermarkets." *Federal Home Loan Bank Board Journal.* November 1974, pp. 10–11.

NELSON, RICHARD L.   *The Selection of Retail Locations.* New York: F. W. Dodge Corporation, 1959.

NICHOLSON, SY, comp.   "Lenders Wrestling with Troubled Real Estate; Some Seek Outside Help to Correct Past Errors." *The National Real Estate Investor,* January 1977, pp. 46–55.

"Planning Financial Quarters: Examining Construction Trends." *Burroughs Clearing House,* June 1979, pp. 12–14 + .

SIEGELAUB, HAROLD, and HERBERT A. MEISTRICH.   "The Lender and the Workout Specialist: Friend or Foe." *Journal of Property Management,* March–April 1978, pp. 93–96.

"Some Tips on Picking a Site for a Branch Bank." *Real Estate Investment Ideas,* April 1972, pp. 2–4.

CHAPTER EIGHTEEN
CORPORATE
CONSULTATION

Corporate America, regardless of the products it manufactures, the services it performs, or the merchandise it markets, must pay keen attention to the real estate it acquires, leases, or sells. Each of these functions can affect corporate earnings either favorably or unfavorably. To enhance corporate earnings without prejudicing the corporation's basic source of income, America's executives should call upon the experienced and dependable real estate consultant to assist them in decision making that involves real estate, for example, decision making on plant relocation, the location of headquarters, rental versus ownership, and the valuation of owned real estate during merger or acquisition proceedings.

A substantial asset of many corporations is their real estate holdings. Thus a major influence on the success of these organizations is the judgment they use in acquiring, managing, and disposing of these holdings. Corporations sometimes find it advisable to diversify their activities into real estate development. In such cases, they can enhance their earnings through the prudent selection and use of qualified real estate counselors.

The real estate counselor is frequently retained by a corporate client that has an in-house real estate department. In most cases, the corporate real estate department confines itself to a relatively narrow area of the company's activities. In a sophisticated real estate economy, the counselor adds a new dimension by providing the client with the benefits of a well-rounded exposure to all facets of the real estate market. Where the corporate client has its own real estate department, the counselor usually works closely with the officer in charge of real estate. Absent such a department, the counselor's client contact may be the "plants and facilities" person or the treasurer of the company. On occasion, the counselor reports directly to the chief executive officer on matters involving major corporate decisions, for example, a move to suburbia from the central business district, or a decision between ownership and renting.

The range of corporate real estate decisions depends in great measure on the line of business with which the company is concerned. This chapter is divided into sections that should cover most of the areas of interest. These are sections on retailing, manufacturing, broadcasting, and professional and service corporations. The last category includes attorneys, accountants, advertising agencies, investment bankers, commercial and savings institutions, and insurance companies. In addition, there is a section on the "conglomerate," a relative newcomer on the corporate scene.

RETAILING

This section is directed primarily to such retailing giants as Federated, Macy's, Allied, the May Company, Sears Roebuck, and J. C. Penney. All of these major retailing chains maintain numerous branches scattered through various areas of the nation. The section is limited to the department store client. It does not attempt to cover such chains as Woolworth, Walgreen's and Lerner's or the chains in particular retailing lines, such as the chain food stores or the chains in ladies' wear and shoes.

Limited Clients

Some counselors have found it advisable to maintain the policy of limiting retail consultation activity to one retainer client. Department stores are a line of business with multitudinous "trade secrets" that are often shared with the real estate counselor so as to properly implement particular assignments. However, whenever the occasion arises, as happens frequently, a competing department store may call on a counselor to handle a specific assignment. It is generally advisable for the real estate counselor to undertake the assignment only if he receives the approval of his primary client, particularly where, as is often the case, the counselor is on a retainer basis.

Most department store clients maintain real estate departments. Nevertheless, they call on the real estate counselor to "backstop" in-house capabilities. Diverse matters constantly arise that fall well outside of the conventional real estate problems that the in-house real estate executive is accustomed to dealing with on a day-to-day basis. For example, a department store opens a branch in a state in which it was not represented previously. The local real estate consultant is called upon by the client to advise it on laws affecting real estate, such as occupancy taxes (taxes on rental paid), the vault tax for the use of space under sidewalks, and assessing practices.

Site Selection

Location is the primary key to a retailer's success. Locational decisions involve not only the store's merchandising and real estate executives but also its real estate economic and marketing consultants. A department store client embarking on a branch store program would have its marketing and economic consultant target those growth areas that either lack adequate department store representation or that offer a particular type of merchandising a strong potential for capturing a reasonable share of the consumer market. Armed with the conclusions of the financial and economic consultant, the department store client will usually ask the real estate counselor to explore the acquisition of land within the targeted areas. The normal requirements might be for a parcel of 100 to 150 acres (large enough to permit the development of a regional shopping mall with about one million square feet of gross leasable area), which would be capable of supporting from two to four anchor tenants. The initial exploration of an appropriate site by the counselor necessarily involves an exploration of pending and potential highway and road changes to ensure the ready availability of the anticipated traffic patterns.

Presite Selection Counseling

Prior to the development of the site, the department store may call on its real estate counselor to invite shopping center developers to either joint-venture the project or purchase the land, with the store retaining a portion of the site for the construction and ownership of its facility. In the latter instance, adequate assurances are required that the developer will construct a center that is large enough to be truly regional in character, with a grant to the department store of a collateral easement for use of the parking lot, openings on the enclosed mall, and so forth. The negotiations and business matters involved in documenting a transaction of this type are more complex than those involved in most real estate transactions. The counselor stands ready to provide his or her client with advice relative to land acquisition costs, the availability and cost of institutional financing for construction of the improvement, the most advantageous joint venture arrangement, tax consequences, and, last but not least, the projected earnings of the proposed regional mall based on the projected gross leasable area and estimated rentals, operating expenses, and real estate taxes.

In addition to providing assistance on new branch locations, the counselor serving the retail corporate client becomes involved in a variety of other situations, including the acquisition or disposition of warehouse and distribution facilities, public auctions or private negotiations for the purchase of various types of property, and the financing and refinancing of property. Both conventional and unconventional requests are commonplace in real estate counseling for department store clients.

The assignments of the real estate counselor might include finding an apartment or home for a transferred executive, purchasing an existing liquor license in a particular community for transfer to the client, and locating temporary warehouse space with unusually high ceilings to house the giant helium floats for the client's annual Thanksgiving Day parade.

In short, the counselor serves the corporate retail client by providing support and advice in the areas where an in-house real estate department needs assistance. Such departments may lack the expertise in the real estate areas involved, or they may lack the time and personnel needed to provide other than day-to-day service. Sometimes it is necessary to shield the client from the marketplace. Counselors are available to provide these and related services.

MANUFACTURING

The corporate client involved in the manufacture of goods usually makes its first call on the real estate counselor for advice in connection with the disposition or acquisition of a plant. This introductory relationship of the counselor and the corporate manufacturing client usually results in a broad variety of assignments, many of which are of a sensitive nature requiring the expertise of a discreet and trustworthy real estate professional. One of the most painful procedures for a manufacturer is closing an antiquated plant that employs a substantial segment of a town's working population and may be the major source of employment for the area in which it is located.

Sensitivity of Plant Closings

The sensitivity of a prospective plant closing almost precludes the client from seeking advice and counsel from within the community involved. Plant closings are corporate decisions that are kept under wraps until a plan has been devised that will mitigate the loss of jobs within the community. The obvious purpose of such activity is to minimize an adverse reaction to the image and the product of the corporate client. The real estate counselor, operating on a regional or nationwide basis, offers the client a variety of plans to avoid the adverse effects of a complete shutdown of the plant. One method is to offer the property to a preselected list of "users" throughout North America and, more recently, even outside the continental limits, on a one-to-one basis without resorting to the conventional advertising in trade and daily newspapers or the broad circulation of a property offering. This method, if handled so as to avoid leaks, provides the possibility of job replacement to the community by announcement of a new occupant for the plant at the same time that the corporate client announces discontinuance of its operation.

The counselor can also explore the possibility of sale to a "converter" who would recycle an old manufacturing plant and create an industrial development accommodating a variety of companies and uses, thereby diversifying the local job market and establishing a stronger community economic base for the community. Through personal contacts or the use of blind ads in industrial trade publications and such media as the *Wall Street Journal,* locating this type of prospective buyer can be accomplished without "surfacing" an intended plant closing.

In matters of this type, the counselor offers the corporate manufacturing client a complete program for plant closing and the disposition of property, for implementation either by corporate personnel or by the consultant. In instances like the one described above, the client will usually ask its counselor to handle the matter. The counselor's planning would include a market analysis that results in a recommendation for "asking" and "taking" prices for the excess real estate and suggestions for disposing of the property and for structuring a transaction on behalf of the client. As a result of such planning, the counselor may be called on to negotiate and finalize a transaction, obviously always subject to approval by the client's executive personnel or its board of directors.

Office Relocation Decisions

Additional assignments that result from the counselor's professional approach to an initial assignment from a national manufacturing client frequently include providing the client with advice as to the relocation of its home office, its corporate headquarters, or auxiliary facilities. Corporations identified in the Fortune 500 may have office space requirements of as much as 500,000 to 1,000,000 square feet of net rentable area. Users of space in this magnitude now seek professional real estate advice on a fee basis. Changes that have taken place in this segment of the real estate industry make it advisable to obtain knowledgeable and objective advice, which is best furnished by the professional counselor. Rental rates are only one of many factors that enter into space decisions in these instances. Each property is compared according to each of the following fourteen items. Other features of comparison are floors, the position of stops on the elevator banks, the availability of public transportation, and the available parking for each 1,000 square feet of leasable space.

1. The signing for building identification (for example, the Pan Am Building).
2. The extent of "work letter" or office finishings to be provided by the landlord. In most instances, the landlord gives the tenant an allowance to finish its space (partitioning, carpeting, etc.). The greater the work letter in dollars, the less the client has to spend to finish its space in the fashion to which it is accustomed.
3. The escalation provisions for computing increases in operating expenses and real estate taxes, the base year to be used for the computation of escalation, the use of actual operating expense escalation as opposed to a "Porter wage" formula, and/or the inclusion of an index for escalation or additional escalation.
4. Possible repainting during the lease term.
5. The renewal options following an initial term and the basis for establishing rentals during option periods.
6. The right of first refusal to purchase the building.

7. The takeover of existing space by the prospective new landlord until the expiration of the new tenant's current lease commitment.
8. The right of first refusal on contiguous or additional space in the building.
9. Security measures, particularly after the usual business hours.
10. The adequacy of elevator service.
11. Cleaning standards.
12. Provision for and the cost of such items as heating and air conditioning after normal office hours (8:00 A.M. to 5:00 P.M. on weekdays and a half-day on Saturday).
13. Subletting privileges, with the tenant having the right to profit on subletting and/or sharing the profit with the landlord.
14. In communities where the corporate client has never previously leased space, it is customary for the real estate counselor to provide the client with a report setting forth the range of rental rates for various types of buildings in different parts of the municipality.

The real estate counselor who has been engaged to assist the client in office relocation decisions provides a variety of services for the client. These require the following:

1. An analysis of the client's growth projections during the next fifteen to twenty-five years in five-year segments so as to evaluate potential space needs.
2. A study of personnel profiles for locational purposes so as to obtain commuting patterns for all segments of the staff—clerical personnel, professionals, "creative" people, and middle and senior management.
3. Where the home office is to be owner occupied, a review of the client's present lease commitments that assesses occupancy costs as a rent equivalent, taking into consideration charges that are involved in the ownership and management of real property (allowances for stabilized maintenance, real estate taxes, operating costs, insurance, debt service, etc.).

Armed with this information, the real estate consultant usually reports in writing to the chief executive officer, setting forth his conclusions and recommendations. These could include advising the client to remain at its present location, to seek new space with adequate insurance for future needs, to acquire property for its own use either in an existing building or in a building that is to be developed, to purchase building space on a condominium basis, or to move back office space to less expensive areas of the municipality or to suburban locations.

If the client selects one or more of these alternatives, the counselor is then called on to implement the client's decision. The assignment may well require the counselor to use the skill of other professionals such as architects, engineers, or space planners, and even to provide assistance with respect to moving.

To successfully conclude such an assignment, the real estate counselor has to be available to the client's attorneys for consultation and review of all business matters incorporated in the papers required to consummate a transaction. Actually, an assignment ordinarily requires ongoing contact with the client and is not completed until the client moves in and takes possession of the property.

BROADCASTING

The advisory functions of a counselor serving a broadcaster headquartered in one of the nation's large urban centers can touch almost all facets of the real estate industry, ranging from residential to studio facilities. However, the preponderance of the counselor's activity is usually in commercial real estate, including office buildings and the various types of facilities involved in the broadcasting industry, such as studios, sound stages, rehearsal halls, and warehouse and storage facilities.

Typically, broadcasters with major concentrations in the large urban areas require large blocks of office space to house creative and management personnel. Despite the fact that many large broadcasters own "home office" buildings in their principal areas of operation, the growth of this field has caused most broadcasters to seek additional space. The counselor retained by firms in the broadcasting industry is called on by the client to conduct space studies, to analyze the cost of existing facilities, and to explore possibilities for additional space. In this connection the client must advise the counselor which, if any, of its myriad departments can be separated from its principal operation without causing undue hardship to its other operations. For example, NBC, CBS, and Capital Cities / ABC are located within three blocks of each other along one thoroughfare in a large northeastern city. Day-to-day interaction between the executives of the "friendly" competitors is a decided advantage to all three networks. Placing the creative staff and the senior people outside this small "club" area would impair their effectiveness. Conversely, and particularly in this age of sophisticated electronic equipment, there is no need to place the accounting department, except perhaps for top executive pesonnel, in space that costs more than $40 per square foot. Such departments, which sometimes use as much as 40,000 to 60,000 square feet of space, can be housed in one of the less expensive parts of a central business district as rentals as much as 50 percent lower than the rentals charged for prime office space.

Given an adequate understanding of the corporate operational problems, the counselor provides his or her client with a broad array of alternative areas for "secondary" space requirements, all of which would be outside the central business district (CBD) core. The counselor's recommendations would include information on the availability of space; on competitive rental rates with escalation provisions for operating expenses and real estate taxes; on the extent of the landlord's leasehold improvements to the space such as partitioning, lighting, and floor coverings (commonly referred to as "work letter"); and on the possibilities of options to renew. The counselor would advise the client of his reasons for preferring specific properties within each of the geographic alternatives.

The client almost universally follows the counselor's recommendations. The counselor is then called on to consummate a transaction and to negotiate the acquisition of space at a rental rate or a purchase price that is usually significantly below the owner's asking rate or price. At the conclusion of negotiations the counselor again has to work closely with the client's attorneys in connection with

FIGURE 18-1   Capital Cities/ABC Building in New York City. Photograph by Martin Barkan, courtesy of James Felt Realty Services, New York, New York.

a rental agreement. Further, he reviews and assists them with the business terms of the lease, which in today's real estate economy represents a complicated legal document incorporating all of the concerns that have been discussed above.

Office space problems generally take up a great deal of the counselor's time in the broadcasting industry. Yet problems with warehouse space for the storage of props and scenery or with the construction or leasing of sound stages are also quite important to the real estate counselor who represents a major broadcaster. Although the West Coast continues to be a major area for TV talent, the East Coast, and particularly New York City, is regaining its former prominence as a center for TV production, particularly in the field of the soap operas. The preeminent legitimate stage presence in New York City provides a large pool of fine actors who are available for roles in the highly profitable soaps.

Broadcast journalism has also expanded significantly in recent years. This trend has caused the industry to maintain large installations in areas of the nation where news is "made" almost around the clock. The most important of these areas are Washington, New York City with its financial headquarters concentrations and the UN headquarters, and California or Camp David when the president is on vacation. The real estate counselor serves the client in these areas through home and branch offices and through correspondents in cities where the counselor does not maintain offices.

As the broadcasting client's space inventory continues to grow, the counselor takes on additional tasks, particularly where there is no in-house real estate department. These responsibilities may include preparing lease summaries for the bookkeeping department and monitoring expiration dates for leases or renewal options for the company treasurer or the person in charge of facilities. The counselor may also be called on to devise a tickler system for in-house use by non–real estate personnel charged with the responsibility of following up on such matters.

PROFESSIONAL AND SERVICE CORPORATIONS

In recent years the large urban centers of the nation have become oriented to service industry employment rather than to manufacturing employment. For example, in past years the principal employment opportunities in many eastern cities were found in manufacturing, often in multistoried loft structures. This manufacturing emphasis no longer exists. Currently, jobs in the service and professional categories (law, accounting, advertising, banking, insurance, and real estate) make up the largest segment of the job market in these cities, a far cry from the conditions that prevailed in 1945. In actual numbers of jobs, the losses in manufacturing have generally been more than made up by the growth of the service industries. Those areas of the country in which manufacturing employment has increased have had necessary increases in the service categories as well. However, these are minor except for major Sun Bélt concentrations that affect all areas of employment.

Growth in Office Space Demand

The growing trend of white-collar employment growth was music to the ears of the developers of residential and commercial space, except for specific areas of the nation such as the energy corridor. Each year there has been a growth in the demand for office space to house professionals and senior and middle management persons employed in the service industries. Furthermore, these employees must be housed in safe and decent housing with reasonable proximity and convenient access to places of work.

The space needs of the legal profession have escalated to proportions hardly imaginable five to ten years ago. Many of the larger firms (more than a hundred lawyers) require as much as 150,000 to 200,000 square feet of space, and more modestly sized firms need 60,000 to 80,000 square feet. At first blush, these requirements seem mimimal in relation to the requirements of the larger space users. However, these tenants are beginning to express concern about the effects of current market rentals on fees. A 200,000-square-foot unit at a market rate of $40 per square foot for preferred locations results in an annual rental of $8 million per year or $80,000 per attorney, assuming a staff of 100 lawyers. However, the base rental in and of itself hardly tells the entire story in today's office building rental market. In New York City the rental rate does not include electricity or the effect of escalation provisions. The charges for electricity range from $2.50 to $3.00 per square foot, depending on the building's facilities. The charge approximates $2.50 per square foot where each tenant's consumption is metered and is now approaching $3.00 where the charge is based on "rent inclusion." In the latter instance, the electric charge is an add-on to the rent and may be increased for increased usage or for rising costs to the owner.

Rent Increase Issues

The escalation of real estate taxes and operating expenses has resulted in substantial annual increases in occupancy costs in many of our major cities. In some cities landlords and developers of office buildings have been using two methods for computing these charges—"direct pass-through" and a formula tied to the wage rates of building services employees. Under the direct pass-through, which is widely used nationally, the tenant pays its proportionate share of the increased costs of operating a building over such costs in the "base year," customarily the year in which the tenant takes possession of its space. This practice was superseded by the "Porter wage formula," in some instances because of disputes that arose as to the charges or expense items to be included in the escalation computation under the direct pass-through method. Tenants were constantly taking issue with the landlord's definition of operating expenses. Many landlords substituted the Porter wage formula to avoid this hassle or because they perceived it to be more profitable. This appeared to be a reasonable solution to the problem of avoiding controversies, and initially the landlord and the tenant were prepared to accept the new plan, particularly when the ratio was 1 to $\frac{1}{2}$ (that is, as Porter wages for office buildings increased one penny per hour, rent was increased by one-half penny per square foot). Over several years, however, that initial relationship of 1 to $\frac{1}{2}$ shifted steadily to today's standard of 1:1. In addition, particularly during tight markets, landlords instituted increases over the base rent geared to CPI increases in the cost of living, with a resultant escalation above that provided for operations expenses and real estate taxes. In many new buildings in large urban centers, the base for escalation is predetermined by the owner at levels intended to fix the owner's expense for operations and real estate taxes. These levels have been developed unrealistically and have resulted in initial additional occupancy costs ranging upwards of $2 per square foot.

Lease Negotiations

The use and effect of complicated lease provisions are difficult for the layperson to properly evaluate. This has led many large space users to retain real estate counselors to assist them in lease negotiations. In this area of work the counselor normally performs the following functions:

1. Suggests the formation of a "space committee" that would be responsible for making decisions and formulating policy in connection with a contemplated removal to new and expanded offices. Centralization of authority is necessary for a counselor to effectively interact with a client in this regard.

2. Acts as the client's representative in all matters pertaining to space needs. The counselor accepts full responsibility for acting as the client's representative, and in order to avoid confusion suggests that all inquiries from brokers or developers be referred to himself. This type of arrangement serves a threefold purpose: (a) it permits the counselor to act as a buffer between the real estate brokerage community and the client; (b) it protects the client against brokerage disputes; and (c) most important, it permits the client to focus on its business or profession instead of diverting its energy to coping with its space needs, particularly where executive personnel would spend inordinate amounts of time in an area with whose problems and pitfalls they are unfamiliar.

3. Develops alternatives to a conventional leasing arrangement that solve space needs while satisfying investment objectives (for example, purchase of a building, acquisition of a portion of a building on a condominium basis, or joint venture development of a building.

4. Attends all meetings of the space committee and provides required reports and recommendations from time to time.

5. Assists the client in selecting an architect or space planner to design a layout for the proposed space before a final space selection is made. This ensures the practicality of the space utilization for the client's purposes.

6. Consults with the client's legal counsel on all the business terms of the lease.

CONGLOMERATES

Within recent years many public companies have diversified their operations by acquiring corporations that are completely unrelated to their principal line of business. These acquisitions are undertaken for a variety of reasons, such as increasing and ensuring earnings, protecting earnings against dramatic changes affecting a company's principal line of business, moving into new growth markets, and acquiring operations that fit into the company's mix of operations.

"Due Diligence" Effort

As a publicly owned company, the acquiring entity is required to undertake various studies, all of which, for want of a better term, might fall within the catchall category labeled "due diligence." As part of the due diligence effort, the acquiring entity will in almost all cases require the services of a real estate counselor (in addition to a battery of legal people) to satisfy the requirements of the Securities and Exchange Commission and to evaluate the real estate assets that are to be acquired as a part of the transaction.

In this connection, the counselor usually is called on to inventory all real estate assets, including properties held in fee and long-term leasehold estates, in order to help establish policy with respect to these holdings. Advice sought by the takeover company ranges from valuation to a program for disposition and marketing of excess real estate.

A major conglomerate based in the eastern United States recently engaged a real estate counselor active on a national basis on an annual retainer. Within a year the counselor was called on to perform a great variety of functions, a partial list of which is briefly itemized below:

1. To value more than fifty parcels of real estate throughout the United States and Canada.
2. To establish asking and taking prices for all real estate that the company determined to be in excess to its needs and to prepare and handle a program for disposing of these properties.
3. To engage local real estate brokers on a full-commission basis to sell the properties, with all negotiations conducted by the counselor, subject to approval by the client only after all details of the transaction had been arranged—with the counselor keeping the client advised on a day-to-day basis of all serious negotiations.
4. To consult with the client's counsel on all the business portions of sales contracts and to assist the client's counsel in all problems through closing.
5. To negotiate with landlords or their agents for the renewal of office leases involving in excess of 250,000 square feet of office space.
6. To offer for sublet excess office space resulting from the merger or acquisition. Once again, the counselor encouraged full participation by the brokerage community so as to obtain the best results.
7. To secure new office space in a major East Coast city for use as a regional "home office" for company headquarters.
8. To engage auctioneers to dispose of excess machinery and equipment in manufacturing plants.
9. To work closely with the client's Communications Section in the preparation of marketing brochures, newspaper advertising, and so on.

CONCLUSION

For years the American business community disregarded the inherent value of its real estate. Balance sheets reflected values based on initial acquisition cost and capital investment—less depreciation. Such balance sheet numbers failed to reflect the current value of land and buildings. One prominent real estate counselor built a very successful career by making companies aware of their hidden real estate assets. In more recent years, as changing investment goals and expansion of the corporate economy have made business more complex, chief executive officers and financial officers have become aware of the profit potentials in these hidden assets. As a result of this trend, the real estate counselor has become an important team member in the business and financial communities.

The participation of companies in the expansion of the real estate industry has enlarged the role of the real estate counselor. He has had to become fully aware of the financial structure of companies and of their long-term objectives. Without that awareness he could not properly fulfill his role as adviser. Given the increasing importance of real estate to the corporate client, the role of the real estate counselor as an adviser to business may be expected to become even more important in the future.

SELECTED REFERENCES

CAMPBELL, ROBERT E.   "Consultant's Role in Management of Corporate Real Estate." *Journal of Property Management,* July–August 1974, pp. 171–75.

"Easing Relocation Shock." *Industry Week,* August 2, 1976, pp. 50–53.

NELSON, RICHARD LAWRENCE.   *The Selection of Retail Locations.* New York: F. W. Dodge Corporation, 1958.

"Real Estate Consultants—Troubleshooters for American Business." *Real Estate Forum,* August 1972, pp. 40–47.

"Real Estate Counselors Solve Problems for Small Owners and Giant Corporations." *Properties,* February 1969, pp. 32–33

CHAPTER NINETEEN
GOVERNMENT AGENCY COUNSELING

Professional real estate counselors cultivate and maintain continuing relationships within their profession that result in immediate availability of specialized service, research and knowledge. This unique characteristic enables them to produce effective solutions for government much quicker and less expensively than government can secure without this extensive talent.

Services of real estate counselors are particularly valuable to government agencies as market-oriented advice that is seldom available from within government, at least to any extensive degree. However, to the extent that public agencies possess this type of expertise, there is appreciation and understanding of the private sector's capability for effective dealing with the often complex real estate issues related to funding, analyses of alternative programs as to consequences, and the implementation of solutions within policy parameters that are acceptable to both public and private sectors.

The real estate counselor who is trained in and apprised of government constraints and objectives with respect to improvements in the economic, legal, political, physical, and social environments is sensitive to the value of developing public-private partnerships, promoting policy coordination, and recognizing the influence and need for objectivity with special interest groups.

Real estate counselors not only help government in solving real estate-related problems but also provide government with expertise related to the determination of objectives, programs (and funding), and places (location) and help ensure success through the proper analysis of timing, probably the most difficult and critical of decisions.

GENERAL ACTIVITIES

Community Planning and Zoning

Real estate counselors are most frequently involved with local government agencies in providing market-oriented advice on questions of community planning and zoning, community revitalization, real estate assessment practices, and government property needs. Bridging the gap between counseling's private market orientation and government's public goals requires a recognition of common ground that is fundamental to the fostering of an efficient and effective private-public partnership within ever-changing urban environments.

The real estate counselor and land use planner (private or public) are similarly concerned with future patterns of urban growth, the quality of development, and land use relationships as they influence private investment and public funding decisions, priorities, and risk. In this context, the real estate counselor is able to assist local government in such matters as preparing community development programs. The counselor may participate in shaping sound planning policy as a guide to decisions affecting future growth and development. He or she may also supplement public planning and zoning recommendations with market expertise and may analyze the probable effectiveness of alternative funding priorities for projects likely to influence timing and commitment by private investors. The real estate counselor can also prepare market-sensitive studies and projections that address risk management considerations related to infrastructure costs, bonding, regulatory enforcement, and workable private-public partnership agreements.

Implementation of Comprehensive Plans

A number of states now require consistency between local planning and zoning, most notably with a view toward the establishment of equitable practices in plan implementation. Land use zoning is typically regarded by the courts as enforceable when it is supported by planning policy consistent with an adopted comprehensive plan. A comprehensive plan should contain general physical plan elements, each having a summary of relevant baseline data and analysis and a statement of goals, objectives, and key policies on land use, community design, transportation, recreation and the environment, public facilities, and services and energy. These plan elements provide a decision-making guide on matters affecting the future of a community and may have political overtones. Comprehensive plans are normally adopted by a city council or a county board of commissioners "in concept," allowing departmental project plans to be prepared and updated so that proposed public agency projects can be set with priorities that are coordinated and reviewed in light of specific public needs, financial capabilities, and the private incentives needed to maximize project effectiveness.

Highway construction, utility extensions, and incentives to basic industry have proved successful in promoting orderly cost-effective patterns of urban growth that are consistent with the concepts outlined by an adopted local comprehensive plan. However, developing public capability to meet capital infrastructure and service costs for community development within a given time frame requires planning that is sensitive to economic conditions and to the implications of bonded indebtedness which typically are not addressed by comprehensive plans. Therefore, it is often the practice of local jurisdictions involved in capital-intensive development projects to update project plans every several years. A twenty-year local comprehensive plan may only require updating every five to ten years, depending on the existence of relevant five-year project plans and on the pattern, magnitude, and intensity of local urban growth.

The relationship between planning and zoning is generally imprecise, thus raising questions of right versus privilege and sacrificing predictable flexibility to both changing market conditions and changing public need. A local comprehensive plan provides conceptual guidelines for a master plan (which includes criteria regarding natural constraints and amenities, generalized land use arrangements, population and housing density maximums, and the determination of public facility and service responsibilities), which, in turn, is used as a guide to more specific decisions on land use zoning and subdivision development. Zoning is ultimately established within a proposed neighborhood or district for specific categories of land use activity, at densities not exceeding those prescribed by the master plan and in a fashion that is intended to foster local standards of land and building use at minimum public cost. Land subdivision (or platting) is similar to zoning in design orientation, though it is most often accomplished following the rezoning of land out of holding status, which is done prior to (or at the time of) the approval of the development plan.

In plat planning attention is paid primarily to gaining the maximum amenity-value potential of each proposed site and to properly timing final plat approval in relation to market demand. The elements of subdivision design that receive particular public scrutiny include the final engineering considerations for streets and utilities, school and park dedications, drainage, and lot configuration as well as the grading, revegetation, landscaping, use buffering, and other measures that are intended to foster a local standard of site development at minimum public cost.

Competent independent real estate counsel is obviously imperative throughout the process of short- and long-term planning in the use and succession of uses of real estate, because of the specific type of expertise that is required to achieve equitable treatment, security of property values and environment, and protection of the general welfare.

Budgeting of Capital Improvement Programs

A government budget is the financial expression of a composite of planned public agency programs that describe (either by object of expenditure or by function) how revenue dollars are to be allocated, based on political decisions of optimum public benefit. Budgeted capital improvement funds are disbursed among agencies whose combined program expenditures produce community facilities and services, the effectiveness of which is measured by various concepts of the general public welfare. Though seldom given equal consideration, the basic features of budgets for capital improvement programs include middle-range and end-objective planning (of priority programs), centralized management review, and a policymaking (control) framework that is aimed at management's effective use of funds within a given operational time frame.

Probably the greatest difficulty in the structuring of a planning-programming-budgeting process for public agencies is establishing consensus on a clearly defined problem. This is due not only to the complexity of analyzing major program policy options for funding but also to the fact that the private sector is typically relied on to remain sensitive to the beneficial output of public programs under changing economic conditions.

In recent years the application of economic analysis to public sector decision making has focused on program budgeting that recognizes direct linkages between planning, programming, and budgeting processes. This management systems technique is used at various levels of sophistication in administrative decision making and is responsive to computer applications. Its value in planning is that of providing analytical capability for the review of programs and objectives within a comprehensive policymaking framework, as well as a politically acceptable mechanism for translating comprehensive and program plan objectives (and general policy statements) into specific policy appropriate for effective public administration. Orientation of program budgeting is toward shaping policies on expenditures, rather than on taxation and debt.

Too often, feedback from the private sector to the public sector on changing economic conditions lacks analysis of economic implications directly affecting the efficiency of programs, policies, and funding. Such feedback during budget hearings may be after the fact, or, as is often the case, may not be given within the context of fostering the long-term economic stability of the community. There are certain political advantages to funding public programs that provide short-term visible benefits. Thus, several fundamental problems concerning waste of public funds and lack of communication may exist between the private and public sectors of a community. The real estate counselor is in a strong position to strengthen public-private coordination toward the improved effectiveness and efficiency of local public expenditures, particularly where there is public disclosure and information relevant to the economic soundness of public projects.

Policy Impact Analysis

Translating goals into policy has remained a long-standing administrative problem, possibly due to the nonspecific time frames typical of local plans, uncertainties in project funding, and the insufficient economic and financial expertise of local public administrators. In recognition of the fact that the police power has inherent deficiencies in fostering the general public welfare, state-of-the-art zoning administration has evolved within the framework of land use planning to allow increased flexibility in land use regulation, which, in turn, has allowed land use policies to be shaped by citizen input on quasi-judicial matters affecting future administrative action. In this context, expert testimony at public hearings on local economic trends and investment potentials relating to location, design, and timing of planned development can contribute to the long-term economic stability of a community and to protection of the interests of the various groups affected by planning and zoning decisions.

Effectiveness of comprehensive plan implementation is strongly influenced by the position of the planning process in its decision-making environment. Traditionally, the relationship between local comprehensive plans and economic reality has been somewhat remote, with real estate counseling (to the extent that it was attempted) during comprehensive plan formulation begin heavily laden with economic assumptions. Conversely, local agency projects such as downtown redevelopment (now termed ''urban enterprise zones'') and neighborhood revitalization have realized notable success when a market approach has been incorporated into the planning process during the plan formulation stage rather than after the development of plan implementation problems involving the feasibility of design alternatives, investment risk, and private commitments.

Economic speculation and the counselor's risk of tarnished credibility are minimized within a legal-administrative framework for comprehensive planning where local plan formulation is approached through goal-oriented policymaking on a case-by-case basis. This approach, though often controversial, gives the real estate counselor the opportunity to address general economic conditions and specific market-oriented planning policy issues related to private planning and zoning proposals. In combination with a relatively high level of public participation, policy planning can over time produce an increasingly predictable pattern of decisions that evolve as a comprehensive working plan document. Many jurisdictions have applied this concept in updating existing plan documents and in shaping policies to guide administrative decisions that affect private investment and market competition as well as the economic growth and stability of the community.

Due to interrelationships among urban subsystems, a specific project having primary economic impact on a targeted recipient group can also be expected to have secondary economic impact either because of proximity of location or because of mutually reinforcing activity. Extended public-private partnerships may be capable of realizing greater cost effectiveness in public program expenditures through the selective use of subsidized private cost reductions. Such joint efforts could result in the improved design and construction of new street improvements and street lighting, seed money for private financing, tax ceilings on upgraded improvements, and the revaluation of low-interest loan accounts within special improvement districts.

Counseling advice on specific projects may be properly given within the context of the economic impact of local public decisions and private-public partnership arrangements. In-house assessment in terms of the interdepartmental and intergovernmental coordination of planning policy and project modifications may be left to public officals.

Preparation and Review of Master Plans

Generally, a master plan for the development of a major land area within a community is intended as a means of evaluating the relationship among proposed land uses at prescribed densities as well as the adequacy of support facilities and services to meet the needs of anticipated population and housing. A master plan, though still very general, is distinguished from a local comprehensive plan by its level of specificity. Master plan considerations relate to the physical parameters of development and amenity-value potentials, the character of proposed neighborhoods, opportunities for the self-sufficiency of employment centers, and conceptual land use arrangements. A master plan also considers population and housing density maximums, the location and capacity of major streets and utilities, front-end capital requirements, and the time frame for development phasing and land absorption in the marketing of either raw subdivision land or platted sites with streets and utilities, but usually not in the marketing of turnkey sites with buildings already developed.

For counseling purposes, the major utility of a preliminary master plan is as a tool for the analysis of land use potentials. Emphasis is given to various anticipated net future benefits to the landholder that are related to market timing, predicated on expected development and on future density criteria.

Certain economies of scale are available to invester-developers of large tracts of land having suburban subdivision potential. Such economies include reduced unit costs of master planning, zoning, platting, street and utility extensions, and marketing, as well as increased amenity-value potential that is made available by the design flexibility of larger land parcels. Counsel is especially valuable in the planning and timing of land parcels with unique physical attributes. Such parcels may become liabilities if they are poorly treated, or they may become key assets if they are employed in market-wise fashion.

The fitting together of neighborhood master plans into a pattern faithful to a desired community image requires a knowledge of the forces in the real estate market that create the effective demand that results in successful development. Anticipating growth through the use of logic concerning the access, topography, and availability of utilities is, however, not enough. Many well-considered long-range community plans have been mutilated because the unavailability of major land parcels at the anticipated time altered or spoiled the "orderly" development that would have maximized the "general welfare." Other community development goals break apart because of inflexibility in the face of changing market conditions. Since society's needs and desires are dictated by changing political, economic, and social conditions that emanate from all levels of local to world affairs, the market is quickly altered and the best-laid plans, of course, go awry. Thus, inside knowledge of the market, the plans of major landowners, current market demands, the depth and breadth of the market, trends in such matters as affordable housing density, the tolerance of tax levels to support schools and parks, and practical solutions in development plans of needs for personal security—all of these ingredients should be part of the recipe for master plan review.

From a government planning viewpoint the selection of suitable uses of land must encompass, in addition to influences and efforts on neighboring and community welfare, the practical matters of market need and, in particular, demand related to timing. No net community benefit comes from sterilizing the use of a land parcel with zoning that is unacceptable to the market, even though a pocket of neighboring owners may relish an opportunity to temporarily usurp the rights of others to develop or use their land. The avoidance of confrontations between neighbor and developer requires understanding of both viewpoints plus practiced communication by an acknowledged real estate authority.

Master planning also often serves as an important ingredient for securing annexation with necessary zoning at achievable land use densities (subject to future revisions), for obtaining public and quasi-public commitments to serve an area with utilities, and for coordinating planning so as to achieve properly timed subdivision and marketing with adjacent properties.

Anticipating the probable rate of land absorption in new subdivisions is important for planning and zoning decisions and for decisions on municipal services (police, fire, schools, arterial highways). Unnecessary taxpayer burdens result from overoptimistic land absorption guesses, and the provision of inadequate land for development creates excessive price levels and indirect damages by discouraging new business and industry. Measuring the rate of land absorption is a principal product of many private real estate consultants versed in the economic effects of the under- and oversupply of a particular land use activity and of market timing.

Zoning Impact

The ever-present dread of neighborhood property owners is that rezoning and zoning variances will depreciate the value of their property either directly or by setting precedents that lead to further property use variances. Capable market investigations that compare property values under similar circumstances may allay such fears if these investigations are well documented by an accepted independent authority.

The applicant for a zone change or variance bears the burden of proof for demonstrating that unique or changing circumstances have created economic hardship that is likely to continue unless remedial local public action is taken. Precedent, feasibility studies of alternative future uses, and capable market investigations that compare similarly situated properties subject to different zoning regulations may provide evidence to justify a requested zone change or variance, though specific design and use conditions based on the applicant's intended future property use are often attached to such approvals.

The inflexibility of outmoded land use ordinances has generally contributed to design obsolescence in private development, often precluding realization of the amenity-value potential of sites subject to uniform lot size, setback, density, and other use restrictions that influence both subdivision layout and building design. Once established, site-specific land use zoning seldom remains responsive to the pressures of urban growth, because such pressures tend to alter (from existing zoning) the appropriate development of land committed to long-term future use. Market assessment of a proposed development at a given location, made in view of urban growth trends and projections, provides a meaningful basis for estimating the degree of private investment risk that is related to land use development based on realistic zoning alternatives.

Recognizing the potential for conflicts among development projects and consequent land use activities over the economic life of a neighborhood, many planning and zoning administrators have initiated community-wide rezoning of land from generally restrictive to selectively more flexible planned development districts. Although involuntary rezoning constitutes an involuntary exchange of development rights, overall comparability of the values involved in such modification of enforceable restrictions may be necessary in order to avoid a public taking.

The real estate counselor may be asked to provide expert testimony toward establishing reasonable administrative criteria for development plan review and approval, particularly where such policymaking is not limited to the confines of a political question. Voluntary rezoning to permit more intensive land use in planned development districts is typically reviewed in light of a larger area's adopted master plan and has proved successful in protecting the market value of existing improvements and their potential for upgrading. Such rezoning can increase design flexibility in new development, provide adequate buffering of otherwise incompatible land uses, reduce anticipated long-term public expenditures for neighborhood redevelopment and public safety, and maintain the local tax base.

Design flexibility in planned land use zones requires the private owner-developer to secure local public approval of his or her proposed development plan. Planned commercial zones typically require a unified control document supplementing a development plan, where owners of several contiguous sites included within one development plan share common elements such as off-street parking, curb cuts, and signage, yet retain individual ownership of separate sites and buildings.

Community Revitalization

A local public agency may designate a redevelopment area based on a wide variety of criteria relating to economic and financial potentials among project alternatives, the availability of nonlocal funds, and plan objectives aimed at reducing adverse urban conditions and blighting influences. The redevelopment administrator is allowed considerable discretion in identifying existing and probable future redevelopment need and in selecting redevelopment project priorities. For these purposes, neighborhood change indicators such as demographic data, household income, retail sales, school enrollment trends, other service delivery statistics, property tax information, and a neighborhood conditions survey are typically used and sometimes graphically mapped for public hearings.

A local redevelopment agency may seek objective advice supported by reliable market data from a recognized authority in prescribing economic prerequisites and methods of improving the viability of revitalization project proposals and the rehabilitation potentials of residential and nonresidential areas as well as the levels and types of public assistance that are likely to be sufficient for attracting site-specific private investment within a selected target area. Having identified the redevelopment problems and objectives, the fundamental task of the real estate counselor is to advise the redevelopment administrator on how to balance publicly desired project characteristics with the level and magnitude of economic revitalization that is projected as achievable in the market during project implementation. Specifics are helpful and are likely to entail the selection of a workable project alternative, the creation of a properly timed market-sensitive program, and a gradual fine tuning of the adopted strategy in a fashion that manages risk among the private and public interests that enter into redevelopment project commitments.

Although most discretionary public funds for local redevelopment come through federal block grant allocations, some local agencies have been able to invest a greater proportion of their discretionary monies into public capital improvements by directing federal loan subsidies to eligile private investors through a local nonprofit development corporation. Other measures oriented to risk management in private-public redevelopment partnerships include performance contracts, reinvestment of local low-interest redevelopment loan funds, temporary property improvement tax ceilings (possible on a contractual basis), earmarked special improvement taxes, and local redevelopment loan guarantees to mortgagors not holding an interest in potential equity gain on property benefiting from public capital improvement expenditures.

Economic development has become a joint concern and goal for government and private business. Public entrepreneurship, through the coalition of public and private entities, is the new blueprint for revitalizing lagging economies in many areas.

Real Estate Assessment

Assessors are generally charged with a responsibility for uniform and equitable valuation of real estate as a tax base by mass appraisal methods. Valuation formulas are typically directed through state legislatures with various percentages of value assessments for different classes of property. Although these directives may say to the assessor that all of the many valuation factors and processes should be applied, the safe practical method used to date for assessed valuations is a fixed date of replacement cost analysis combined with depreciation charges to building improvements related to age. Land values are similarly assessed by mechanical processes to the maximum extent. The assessor's goal is to minimize local complaint by demonstrating equity in property classes and individual properties. The assessment goal at the state level is equal value relationships among counties for fair flows of tax monies.

Private specialists in real property valuation are substantially engaged each year to analyze the fair assessed value of properties that, for various reasons, do not fit the mass appraisal mold. Situations of this kind frequently include individual property peculiarity such as a long-term below-market lease or a given right of use for a specified time to a charitable organization. Economic cycles on a local basis may result in temporarily depressed values for warehousing at one time, for general office space at another time, and for apartments at yet another time. Or a whole industry such as steel might suffer nationwide to such an extent that local taxes, as a matter of equity, should be adjusted by assessment related to individual independent valuations.

Real estate consultants are frequently relied on in such matters to assist in presenting individual tax appeal cases as well as in counseling assessors. General overall knowledge of a community, an industry, or local political vagaries may have as much impact on assessment adjustment as does a well-documented appraisal. Consultants in this field have knowledge of state law concerning factors of valuation, the general intent of effective legislation, and differences between the terminology of the real estate investment industry and that of state legislators. They have experienced and understand the assessor's zealous position with regard to overt special individual treatment of one property, and they also understand the makeup of assessment appeal bodies and their impatient need to have valuation reasoning presented with the layperson's logic.

SPECIFIC GOVERNMENT NEEDS

Professional real estate counsel is of benefit to government and taxpayer alike when it is used to improve the planning, acquisition, disposition, and use of real property by government.

Administrative and Operating Facilities

The development of government office space or government storage or maintenance facilities on skillfully selected sites can stimulate private investment on neighboring property, which is in the community interest of creating a greater tax base or revitalizing a business district. Also, government is frequently well advised as to when and where it should rent space, in lieu of purchase, particularly when that space is located within an area of excess market supply and fragile property values.

Streets and Highways

Decisions on the location, types, and access rights of new streets and highways have creative or destructive impacts on private property that are obvious to the professional real estate counselor. Local planning agencies are privy to announced plans of projects and resultant arterial and street requirements, but private consultants provide added information concerning probable additional impending development that is critical for the coordination of highway network planning. Acquisitions of rights-of-way also require expert knowledge concerning their probable impact on the valuation and development of other property, how to minimize right-of-way costs by avoiding property severance and/or trading for use privileges (zoning and access rights), and how to acquire existing access rights with a minimum of pain and expense to both parties.

Schools

Ever-changing student and faculty needs that respond to changing standards of business, industry, and society result in demands for continuing surveillance of the facilities of public and private schools. The real estate counselor is often needed to resolve questions surrounding the acquisition and disposition of property and negotiations with neighboring landowners on such matters as expansion and zoning change, and the need to adapt space to change often requires the team play of the architect, builder, academician, and real estate counselor.

Private schools are often beneficiaries of real estate gifts. Giving may be encouraged and enhanced if the donee makes professional counsel available to the donor. Such counsel usually involves not only providing real estate knowledge but also providing advice with regard to related legal and tax accounting sources. Real estate counsel also assists private colleges in programming the use of real estate gifts. Such decisions relate to questions regarding the most profitable or beneficial use and the timing or manner of marketing, particularly with lands that are in use transition or that are in a maturing process.

Counsel to public school administrators regarding site selection is particularly valuable when a knowledge of the success potentials of community-wide development plans is needed. The absence of such counsel usually leads school administrators to carry forward in the direction of previous growth, frequently failing to heed impending economic and social change. Public school systems also require advice on the disposition of excess and obsolete property and on market timing, use restrictions, and effective marketing methods.

Parks

Parks, like schools, usually have a strong social and value impact on adjoining property, but that impact is not always beneficial. Location studies and analyses of need and probable resulting effects are of considerable importance to society, government, and business alike. Floodplain zones are especially useful for the creation of recreational and open space—a potential conversion of community liabilities to assets. Private owners of floodplain lands in many instances attempt to force a dangerous use or a litigious development precedent that might well be circumvented with local government cooperation by trading developable excess public land to private owners for marginal floodplain land that is converted to parkland.

Public Utilities

Thorough study and professional market-oriented advice is cost effective for public utilities in their long-range planning of main service facilities, as is advice on the price, timing, and methods of acquiring and disposing of excess property.

State Government

State government agencies are more likely to achieve palatable solutions in the processes of property acquisition, conversion, and disposition if they avail themselves of direction from the professional counseling field. A decision between litigation and settling with a compromise purchase price, for example, may hinge on the potential cost of setting a domino effect precedent that private business and local society may be better equipped than government to foresee. Advice of a parochial nature is frequently invaluable to legal counsel preparing for condemnation and damage trials. And the professional real estate counselor may be an invaluable expert witness because he or she is usually a person practiced in communication who is able to reduce the mountain-size problem to a molehill and to express the client's interest in dispassionate and reasonable terms.

Federal Government

Local real estate knowledge, although greatly needed, is too seldom used by federal government agencies, perhaps because of the tyranny of regulations and funding structures. However, few needs are as obvious as good grass roots advice for the Department of Housing and Urban Development and the Veterans Administration on local market conditions and on the disposition of foreclosed property. The military services, the General Services Administration, the U.S. Postal Service, and the Department of the Interior are equally poorly equipped to function successfully in acquiring, managing, and disposing of real estate without a strong infusion of local knowledge into the decision processes. Acceptance of this vital ingredient for sensible and beneficial decisions is gaining ground through the use of recognized professional real estate counsel. The many real estate activities of federal government agencies where such counsel is needed include

1. Site selection (and acquisition) for building, the training of army troops, and the development of waterways, reservoirs, parks, highways, and postal facilities
2. The selection and disposition of surplus property
3. The trade of public for private lands where benefits are mutual
4. The adaptation of federal regulations to local needs
5. The management of Indian lands for long-range value
6. The management of public grazing lands and of commercial facilities in public parks
7. The common property management problems of administrative, cultural, social, and maintenance facilities

Growth of professional quality and quantity in the real estate counseling field is resulting in benefits to government and the public from wiser use of real property. All concerned are gaining increased rewards via improved decision making.

SELECTED REFERENCES

FISCHEL, WILLIAM A. *The Economics of Zoning Laws: A Property Rights Approach to American Land Use Control.* Baltimore: John Hopkins Press, 1985.

FOSLER, R. SCOTT, and RENEE A. BURGER, eds. *Public-Private Partnerships in American Cities.* Lexington, Mass.: Lexington Books, 1982.

GIBBONS, JAMES E. *Appraising in a Changing Economy: Collected Works of James E. Gibbons.* Chicago: American Institute of Real Estate Appraisers, 1982.

LEVINSON, P., S. MAZIE, L. LEDEBUR, M. BENDICK, Jr., and D. RASMUSSEN. *Industrial Incentives in Local Economic Development.* Washington, D. C.: The Urban Land Institute, 1981.

PECHMAN, JOSEPH A., ed. *Economics of Policymaking: Selected Essays of Arthur M. Okun.* Cambridge: MIT Press, 1983.

PETERSON, JOHN, E., and WESLEY C. HOUGH. *Creative Capital Financing for State and Local Government.* Chicago: Municipal Finance Officers Association, Government Finance Research Center, 1983.

RASMUSSEN, D. W., M. BENDICK, Jr., and L. LEDEBUR. *The Cost Effectiveness of Economic Development Incentives.* Washington, D. C.: The Urban Land Institute, 1982.

SO, FRANK S., ISRAEL STOLLMAN, FRANK BEAL, and DAVID A. ARNOLD. *Practice of Local Government Planning.* Washington, D. C.: International City Managers' Association, 1979.

WHITE, JOHN ROBERT. *Real Estate Valuing, Counseling, Forecasting: Selected Writings of John Robert White.* Chicago: American Institute of Real Estate Appraisers, 1984.

CASE STUDIES

Governor's Task Force on Science and Technology. *Economic Revitalization Through Technological Innovation.* Volume II, January. Raleigh: North Carolina Board of Science and Technology, 1984.

JOHNSON, ROBERT A., SEYMOUR I. SCHWARTZ, and STEVE TRACY. 1984. "Growth Phasing and Resistance to Infill Development in Sacramento County." *Journal of the American Planning Association* 50 (Autumn): 434-446.

RODDEWIG, RICHARD J., and JARED SHLAES. *Analyzing the Economic Feasibility of a Development Project: A Guide for Planners.* Planning Advisory Service Report #380. Chicago: American Planning Association, 1983.

FIGURE 9–2 SUMMARY OF ASSUMPTIONS AND ANALYSIS
(See Chapter 9, page 125.)

INFLATION	1.05	DEPRECIATION SCHEDULE (BL) ...	31.5
ANALYTIC YEAR	0	PURCHASE PRICE	650000
MONTHLY RENT YEAR ONE	5666.66	DEPRECIABLE AMOUNT	650000
MONTHLY RENT/ANALYTIC YEAR ..	5666.66	ANNUAL WRITE OFF	20634.92
PURCHASE PRICE	650000	MONTHLY BASIS	1719.58
DOWN PAYMENT	130000		
MORTGAGE INTEREST RATE	9.50%		
TERM IN YEARS	25		
RESALE VALUE GROWTH RATE	1.05		
REAL ESTATE TAX MILL RATE	0.025		
EQUALIZATION RATE	1		
INCOME TAX RATE	0.34		
INTEREST RATE (DN PMT)	0.07		
GROWTH OF R.E. TAXES	1.05		
RENTAL AREA	4250		
PURCHASED AREA	4250		
R.E. SALES COMMISSION RATE	0.05		
SPECIAL CHARGES	0		

Monthly Analysis

Twelfth Month Of Year	One Year	Five Year	Eleven Year
Principal Payment	465.20	679.24	1198.39
Mortgage Interest	4078.02	3863.98	3344.83
Mortgage Payment	4543.22	4543.22	4543.22
Plus Real Estate Tax	1300.00	1659.17	2117.56
Less Income Tax Savings @ 34%	1828.53	1877.87	1857.21
After Tax Cost	4014.69	4324.52	4803.57
Less: Equity Accumulation	465.20	679.24	1198.39
Plus Lost Interest On Down Payment	758.00	758.00	758.00
Effective Cost	4307.49	4403.28	4363.18
Rental Payment	6412.5	6412.50	10793.25
After Tax Rental Payment	4232.25	4232.25	7123.55
Ratio: Cost/Rent	1.02	1.04	0.61
Monthly Depreciation	584.66	584.66	584.66
Cost After Depreciation	3722.84	3818.62	3778.52
Ratio: Cost/Rent	87.96%	90.23%	53.04%
Appreciation Benefits	2247.45	2636.70	3350.57
Economic Cost After Appreciation	1475.39	1181.92	427.95
Ratio: Cost/Rent	34.86%	27.93%	6.01%

INDEX